ENTREPRENEURIAL FAMILIES:
BUSINESS, MARRIAGE AND LIFE IN THE EARLY
NINETEENTH CENTURY

Studies in Business History

Series Editors: John Singleton
                      Francesca Carnevali

Titles in this Series

1 The Modern American Wine Industry: Market Formation and Growth
in North Carolina
Ian M. Taplin

2 Multinationals, Subsidiaries and National Business Systems: The Nickel
Industry and Falconbridge Nikkelverk
Pål Thonstad Sandvik

Forthcoming Titles

The Optical Munitions Industry in Great Britain, 1888–1923
Stephen C. Sambrook

Rockefeller Philanthropy and Modern Social Science
David L Seim

ENTREPRENEURIAL FAMILIES:
BUSINESS, MARRIAGE AND LIFE IN THE EARLY NINETEENTH CENTURY

BY

Andrew Popp

Routledge
Taylor & Francis Group

LONDON AND NEW YORK

First published 2012 by Pickering & Chatto (Publishers) Limited

Published 2016 by Routledge
2 Park Square, Milton Park, Abingdon, Oxfordshire OX14 4RN
711 Third Avenue, New York, NY 10017, USA

First issued in paperback 2015

Routledge is an imprint of the Taylor & Francis Group, an informa business

BRITISH LIBRARY CATALOGUING IN PUBLICATION DATA

Popp, Andrew.
Entrepreneurial families: business, marriage and life in the early nineteenth century. – (Studies in business history)
1. Entrepreneurship – Great Britain – History – 19th century – Case studies.
2. Family-owned business enterprises – Great Britain – History – 19th century
– Case studies.
I. Title II. Series
338.7'0941'09034-dc23

ISBN-13: 978-1-138-66173-8 (pbk)
ISBN-13: 978-1-8489-3236-4 (hbk)
Typeset by Pickering & Chatto (Publishers) Limited

CONTENTS

Acknowledgements   vii

Introduction: An Unlimited Partnership   1
1 'Did You Really Think Your Letter Would Prove Too Long?'
   Epistolary Lives   9
2 John Shaw in Business   23
3 John and Elizabeth in Love   41
4 'Our Present Adventure': India and Beyond   59
5 'To Work Hard for a Larger Family': Managing Work and Family   77
6 'The Whole Circle of Our Acquaintance': Networks and Sociability   95
7 'Happiness (in Earthly Things)': Getting and Having   111
8 Conclusion: The Life They Made   127
Epilogue   133

Notes   141
Works Cited   177
Index   183

ACKNOWLEDGEMENTS

My greatest debt is to John and Elizabeth Shaw. I hold them in the greatest respect, even affection. They represent for me the quiet dignity of ordinary life. They have been an important part of my life for a number of years and without their testament I could not written this book. My engagement with their story has had a profound effect on me and I hope that is reflected in my efforts to write about them. I also feel that I have a duty to Elizabeth and John. I did not have their permission to write their story, to reveal to the world the most intimate aspects of their lives. It is easy to believe that any ethical issues are negated by the passage of time, but it cannot be that simple. All I can offer is an attempt at drawing on my own resources of sympathy and humanity.

Second, I owe an enormous debt to John Malam, without whom this book would not have been written. It was John who, at a meeting of wonderful serendipity, first told me of John, Elizabeth, and their letters. John had been instrumental in saving important aspects of the Shaw archive from neglect and even destruction and had spent much time in carefully gathering, collating, and finding a home for a wealth of documents. He did a great deal of careful research and arranged and paid for transcriptions of the letters to be made. All of this he shared with me with unstinting generosity. As an author of non-fiction works for children, most of them historical, John exemplifies that desire to share knowledge that should be at the heart of all scholarship. John's own work built on pioneering research undertaken by Geoff Hancock in the 1970s. As ever we are reminded that all scholarship is a collective endeavour.

Of course, I must thank John Singleton and Francesca Carnevali for having the courage to commission this volume and Ruth Ireland for her editorial support. The staff of Wolverhampton Archives and Local Studies proved unfailingly helpful on my many visits. I wish also to acknowledge with gratitude the generosity of Leif Melin and others at the Centre for Family Enterprise and Ownership (CeFEO), Jönköping International Business School, where my time as a Toft Visiting Professor in Family Business afforded much valuable space for writing and the exchange of ideas.

Academia, at its best, remains a community. I have received much help and support from my fellow historians. Some of these were old and trusted advisers, such as John Wilson. John cast his eye over much of the book; as ever his opinions were due the greatest respect. He is just one of a fantastic team of business historians at the University of Liverpool Management School (ULMS) that includes, or has included, Rory Miller, Stephanie Decker, Rachael Vorberg-Rugh, and Simon Mollan. It has been a pleasure to be part of this group. Also at ULMS, my intellectual horizons have been dramatically widened, and for the better, through working with Robin Holt, Mike Zundel, Garance Marechal, and others. I gratefully acknowledge the wider support afforded me at ULMS, in particular the granting of a period of research leave.

Equally generous and valuable help came from further afield. Martha Hanna responded with enormous enthusiasm to my initial 'cold-calling' email and provided much advice and encouragement, as well as the inspiration of the story of 'her' own couple, Paul and Marie Pireaud. Denise Z. Davidson also provided very valuable feedback on several chapters. Kolleen Guy deserves some very special thanks. She enabled me to believe in the value of what I wanted to do and her love and mastery of the historian's craft provided a model to emulate. In particular, she gave me the concept of John and Elizabeth's entrepreneurial marriage and life as an 'Unlimited Partnership', a brilliant distillation of all I set out to achieve. Mary Rose, who has played a vital role in developing the history of family business, read a complete draft. Her comments and approval were invaluable. From the world of family business studies Ellie Hamilton also read a complete draft and did much to convince me that I might be doing something right. I have presented work relating to John and Elizabeth at more conferences and seminars than I care to recall; I thank the audiences at those events for their attention and input. Similarly, I thank the editors and referees of those journals where articles on John and Elizabeth have appeared; they include, *Business History*, *The Journal of Historical Geography*, and *Entrepreneurship and Regional Development*. Robert Lee and Christina Lubinski, Paloma Fernández Pérez, and Jeff Fear have been kind enough to include related chapters in edited collections. The influence and support of Phil Scranton has been an important constant.

Life has delivered blows and challenges in recent years and writing about marriage has a particular personal resonance for me. Those difficulties have been made so much easier to bear by the wonderful friendships I have developed in the business history community. I remember with particular fondness – and only occasional embarrassment – many good times spent with Francesca Carnevali, Lucy Newton, Teresa da Silva Lopes, Susanna Fellman (and many others); partners in crime at conferences the world over. Cheers!

Ultimately, though, this is a book about family and its endurance, its affections, its strengths, its value, and its importance. If my greatest debt is to John and Elizabeth then undoubtedly my greatest thanks go to my own family. It is they who give meaning to everything I have tried to do here.

Andrew Popp
June 2012

INTRODUCTION: AN UNLIMITED PARTNERSHIP

'Hearts in union mutually disclosed'[1]

Making a Life

Late in the afternoon of Sunday 22 April 1832 John Shaw, a hardware merchant, sat down at his home in Wolverhampton, in the English midlands, gathering his thoughts and feelings so as to write to his beloved wife Elizabeth, 'My dear Liz,' then visiting her family in Colne, some 113 miles to north in the heart of industrial Lancashire. The day found him in a reflective, perhaps even pensive mood; his fleeting emotions ranging back and forth across past, present and future:

> I got your [letter] … at the top of which I find a calculation of the years we have been married which appears quite correct although I was not aware it was nineteen years past – how quickly has time flown and should we be spared for another such period I suppose it will not appear to have been much longer. I much fear neither of us [is] sufficiently grateful and thankful for the protection and success we have so abundantly enjoyed during so long a period and hope and trust we may be more so in the future.[2]

The nineteenth-century businessman of popular culture and myth is a gritty, bluff, no-nonsense character. Resourceful rather than romantic. The entrepreneur of academic writing – and he is another decidedly gendered figure – is variously a decisive, risk-taking, and, increasingly, creative agent. We are rarely asked to imagine that either character has much of a personal life, let alone an interior life. In this study I will explore the historical experience of entrepreneurship and family business in the context of a central and basic human question: how do I make a life?

The modern self, relatively unfettered and living in a world increasingly rich in resources and propensity, working with a previously unseen openness to innovation and change, has the luxury to ponder a series of questions: what is valuable and worthwhile to me; what would constitute a whole and satisfying life; what means and practices might produce such an end; how might the relationships

I form sustain this vision of how to live.³ Adopting a focused micro-historical approach we will see how two people, John and Elizabeth Shaw, together, worked out their answers to those questions in the first half of the nineteenth-century. Of course, as well as working out how to make a life most of us also have to work out how to make a living. John and Elizabeth Shaw chose family entrepreneurship – family business foundation and ownership – in answer to this particular question. But in apparently privileging entrepreneurship and business by making it the focus of my enquiry I do not argue for the centrality of economic rationales and imperatives. Rather, perhaps counter-intuitively, the aim is to de-centre or, instead, re-humanize the economic by considering it in the context of those questions outlined above, from which it is so often divorced in our studies, and which, emphatically, I believe are foundational. For John and Elizabeth Shaw their entrepreneurship and family business existed in service to a greater set of priorities that ordered their decisions and choices as they followed the project of trying to make a life that they could consider good. Thus we reclaim entrepreneurship, especially when expressed in a family context, as an intensely human, perhaps even humane, art.⁴

The Individual in the World

The choices available to John and Elizabeth as they made their lives were not unlimited. They operated within structures that were both deeply rooted and undergoing sometimes dramatic, unsettling and uncertain processes of change. They were situated in ways that were both more and less privileged in this respect than others amongst their fellow British citizens. Even as individuals, they did not each face exactly the same set of possibilities and barriers as the other. In theoretical language we would consider their agency as constrained; their priorities, desires and ideals had to be worked out through the means available, an availability structured by a wider set of social, economic and political institutions and forces. This means that the choices they made, though undoubtedly intensely personally felt, also reflected a much wider picture. This is part of the value of their story. Their solutions were theirs and theirs alone but they bore, indelibly, the imprint of a much wider world. And for that reason the hope is that their story will be one of wider resonance and significance.

What did it mean, for example, to be born either a man or a woman in late eighteenth-century England? How was the economy structured so as to provide, or deny, resources and opportunities to those differently positioned (socially, geographically)? What societal norms prevailed and why and with what force? How was the polity and the public realm structured? At this time, for example, dissenters and non-conformists such as Elizabeth and John were barred from entry to politics and the professions, simultaneously restricting and focusing their opportunities and their ambitions. As clearly coming from the 'middling sort' in society what cultures and values did they bring to their enterprise?[5] What scope was there for fashioning a satisfying private life that was, equally, emotional, intellectual and material in its forms? This study will then, of necessity be multidisciplinary, drawing in particular on recent researches in business, social, gender and cultural history.

As already suggested, this couple made their life in a world in flux. Both were born and came to maturity and adulthood, to that point in life when those choices we have been talking about became both meaningful and pressing, during what is often thought of as the 'classic industrial revolution' period – the fifty or sixty years following 1770. Recent decades have seen historians seriously revise our understanding and our vision of the industrial revolution. Subtlety has entered the picture, the dramatics downgraded. We are told, convincingly, that growth was slower and patchier than we thought; change, whether organizational, institutional, or technological, piecemeal and incremental. Even if adjustments and accommodations were made society didn't always experience change as radically dislocating. Continuity provided a counterweight to change. Indeed, as we shall see, John and Elizabeth themselves rarely commented on those elements those of us who followed have come to see as emblematic of their age; the factory system, radical new technologies, such as the railways, urbanization, social and political unrest, a widening of the franchise, war and empire – though all of these forces and events touched their lives. In this sense their life-world seems, from the evidence, if not hermetically sealed then relatively insulated.

But there can be no doubt that the world they left, at every level from their own lives up, was very different from the one into which they had been born. John, the son of a Staffordshire farmer, died in 1858 a very prosperous man; the very model of the successful Victorian. He could rightfully claim this as a just reward for years of hard work – and that quintessential entrepreneurial quality; risk-taking – and, no doubt, this deeply religious and pious man would have asserted that his greatest debt was to Providence and God. But he was also clearly canny in taking advantage of the opportunities offered by a society that was at once wealthier, better connected (internally and externally), and increasingly oriented to and comfortable with the idea of consuming and having, making and accumulating

Indeed, the Shaws did not simply react to or use to their own ends these wider shifts; instead they were actively part of the process, engaging in what Spinosa, Flores and Dreyfus have called 'history-making',[6] by which is meant a kind of entrepreneurialism defined as the 'disclosing of new worlds' – a capacity for 'regularly and as a matter of course seeing yourself and the world anew.'[7] John and Elizabeth time and again demonstrated this capacity, whether in a bold move to extend the business to India or to re-imagine their respective roles within the domestic space

Elizabeth and John were thus no mere pawns of a set of ungovernable and impersonal forces. They actively internalized, used, shaped and lived by a set of views and understandings they took from the world in which they found themselves. The changes we have briefly surveyed constantly opened up – and closed down – new and old 'spaces' for acting and being. These were two active, intelligent and engaged individuals. Our evidence allows us to eavesdrop as they mapped out and negotiated a path; puzzling out, as though through trial and error, solutions that would work, or that would at least do. What priorities ordered their understanding of what was both possible and proper?

An Unlimited Partnership

This is a story about relationships. It is a love-story even. John and Elizabeth's world view was dominated by their relationship to God – a relationship that was experienced as real and immediate, not distant and abstract. They looked to theology as guide to help them to interpret and act in the world. So powerful and important to them was Christian theology, in all its detailed minutiae, that differences in belief that seem relatively insignificant to the modern observer nearly strangled their 'connection' at birth. They saw their lives as unfolding according to God's will. References to Providence are legion. Salvation, to be reached only via a very strait gate, was the ultimate, indeed, the only end. As a frame of reference for making choices a non-conformist Protestant world view needs to be taken very seriously indeed; in particular it cannot be reasoned away as merely a 'discourse' amenable simply to textual analysis.

But the most powerful earthly expression of God's love was found in human love. The Shaw's greatest life project – on this earth – was their marriage. It was first and foremost this which their entrepreneurship existed to service, sustain and nourish. And in turn it was love and marriage that made entrepreneurship – and worldly success and comfort – meaningful. Their entrepreneurship was but a means to an end. It was through this work that John and Elizabeth made for themselves a space in which to build and dwell. That is why I have chosen to think of this as a study of 'an unlimited partnership.' That concept is a way to get at the inextricable weaving together of forces we normally see as, at best, only distantly related: love and marriage, on the one hand and entrepreneurship, organization-building and economic decision-making on the other.[8]

Business history has devoted considerable effort to tracking the evolution of forms of business organization. Despite revisions this historical effort remains a largely Whiggish endeavour; from simple to complex, from constrained and limited to fertile and expansive. Significant in this shift is one from unlimited to limited liability. The limited liability form of corporate organization is one that by controlling for risk, depersonalizing ownership and allowing for the removal of fetters present in earlier, more 'archaic' forms of business organization (thus, for example, allowing access to much wider sets of resources, especially financial capital) seemingly cut or, at the very least, attenuated the link between the firm and the human actors it contains. The modern business firm became much more than sum of the people it was comprised of. But even today most entrepreneurial firms, just as John and Elizabeth's was, are built on a foundation of personal ownership and management. Probably the majority of them are by any definition family firms. Recognition of this behoves us to reintroduce human drama to the story.[9] The aim is not then simply another examination of how family structures, or religious beliefs, might have impacted business strategy and firm history, as though the latter concerns were prior to the former, but instead a much fuller reintegration of these spheres.

And, as already suggested, for John and Elizabeth, this human drama was richest and most fully realized in the form of their romance and marriage. Here 'unlimited partnership' has a second, equally important set of resonances. This was a partnership in multiple senses and, most importantly, these dimensions were 'unlimited;' they overflowed into one another; the boundaries between them were ill-defined and permeable. Categories that historians are used to working with; economic/non-economic, public/private, efficient/affective, male/female, dissolve and crumble as we come to know this story.

Ordinary Lives

Edward Berenson has written of micro-history as the reading (and writing) outwards, towards wider concerns, 'through one exemplary event or person.'[10] John and Elizabeth Shaw exemplified nothing but the ordinary. Their lives were almost wholly unexceptional and uneventful – at least in the sense that we would normally consider historically significant. Certainly together and with their partners and sons they built up a successful business that remained in independent existence for more than 160 years, though it is hardly to be found in the annals of British business history.[11] They were not spared their measure of tragedy but for the most part their lives were ones of quiet contentment, sometimes even joy. Even their tragedies were the ordinary stuff of bereavement. Dull and provincial, far removed from metropolitan glamour in bustling, grimy Staffordshire, might sum them up. But in their very ordinariness they exemplify the lives of many more that lived as they did but for whom no historical record now exists, those condemned to silence by the archival gaps or the condescension of history and historians.[12] The evidence we have for the Shaws allows entry into the rich warp and weft of their quotidian lives and thus it also allows that

'reading outwards' suggested by Berenson to the dilemmas, challenges and possibilities thrown up by the mesh of interlocking economic, social and cultural
change that characterized England in the first half of the nineteenth-century.[13]
Through the lens they provide we are better enabled to shift a series of important
debates, from the relationship between family and business to the construction
of gender within both public and domestic realms, from the abstract to the very
concrete, to witness how wider forces were negotiated between two people as
they lived their lives together.[14] Crucially given the length of time covered by the
sources, we are afforded an almost unique perspective on these issues across the
best part of long, whole lives.

Structure

This is not a biography, thus its organization is largely thematic rather than
chronological or narrative-based. Moreover the sources, though very extensive,
are too incomplete too allow for the construction of a satisfying biography.
Chapter 1 will deal with the most important aspects of those sources and the
opportunities and challenges they present us with. A wide range of archival
sources, including conventional business history sources, will be used throughout this study but at its heart lie more than 200 intimate letters between various
members of the Shaw and Wilkinson families. More than one hundred of those
letters are between John and Elizabeth and they cover the years 1811 to 1839;
that is from courtship to middle age.[15] We will examine the nature of letters as
a source, their silences and their elisions as well as their strengths and virtues.
We will see the role that letters and letter-writing played in John and Elizabeth's
lives, the constitutive force of writing, their attitudes to it (including as men and
women). We will also examine how other historians have used letters as a source
in their own writing. I believe that letters have a particular ontological quality
somewhat different from that of diaries and, especially, memoirs and that those
qualities demand we take the subjective experience of our subjects seriously. Letters are of course relational, they must flow between at least two people; that
quality crystallizes this study's focus on the unlimited partnership between Elizabeth and John. At the same time letters also have a particular relationship to
time; they allow us privileged glimpses of the unfolding of life, of the unknowa-
bleness of the future, of the slipping away of the past. They have a richness and
an immediacy that provokes a desire to set Elizabeth and John in their time and
place and to follow them as they live and grow. I am unashamedly engaged and
captivated by their story and present much of it in their words.

Chapter 2 will present a brief history of the firm founded by John Shaw
around 1800. I think of this study as one essentially rooted in the discipline
of business history. It is thus important we understand the firm, what it did,

and how it grew. This was a classic family firm emerging out of a, for the time, entirely typical partnership. As a factor John Shaw did vital economic work as an intermediary between buyers and sellers, integrating markets, manufacturers and consumers. This chapter will also locate the firm in the context of a brief economic, social and cultural history of the first half of the nineteenth-century. Chapter 3 is in many ways the still centre around which the book hangs together. It explores in depth the Shaws' marriage, particularly how it came to be through a prolonged and sometimes difficult courtship, much of it conducted by letter.[16] John and Elizabeth's struggles over the three years of courtship are the historian's gain, for it led to them very carefully debating, explaining and refining their values, priorities and choices; their understanding of what it meant to be in love and to be together; what it was that they wished for together and individually. Thus with care we can come to a much clearer understanding of how and why they ordered their world as they did. This chapter is central because, we assert, it was marriage, love and family, as they understood and experienced those concepts, which provided the foundation for everything else they did – business especially. Business was entered into as allowing the expression of virtue of industriousness but pursued as a duty and means to provide for loved one.

In 1834 the partnership of Shaw and Crane, as the firm was operated between 1815 and 1848, took the almost unprecedented and unpredicted step of opening an entirely new operation in Calcutta. This adventure, as the partners themselves thought of it, will form the subject of Chapter 4. This is essentially a story of the dynamic interactions between firm and family, of waning energies and ambitions renewed, reawakened and given a fresh expression. It is also an exploration of how the firm was part of a wider world, of empire and international trade most obviously, but also the web of connections and institutions that made it possible for a small Black Country firm to take this barely credible step. And, ultimately, it is at the end a tale that plays out as tragedy, urging us to bring back real emotions to the very centre of our studies of family business.[17]

We should beware the temptation to romanticize John and Elizabeth, their lives and their marriage. Entrepreneurship placed great demands upon them – particularly prolonged and painful separation as John undertook long selling journeys around northern England (though it was of course that separation that generated the correspondence on which the historian now depends). Chapter 5 will examine how they coped, what roles they took, how the work was divided. It will bring gender to the fore, alongside notions such as the public, the private and the domestic and will thus engage with debates current in gender, women's and social history. What is revealed will, I hope, sometimes confound or complicate our expectations – but also delight us with a touching portrait of family life.

Family was a far from nuclear concept in this period. In Chapter 6 we will see how John and Elizabeth interacted with the others through circles of family, friendship and sociability, the ways in which these relationships sustained them, and how they grew and changed. This was a largely warm, convivial and nurturing environment. It is often contended across a range of literatures that such circles and networks overlapped to a great degree with more instrumental or economically oriented connections and networks, whether in the form of business finance from other family members, trusting relationships with customers and suppliers, or cooperative endeavours with other entrepreneurs in the local and wider economy. These dimensions of their networks will also be the subject of this chapter.

Finally, in Chapter 7, we will turn to the material world John and Elizabeth inhabited, the homes in which they lived, the things they surrounded themselves with and how they thought about them. Doing so also forces us to think about values and aspirations. The picture that emerges is a complex one. Elizabeth and John began life with a religiously inspired ambiguity towards material possessions and, in particular, the temptations of fashion and display. A modest appearance and way of living denoted for them a properly humble Christian disposition. Over their lifetimes, however, they became decidedly wealthy through business success. Thus the chapter will explore how they came to terms with that transition in their fortunes and, in particular, how John disposed of his wealth at death.

Chapter 8 will present a conclusion that will relate this very specific, focused and detailed story to wider concepts and theories in the literature. In particular we will explore the intersection between family, marriage, business, gender and class. A short Epilogue will briefly sketch the subsequent – and long and distinguished – history of the firm of John Shaw and Sons.

1 'DID YOU REALLY THINK YOUR LETTER WOULD PROVE TOO LONG?': EPISTOLARY LIVES.

'Did You Really Think Your Letter Would Prove Too Long'[1]

Introduction

'the receipt of my letters cannot afford you more pleasure than I do experience in writing to you – It is I can truly affirm of my pleasures the first and the greatest'.[2]

Letter writing was central to Elizabeth and John's lives for more than three decades. Their correspondence was a necessarily mutual endeavour that demanded willing commitment from both of them. They became, in a most memorable and apt phrase, 'Coscribbler[s]'.[3] They wrote their marriage into existence across three often difficult years of courtship conducted through correspondence, they sustained and nurtured that marriage through letter-writing, they offered one another succour and support across long pages, shared news and gossip, took decisions, worried out problems and evoked memories. Letter writing combated absence and dwelt in and built intimacy at a distance. Writing and receiving could deliver great pleasure – 'Need I say the contents of [your last] have given me an infinite deal of pleasure. It has once more made my prospects happy and pleasing ... and removed from my Breast such an [*sic*] heavy load it never before experienced'.[4] Sometimes, though, they pained one another greatly with a mis-thought or expression or a misread word, an imagined neglect, or a post missed or misdirected. They wrote at snatched moments in the back rooms of shops in Rochdale, from home or warehouse, propped up in their sick beds and in the bedrooms of a hundred different inns. They wrote when they could, but above all at night, lit by candle,[5] as the only time of day that afforded the space for repose and reflection, the rest of their hours filled with the pressures of daily working and household life.[6] They complained of or apologized for their writing materials, or of the need for hurry to catch the post, and yet through it all they created hundreds of letters, page after page, thousands upon thousands of words. Letter-writing was for them an act of love and devotion.

They came of age, and to their own experience of correspondence, towards the end of what is now sometimes seen as a golden age for letter-writing in the seventeenth and eighteenth-centuries, a time that witnessed a deluge of letter-writing manuals and produced some of the greatest epistolary collections (such as that of the Marquise de Sévigné) and epistolary novels (most notably Samuel Richardson's *Clarissa* and *Pamela*, first published in 1740 and 1748 respectively, and Pierre Choderlos de Laclos' *Les Liaisons Dangereuses*, first published in 1782). But whereas those epistolary novels depicted letter-writing as an art full of guile and danger (particularly for young women) Elizabeth and John, though both were certainly well educated and well read for their class,[7] wrote with a degree of artlessness, directly and spontaneously, as an everyday craft. Instead of suggestion, they privileged honesty and were all too aware of the snares that correspondence might lay in their path; in one letter early in their courtship John reminds Elizabeth that in her last 'you request me not to write such another as I did then' and responds that 'I could not do otherwise when the mind is ever charged and the heart feels just ready to break will it not speak its sorrows – should I not have disembled [*sic*] had I done otherwise indeed I could not do otherwise'.[8] The result is a remarkable series of documents, alternatively workaday, mundane, prosaic, but also intelligent, intimate, heartfelt and profoundly moving. The collection is particularly notable for the way it is sustained across several decades, for the class from which it emerged, and for the extent to which it is two-handed, many responses from both authors surviving. This chapter has two main purposes; to explore Elizabeth and John's experiences of and approaches to letter-writing, encompassing their varied experiences as male and female subjects, and to consider how their letters can be used as a source for writing history.

Writing Letters, Writing Lives

It is fortunate for the historian that Elizabeth and John frequently used their own letters as an opportunity for reflection on the meaning, importance and practice of corresponding – notably the majority of letters open with some brief comment on when one or the other last wrote or was expected to write, or on what was written. Writing to each other was a cornerstone of their lives together and apart:

> I cannot describe to you the feelings and sensation of my mind on receipt of your letter at this place which is just come into my hands. Oh my dear Girl since you cannot for a moment conceive my silence could in any way be attributed to want of affection ... [or]

that you are absent from my mind as I declare to you that you are and have been more upon my mind than ever and I can attribute my not writing earlier to anything than what I named to you in my last ... I hope I shall in some measure stand acquitted of neglect in [not] writing when I say your last letter was only to hand at Carlisle ten days as it was answered at Richmond – not well knowing the fresh ground I was going on I had given you too much time to answer my letter and which made it appear so long ere you got a reply – but had I had the most distant idea that the time would have had such an effect on your mind be assured my dear love it could not have happened – you should have had a dozen letters in the time – I can assure you it gives me as much pleasure to write to you at all times as it can give you to hear from me and do not – I pray do not my dearest love – entertain a thought that it has come from a want of affection – from any disrespect – for anything you said in your last or any source whatever – but believe me – and what language shall I make use of – I hope sincerely hope – never will be wanting to convince you that you are as dear – ah still dearer – than ever to the man who given you all – all his love and affection and would give you twice as much was it in his power to give more. Oh my dear Betsy your letter has punished me beyond anything you can conceive or I can describe ... you will I am confident find a deal of repetition in this letter but I cannot help it – my fond heart is so full that I am obliged to leave off to give vent to my feelings and tears and then I begin again to repeat what I have before said – I shall expect a letter from you to Colne in answer to my last but my dear Girl do not let that suffice – but let me beg and entreat an immediate answer to this to the same place.[9]

This long quotation, from a letter written by John whilst out on the road early in the third year of his marriage to Elizabeth, captures most vividly the profound complexities of their epistolary relationship. The immediate cause of this long, impassioned outpouring of words is the simple frustration and difficulty of coordinating their exchanges as John constantly moved around the country on his selling journeys, sometimes on unknown routes, as in this case. But what lies beneath this letter, and can be felt coursing through it, is a deep current of emotion that had to be directed, mediated and expressed through writing; particularly telling is John's desperate plea to know 'what language shall I make use of'. Almost as powerful is the sense of abasement in the admission of his self-punishment through guilt at the effects of a long if unintended silence.[10] Before closing the same letter John is again unable to control himself and declaims: 'I long to see you – I long again to embrace and fold you to my bosom', but he realizes that he must for now settle for a 'long long letter. It will do me more good than anything'.[11] The written word was but a poor substitute for the other's immediate presence, for facial expressions, the language of bodies and eyes, and of the spoken word back and forth in the give and take of conversation.

Correspondence was then the child of absence. John and Elizabeth betray this simple truth time and time again, often in the most direct and unaffected way: 'Write me a long letter as I have nothing else to comfort me when you are away'; 'I was disappointed in your letter for it is all about your business and nothing about yourself'; 'According to your request I take up my pen to inform you how we are going on in your absence'; 'Believe me I will never grumble at postage from you ... I don't care how often I have a letter'; 'If you will but send me letters often those are the best medicine in your absence ... a letter from you does me more good than anything else'.[12] It is remarkable how often these sentiments are repeated by different authors and yet in near identical terms; for example John's sister Mary expressed in late 1805 her 'Hope that you will not fail to let us have a letter on Monday and write often my Dear Brother – for that and looking forward for your return will be thre greatest pleasure we shall experience while you are absent'.[13] In the face of absence and distance, distance from home and distance in time from the next looked for meeting, letters, their expectation, their arrival, their disappointments, were enough to induce acute emotions, even bodily sensations:

> Your letter not reaching me till this afternoon made me very very anxious indeed ... However yours was very welcome when it arrived. When you are absent your letters are the best present I expect to get ... Well it will be the case with us married folks now – I thought I knew what absence was before it I was married but I believe I never knew rightly what it was till now – I feel as if part of self was torn from me.[14]

Absence and the need to fight it is a simple universal human experience. Martha Hanna's *Your Death Would be Mine* uses letters to tell the story of Paul and Marie Pireaud, a French peasant couple separated by the First World War. If 'physical separation was the painful reality husbands and wives endured as long as the war lasted' then separation in the name of commerce was no less painful. Still, as Hanna identifies:

> Physical separation did not, however, necessarily entail affective separation or cognitive alienation. Indeed, the most persistent message to emerge from the letters of Paul and Marie Pireaud is one not of separation and alienation but of connection and compassion. The concerns and anxieties of the one became, through regular, frank correspondence, the concerns and anxieties of the other.[15]

Intuitively, Elizabeth and John recognized the power and the necessity of this connection. Reflecting on her coming life as the wife of an often absent traveller, Elizabeth consoled herself that 'Perhaps ... we shall enjoy the pleasure of writing often one to the other & it may be we shall often meet in Soul when far distant in bodies'.[16] They understood too the dialogic, relational nature of correspondence; 'receiving letters from *and* writing to you I reckon amongst my greatest pleasures'.[17]

And in combating absence, writing also provided the space for the growth of a shared private intimacy. It is well-known that in contrast to today, letters were in the past often a semi-communal experiences, written with the express intention that they be read aloud amongst circles of family and friends, or even wider groups of colleagues, fraternities and the like.[18] In part this was a matter of practicality at a time of very patchy literacy, but letters could also act to bind various groups together, especially those such as emigrant families almost irrevocably separated.[19] In the great epistolary novels attempts to secrete or smuggle letters, or even to hide the existence of an entire correspondence, is typically seen as deeply transgressive and dangerous to both individuals and society and often provides a critical plot device, one that occasion's the downfall of many a naive young woman. The assertion of the individual self through the carrying on of an unapproved, unacknowledged, or undisclosed correspondence is a defiance of the wider social order, family in particular, that is wilful and corrosive. In *Clarissa* the heroine's refusal to abnegate herself to the desires of her family exemplifies this dangerous trait. The self should not be entirely sovereign but should instead be partially subject to and dependent upon greater structures.

The evidence from John and Elizabeth's correspondence suggests that this view was well on the way to breaking down by the early nineteenth-century. As we shall see in Chapter 3, Elizabeth began her correspondence with John, a young man who from the very outset had made obvious his intention to court her, entirely without her parent's knowledge or permission. Writing itself was an act that required privacy, quiet and seclusion and receipt and reading were likewise moments for apartness from the day-to-day, perhaps to better bridge that absence discussed above. It is true that once John and Elizabeth were married business letters from Henry Crane and personal letters from Elizabeth would often be written on the same sheet of paper but here the overlap stopped at a clearly demarcated line, for Elizabeth seems always to have written last before the letter was sealed and sent.

In one very explicit reflection of her experience of letter-writing Elizabeth directly addresses the necessity of seclusion, not only to reading letters but also to their composition. Notably this letter was composed at a time when their engagement was settled and common knowledge, at least amongst family. And yet the desire for privacy remained very strong:

> You say, you hope, my letters to you do not take me long in writing, but indeed my last, tho' so very short, took me a long time - & if you must ask the reason why – I answer, I could not give you my thoughts free and unrestrain'd because my bro^r came in just as I began to write and continued with me the whole time – (except when call'd into the shop at intervals) & I got so fidgitty [*sic*] as to lose all my ideas and powers of recollection & to make bad worse Miss Buck came a little before post time so I concluded hastily, but, when it was gone, if wishes could have brought it back it certainly would never have reach'd you – but as it did, I have only to beg your pardon for the many errors contain'd in it ... I confess myself quite unable to write a letter when overlook'd and observ'd by any one – & when alone my ideas flow either too fast or too slow – so that I believe I never shall excel in writing. However if you can be satisfied with me in this respect I shall be content.[20]

Writing was clearly a considered act taken seriously and with care, but beyond that it was also private and intimate, not to be overlooked by others, even casually. This view of correspondence as essentially private and intimate translated in to a fear that it might be read by others and its contents thus revealed. Elizabeth, for example, on one occasion assured John that 'You don't need to fear Sarah [a servant] seeing your letters. I believe no one sees what you write to me but you and myself', and at another playfully recounted her resistance to sharing with his sister, who 'pull'd me about and crumpled your letter upon my hand for half an hour I dare say to see it'.[21] Still, if neither John nor Elizabeth wrote for a communal readership then their privacy was sometimes transgressed; in 1828 Elizabeth's mother explained without embarrassment 'When your letter reach't Bury I had left ... a few days before but Sarah thinking it might contain something of importance had the curiosity to peep in at the end of it and seeing something respecting her Father which induc'd her to open it and finding the happy news it contain'd could not be satisfied without brining it over to Colne'.[22] Clearly such prying, whilst unusual, was also forgivable.[23]

It is no surprize that this fear of disclosure was most acute during what was an often delicate courtship, in one letter undated but almost certainly from early 1812 Elizabeth confesses to 'a fear that this letter should fall into the wrong hands. I hope my last had not been scrutinized when you got it'.[24] Sometimes this fear of disclosure led to requests that letters – even their whole correspondence – be destroyed. In particular, during a crisis in their relationship in January 1812, Elizabeth acknowledges that John had correctly 'anticipated my request with respect to my letters in case our connexion is broken – Are you not aware (that in such a case) they would powerfully bring to your remembrance things and circumstances that ought to be obliterated forever from the mind.'[25] We are returned again, most forcefully, to the extent to which letters are so much more than mere means of communication. If they feared disclosure to others then they also trembled at what they had disclosed to themselves and each other.

Still it is not the case that during their courtship either John or Elizabeth felt the need to hide the existence of their correspondence, for example by writing to names or addresses other than their own.[26] Indeed, despite her professed need for quiet and seclusion whilst writing, Elizabeth sat down to compose her reply to John's very first letter in a public part of the home, where she might be and was discovered by her father, thus making the existence of the exchange public knowledge amongst the family. It is hard not to suspect that the act was deliberate, at least in part.

Once married the intimacy of the letter-space was secure enough and deep enough to allow even for frank expressions of sexual desire, as we shall see in Chapter 3. But even before that point was yet reached letters carried with them a certain physicality or materiality. They evoked the absent other, for example in the idiosyncrasies of handwriting, and the letters' material properties developed their own powerful resonance. Letters might then become a spur to remembrance and evocation. Thus, the arrival of one John's letters:

> Found me [Elizabeth] perusing all the letters you have sent me on this journey. I thought how few in comparison of [sic] former journeys – but I had just pronounced the words in my own mind – it must have miscarried he could never forget me for nearly 3 weeks – when Rich'd came in with one – I read it over and over I don't know how many times but I believe Sarah though I was going oft it for she left me to myself for an hour or two and she found me poring over it when she returned & I think I did nothing else all afternoon and evening.[27]

As she continued this rumination Elizabeth eventually touches on the precise value and qualities of their correspondence; 'Altho' your epistle was so full of complaints yet it cheer'd my spirits which perhaps you will say is a paradox ... [but] I don't only wish to know that you are in the land of the living but I wish you to tell me so'. It as if the letter, in the fabric of the paper, or in the sight of his familiar scrawl, *contains* or *is* John.[28]

What did they write of? Foremost, especially during courtship, they wrote of themselves; of their beliefs, aspirations, principles, their emotions, affections and feelings. They conversed on what marriage might mean, on their own failings, weaknesses and doubts. They played and joshed. They relayed news and gossips. Some of this was local and communal; who was courting, who married, who ailing, who dead; who was drunk, who profligate, who flighty; who was bankrupt, who entered a new partnership, who prospered. Much, though, was intimate and domestic; how fared the writer in health, what of the weather, the children, the vegetables in the garden and the produce in the cellar. There was much business; what orders had arrived, what invoices, who had held out for higher prices, how fared the warehouse and were they working properly or idle, who looked for work, who might be hired. But there were also vivid colourful scenes from both personal and greater realms; a dramatic accident to the gig in which Elizabeth rode on the high Lancashire moors; John lost amidst the drunken crowds on Manchester's streets at New Year; a summer thunderstorm in Liverpool; Luddite tumult and the militia quartered on the town; the wedding of brother Thomas to Miss Chafer lovingly described by Elizabeth with meticulous attention to what was worn and what was eaten – a truly staggering feast; but also the news of Bonaparte's Russian campaign and his subsequent dramatic escape from Elba and return to France. They wrote also, as we have seen, of writing; reflecting on its purpose and value and more prosaically complaining of the quality of the materials or of the lack of light or time to write as much or as well as they wished. Ultimately, though, their greatest subjects remains themselves, but not as an expression of egotism but instead its opposite, a fascination with 'us'. Corresponding was central to the creation of what Martyn Lyons has called the 'unity and identity of the authorial couple'.[29] When Elizabeth wrote at considerable length of her brother's wedding in later 1812, John must have upbraided her in his (now lost) reply for in her next she acknowledged that 'My letters to you in general treat of self & I thought a little variety would be very agreeable but it seems you differ in opinion. I certainly feel obliged for the compliment and will endeavour to please in future'. Just as she wanted *him* in the letters she received, then so he wanted *her*.

John and Elizabeth's correspondence was situated in a wider epistolary world. However, though both were certainly avid readers and frequently use their letters to recommend or reflect on particular authors or books they make very scant reference to collections of letters[30] and none at all (that have survived at least) to letter writing manuals. Still both came from tight-knit if somewhat dispersed families and were experienced correspondents, with parents, siblings and friends, before embarking on their own more meaningful exchange. Of course, they did not always match the image of the ideal correspondent; Elizabeth's oldest brother Richard, living in London, peevishly complained 'I wish you to write me a few lines, when my Father writes me, in some part of his paper. I have wished several times for my Brother John to send me a Letter, but he seems unfriendly in not even sending me how he is ... I hope both you and he will give me a line, whenever you have an opportunity'.[31] Similarly John's mother felt moved to add the following post-script to her newly independent son: 'this is the second time I have address'd you. Let me have the pleasure of a long letter in the course of a few days that I may see you do not disclaim my corr[espondence] entirely'.[32] Once married, though most diligent in writing to her husband Elizabeth seems to have struggled to maintain other epistolary relationships. In 1815 she confessed to John that 'I began a letter to Miss Bates a fortnight since but it lies unfinished in my desk. I don't know when Miss Lomont will get a letter ... too'.[33] Sometimes even her own parents suffered this neglect, in the summer of 1828, fifteen years after leaving Lancashire for married life, Elizabeth began a letter to her mother thus: 'I ought to have written to you long ago but when once a thing is put [off] for anything it often gets served the same over and over and this has been the case with this for I have fix'd time after time without affecting my purpose'.[34] According to Vickery this was a frustration common to many married women once marriage brought the duties of household and family, childbearing and rearing especially.

Epistolary relationships also extended beyond immediate kith and kin. Particularly potent seems to have been that between Elizabeth and Miss Mary Lomax. Though few letters between the pair are extant they hint powerfully at the strength of feelings that could run through correspondence between friends. Our first clues lie in the opening sentences of a letter from Miss Lomax from the winter of 1810. She begins by thanking Elizabeth for 'your dear letter', and for 'the box w[ith] all my old letters in it'. She concludes with a plea that 'your new friends wont make you quite forget me – do write soon for your letters are more acceptable to me than ever just now I am very low in spirits'.[35] Elizabeth struggled to maintain her part in this 'unspoken contract between ... writers' for Miss Lomax's next extant letter opens with a lament that 'you were so very long in writing that I began to think you never intended to write again'. Miss Lomax's brother James's unrequited affection for Elizabeth was causing tension between the two friends, a tension worsened by the difficulties and snares of corresponding:

> I thank you for placing the confidence in me that you have and I can assure you that it shall be known to none but myself – your letter I will either return in a cover by the post or keep it safe while [*sic*] I see you – whichever you think proper – this you may return by the post or keep while I see you ... I wish I was with you – the subject is such a delicate one and I both love and esteem you dearly I scarcely know how to write for fear I might hurt your feelings unintentionally – and I am sure I would be very sorry to do either in word or deed. Do write this week and tell me if you get this safe and will send a person that I can confide in to the p[ost] office on purpose with it.[36]

Her next again begs 'I hope you will write me a long letter and soon. Don't be so long as you were before'.[37] By May 1812 the correspondence had reached a point of crisis, Mary Lomax complaining that 'There was a time when I could have thought you would have done anything sooner than have written me such a letter as your last. Let me tell you I thought it a very sharp one ... May you never receive a letter that will wound your heart as your last did me'. She returns to the slights and neglect she felt she had suffered from Elizabeth the previous summer, when 'I thought you never intended to write to me again – I know I am not worth corresponding with'.[38] Despite this self-pity she continues, desperate to find a way to sustain the communication, either in person or by post, all the while seeming to undermine or despair of the possibility: 'this letter is written always and every way but I hope you will excuse it as burn it you must ... I shall not be angry at you if you don't write to me when at Manchester Miss Lancaster will wish to see your letter as I know you don't wish me to let any one see your letter and as much as what you favour me with I will keep them sacred'. This sad exchange stands as vivid testimony to the intensity of emotions correspondence not only channelled but perhaps actually helped to generate.

However, despite these lapses, both Elizabeth and John were no doubt well aware of the proprieties and expectations that surrounded letters and letter-writing. As already noted, the seventeenth and eighteenth-centuries had seen an explosion in literacy, letter-writing and manuals of epistolary instruction and etiquette. One of the most prominent features of the culture so encouraged was the extent to which it was gendered. Still, we should be careful not to mistake the prescriptions and rules of those claiming mastery of the art for the reality of practice on the ground. Indeed, Elizabeth admitted that 'I follow the dictates of affection and not custom in writing to you'.[39]

Men and Women Writing Letters

During the eighteenth-century there emerged a strong cultural belief that letter-writing was a peculiarly feminine art. Shortly after her own marriage in 1854 Charlotte Brontë provided amused reflection on this perceived difference in a letter to her dearest female friend, Ellen Nussey. Men, Charlotte felt, 'don't seem to understand making letters a vehicle of communication – they always seem to think us incautious'. Her husband Arthur, she reported to Ellen, 'says such letters as mine never ought to be kept – they are dangerous as Lucifer matches – so be sure to follow a recommendation he has just given "fire them" – "or there will be no more". Such is his resolve'.[40]

Evidently Arthur was not satisfied that Ellen had made her promise to burn Charlotte's correspondence in earnest and Charlotte is forced to return to the subject again in her next, where she expands upon the differences between female and male correspondence:

> [Arthur] says women are most rash in letter-writing – they think only of the trust-worthiness of their immediate friend – and do not look to contingencies – a letter may fall into any hand. You must give the promise – I believe – at least he says so, with his best regards – or else you will get such notes as he writes to Mr Snowden – plain, brief statements of facts without the adornment of a single flourish – with no comment on the character or peculiarities of any human being – and if a phrase of sensibility or affection steals in – its seems to come on tiptoe – looking ashamed of itself.[41]

Historian Amanda Vickery agrees, arguing that:

> [a] typical letter written by one woman to another in our period might agonize over a child's illness, exchange local news and society gossip, offer opinions on literature and politics and request information about, servants, fashions and consumables; perhaps, by modern standards, a touch parochial in its details. However, read this letter against the archetypal missive sent man to man in the same era and it looks like a national editorial, for a man's letters often chiefly concerned his own illnesses, minor matters of law and local administration, and above all sport – effectively summarized as my gout is still bad; here is the gun dog I promised you; have you finished the will?[42]

Goodman argues with considerable sophistication for the central role of letter-writing for the construction of gendered female selves in eighteenth-century France.[43] Martin Lyons extends the argument to claim that epistolary identities 'inevitably had a gendered dimension' and historians must take a 'closer look at what personal writing signified to both men and women and at how men and women wrote differently, expressed themselves differently, and structured their narratives differently'.[44] Perhaps so: John and Elizabeth were certainly more than aware of their genders and the roles and expectations they demanded, for they discussed them explicitly. Neither Elizabeth nor John were free of society's constraints in this respect. And yet they constantly, unwittingly *and* knowingly, confounded those expectations. Elizabeth's is often the dominant voice; assertive, didactic, leading and shaping the conversation. It is John that is hesitant, shy and full of doubt. He repines for home, softens his voice and searches again and again for affirmation. Admittedly we have little man-to-man correspondence from John, and what does exist is more workmanlike (that being exactly what it is) but still, beyond business, he addresses none of the subjects Vickery identifies as characteristic of male correspondents. He is instead fond and domestic in voice and subject. If the 'letters between Isaac and Sarah [Holden] are not between equals' then those between John and Elizabeth were, at least in their own eyes if not society's.[45]

The ways in which their letters confound crude gender stereotypes and roles are important in foreshadowing how we will come to see and understand each of them as individual, characterful selves, and as men and women negotiating society's structures and expectations.[46] Understanding this is vital to how we can use intimate letters as historical sources.

History from Letters

There is a growing body of historical research employing private, intimate correspondence as its primary source. Much, if not most, of this work lies in the broad field of social history, and in particular gender[47] and family history,[48] and histories of love, sexuality, marriage and the emotions.[49] Still more is related to the construction of class, national and other identities and social structures.[50] Other branches are much more personal, focused on biographical or life-writing approaches, or on psychological studies of individuals or pairs.[51]

Business history remains more cautious about intimate correspondence as a source.[52] Of course, as a highly empirical sub-discipline it has always used business correspondence as an important source of archival evidence. For the most part it reads these sorts of letters in highly unproblematized ways; that is as relatively straightforward records of fact rather than as socio-culturally determined linguistic texts requiring careful handling and interpretation. The most significant exception is probably found in the work of Gordon Boyce, most notably his 2010 study of correspondence amongst three generations of the Bates' family, Liverpool based merchants, ship-owners and bankers.[53] Boyce does explicitly view such letters as socially constructed linguistic texts requiring careful analysis. However, his analysis remains oriented towards core business history concerns such as firm culture and its linkages to performance and efficiency, and in contrast to the techniques characteristic of letter-using social history he readily employs formal and quantitative techniques such as content analysis and speech-code theory. His focus is on the meta-level, on norms and cognitive patterns operating within groups, rather than on the interiority of the subjective individual self. Language reflects (socially constructed) culture – not a legitimate subjectivity. Indeed it is hard to think of any business history that has asked whether the agents its studies even *have* subjective individual selves. A further example is Leos Müller's study of eighteenth-century Swedish merchant Jean Abraham Grill, whose very extensive correspondence, commercial and intimate, is used to explore his sense of self and identity.[54]

Even within this context of growing interest in letters as an historical source John and Elizabeth's extant correspondence is a remarkable body of documents; a sustained, rich and nuanced dialogue. Yet, as Lyons has argued, 'Private letters always reconstitute fragments of experience'.[55] They are not uncomplicated gateways to the soul, the psyche, or the heart; they carry encrypted in them 'tactical objectives' and 'rhetorical ploys'.[56] Never is this more true than of that superficially most open genre, the love letter. At the same time, moreover, most collections of letters are 'accumulated by complicated processes of selection and destruction, and surviving letters offer only fragmentary and vestigial versions of individual experiences and family relationships'.[57] Thus correspondence cannot be read simply as a 'faithful reflection of the past'. Lyons' answer is to focus not on the content of letters but instead on their writing as a 'cultural practice within nineteenth-century society as a whole'; a practice in whose 'patterns ... the mutual expectations of writer and recipient, and the epistolary pacts that unite them ... the rituals they observed, we may better understand what writing meant to nineteenth-century correspondents'.[58] Mark Seymour makes a similar point, noting that whilst 'Personal letters have traditionally provided some access to the private worlds of emotion and feeling ... a great deal always remains inaccessible'.[59] In short, using letters is never easy – and part of their difficulty lies in their very textuality. Historians have learnt to be almost distrustful of texts.

The question is then the extent to which we allow our subjects an active, flowering individual subjectivity? That is, a subjectivity not entirely autonomous from but at least partially beyond or before the impress of socio-cultural forces. Why, as Roper asks, 'has the study of cultural attributes been so difficult to integrate with the study of subjective experience, in a manner that does not reduce the latter to a simple mirror of social constructions?'[60] There remains, I contend, even at the risk of essentialism, a certain irreducibility of the self beyond the social construction of identities and subjectivities (man/woman; husband/wife; entrepreneur/housekeeper). Moreover, letter-writing bears directly on this subjectivity, whether individual or relational, as in an authorial pair such as John and Elizabeth. However moulded by custom, expectation, learnt practices and broad societal norms, corresponding remained a constitutive process. Letter-writers work within norms, but as themselves, as Goodman writes of one her female subjects 'it [corresponding] allowed her to develop and articulate an individual self'.[61] There is no necessary dichotomy between subjective self and wider constructions; for Goodman the correspondents she studies 'understood themselves *both* as individuals *and* as women'.[62]

I wish to chart then a middle way, acknowledging the culturally determined facets of epistolary practice, paying attention, as we already have to the 'conditions that engendered' the Shaw's exchanges, but believing at the same time that there can be too much emphasis placed on such factors as, for example, letter manuals. Such socio-cultural norms, standards and etiquette as the manuals recommended were but poor, inadequate containers for the lived thoughts and emotions of correspondents, which constantly over-spilled the constraints supposedly placed upon them. Similarly there can be too much emphasis on letters as mere channels for analysable discourses of one sort or another. As Seymour warns, over-emphasis on the discursive nature of correspondence might 'paint historians into a corner' where cultural determination entirely obliterates subjective experience.[63] Of course, in reading the letters we need to exercise care, with an ear alert to conditions and context, forces and structures. But still, the possibility of a directness remains. Tosh argues that Isaac and Sarah Holden, each 'passionately committed to the marriage', confronted a 'trauma of separation [that] called for plain speaking, they squarely confronted issues of principle. Personal grievances and longings are here exposed, instead of being muffled by the requirements of taste or tact'.[64] In my experience of reading John and Elizabeth's letters I stand with Tosh when he claims that 'Sometimes the witnesses step boldly into the box and unburden their hearts'. Hearing that testimony demands a respect for the 'integrity of personal experience' and is an avenue to the 'humanistic appeal of history'.[65] In conclusion, Goodman quotes Habermas's dictum that 'Through letter writing the individual unfolded himself in his subjectivity'.[66] This volume stands as a testament to the unfolding of John and Elizabeth Shaw.

2 JOHN SHAW IN BUSINESS

Introduction

John Shaw's business was but one small cog in the machinery of growth and development that transformed England into an industrial and urban nation. He made no great innovation; but with skill, vision and diligence he inserted himself into the spaces for opportunity being opened up in a changing society. He was a classic market-maker; taking and turning to his own account and advantage the gaps and separations between markets of supply and demand that formed between the nation's scattered cities, towns and villages. Every day he made judgements and connections, shouldered risk, and, perhaps above all else, laboured hard to bring together buyers and sellers, claiming profits as a due reward for the work he did in making trade happen. Market intermediation has often been seen as an essentially parasitic activity, creaming off the fruits of others' productive labour. Conservative radical William Cobbett certainly saw it that way, describing middlemen as 'locusts' who 'create nothing, who add to the value of nothing, who improve nothing, but who live in idleness, and who live well, too out of the labour of the producer and the consumer'.[1] So far as John Shaw was concerned, Cobbett was certainly wrong about the idleness of the middleman and modern theory would hold he was wrong also about the function and value of market intermediation. Factoring represented the vital and indispensable yeast that brought ferment and growth to the economic system.

This chapter will trace the growth and development of the business started by John Shaw as a young man at some point in the first decade of the nineteenth-century (by 1805 at the latest). It will give an account of the scale and scope of the firm, its evolving form and organization, of the intellectual, social and moral foundations of those forms, and of the skills, capacities and resources on which it depended. It will give a sense of the way in which day-to-day activities were carried out and, at the same time, of the challenges and risks faced. For the most part, this is a story of caution, of change and growth that happens bit by bit, step by small step. But one event stands out, the formation in 1834, by the partnership of John Shaw and Henry Crane, of the firm of T.E. Thomson and

Co. The birth of this Calcutta-based merchanting and retail house represented a moment of revelatory and revolutionary change and set in train a pattern of growth through diversification that was to be followed down through much of the rest of the firm's long history. The significance of this event to the further growth and development of the firm demands that it be given extensive treatment and thus Chapter 4 will be devoted to this dramatic entrepreneurial act.

We will begin though by setting the economic, business and social context within which Shaw worked to carve out his entrepreneurial opportunities. Here the emphasis must fall on the regionally embedded and regionally variegated nature of English economic growth and development in the late eighteenth and early nineteenth-century. It was regionalization that made the work of factors like John vital.

Regions, Industries and Markets

Industrialization is often thought of as leading to greater homogenization and convergence across regions, nations and societies – and, perhaps, in the long-run, it does. But, industrialization in England emerged from and, for many decades, profoundly intensified a pattern of pronounced regional economic and industrial specialization. The nation became a highly ornate patchwork of industrial districts; some of them famous: cotton textiles in Lancashire, woollens in Yorkshire, pottery in North Staffordshire, coal and iron in South Wales and Teeside, steel, cutlery and edge tools in Sheffield, jewellery in Birmingham. Others have less renown but were no less determinedly concentrated: watches and other fine instruments in Prescot, Merseyside, hatting in Warrington, gloving in Worcester, boot-making in Northampton, chemicals in Widnes, glass in St Helens. No matter what their eventual fates, these industrial specialisms live on in regional and town identities, physical environments, even the fond nicknames of football and rugby teams.[2] As Jon Stobart would have it, we need, if we are to understand industrialization, to highlight 'the importance of geography as a cause as well as a consequence of historical change'.[3] John Shaw's hard commercial travels made him all too painfully aware of this inescapable fact, but the differences were strikingly obvious to most contemporaries. Sharing intelligence with her two sons, one on the road and the other apprenticed in Liverpool, John's mother, Elizabeth, wrote to him to observe how 'From your account of Manchester William thinks it must be like L'pool; there all is of a continuall hurry and bustle, not unpleasing I think to the young and healthy; what a contrast to Penn'.[4] But this was more than just the inevitable contrast between Manchester and sleepy rural Penn (site of the Shaw family home in south Staffordshire). Thus, brother William himself wrote to John to relate how:

Your Old Friend Joseph Osbourn ... says this [Liverpool] is the first place for business in the Kingdom and wishes it had been his lot to have been placed here instead of Wolverhampton. He says the business of Birmingham and Wolverhampton is nothing to this which I am sure is very true. We do quite as much business as any three in Wolverhampton in the retail way and it is a most flourishing town.[5]

At almost exactly the same time, to the north in Lancashire, the family of Elizabeth Wilkinson, John's future bride, were equally alive to the necessity of searching out those places teeming with activity and potential. Elizabeth's eldest brother Richard had moved to London to pursue a career in banking, from whence he reported that 'I find myself more comfortable in London than in the country as there is more Trade, a greater insight into all the different Branches of business, as such much more improvement may be made by a young person in my situation'.[6] Such contrasts and differences as these represented opportunities to be leveraged – by individuals, firms and regions.

Moreover, the forces that promoted specialization were subject to powerful, self-reinforcing dynamics that tended only to deepen and strengthen regional focus. Interlocking functional activities, knowledge spill-overs, innovative activity and its ready emulation, externalized economies of scale and scope – the beneficial system-like effects of many small firms working at related trades in one place – , Alfred Marshall's famous 'industrial atmosphere'; all of these effects worked to generate powerful virtuous circles of regionally centred economic and industrial growth and commitment.

If industrialization did not produce a uniform economic landscape then there is a second, conjoined, myth about the 'industrial revolution': namely that it involved traumatic, cataclysmic rupture with past practices and forms of business activity. Factory and steam dramatically supplanted cottage and the kick-wheel. In fact, some of the industrial districts and economic regions most powerfully associated with industrialization displayed very real, deep-seated continuities with the past. Artisanal skill, workshop settings, human brawn and micro-scale remained the norm. Wedgwood's Etruria and Boulton's Soho, splendid, large new factories both, were the exception, not the norm, both nationally and in their local contexts. For the most part, growth happened extensively rather than intensively. This was certainly true of the Staffordshire Black Country from whence John Shaw emerged to tramp and ride the pitted roads and tracks of northern England. Here, a constellation of hamlets, villages and towns coalesced to form a myriad of centres focused on metal and metalworking. Overwhelmingly organized on a small-scale and in workshops this ferment of industrial activity churned out a vast array of producer and consumer goods: nails, screws, locks and handles, pots and pans, and a thousand other items.

Of course, London – itself host to a mass of micro-clusters around various craft and fashion led sectors – dominated this scene; a great spider sat at the centre of a web of finance, production, consumption, tastes and trends. But its far-reaching shadow didn't stifle the flourishing of newly vital urban centres throughout the provinces. 'Industrial revolution' was matched by an urban renaissance that also provided the seat of 'consumer' and 'retail' revolutions. Provincial did not have to equal peripheral. Tying all of this together was a powerful compulsion, an over-riding need to integrate. As regions found themselves becoming ever more focused and specialized they faced two demanding challenges; to source those products and commodities no longer produced locally and to find evermore outlets for that now being produced in a rich abundance that was far beyond the capacity of the local economy to absorb. Specialization and integration were as inseparable, as fused together, as two sides of the same coin. But this integration did not happen easily or naturally. Moreover, most producer firms were far too small and stretched to contemplate undertaking this difficult work themselves. Further specialization was needed. A massive, and largely under-researched, undergrowth of functions and infrastructure emerged to handle the work of integration; the country banking system, paired with London acceptance houses, quays, wharves and warehouses, carters and canal carriers (never mind the canals and toll-roads themselves), coaching inns and commercial hotels. It was in these spaces that John Shaw operated. And in bringing buyer and seller together he took on a range of risks, physical and financial; profit was his just reward for making sure that the trade necessary to growth happened.

The Foundations of Family Enterprise

John Shaw began his working life around 1799 or 1800 apprenticed to a Mr Sparrow – most likely the William Sparrow and Sons, factors, of 25 Worcester Street, Wolverhampton, recorded in a trade directory of 1818 – for whom he worked as a commercial traveller.[7] His brother William was similarly apprenticed to Henry Pooley and Thomas Walker, ironmongers of Liverpool, in 1801. William's indenture stated that he was to 'neither buy nor sell' on his own account but there is a neat symmetry to the boys' chosen professions, perhaps in the hope that they might at times be able to help each other out.[8] John and William's father was a farmer and maltster but it seems there was a clear determination in the family (almost certainly driven by their mother) to keep the boys out of what were perfectly respectable ways of making a living and a life. Though not immediately obvious, given the family background in age-old agricultural livings, commerce was chosen as the way forward.

The wellspring for this shift, which would eventually take John far beyond his roots, was a yearning, restless maternal ambition that stressed, in equal measures, virtuous hard work, pride and independence. These were then the classic bourgeois and Christian verities of thrift, application, struggle and self-determination and self-improvement. 'Industriousness' was to be the watchword in all that John was to do. There was thus inculcated in John a strong sense of what it was to be a man in the world – and in the eyes of the world. They were not always lessons that John took to easily, for his mother's letters hint at the shock and dislike John felt at being plunged into working life on the road as Mr Sparrow's apprentice. In these letters from his mother John is constantly urged onward, his spirits bolstered through an admixture of stern admonition and tender parental affection. They evince a view of this earthly world as one of challenge and temptation:

> We much wonder you dislike travelling; pluck up your spirrits; put on a proper degree of modest assurance; and be what I hope to see you; an active tradesman; and a noble virtuous character; then shall Glory in my child; tho' plung'd in ills and exercis'd in care, yet never let the noble mind despair that a gracious God by his preserving Grace may conduct you in innocence and health to the bosom of your family; is your affectionate mothers dayly prayer.[9]

The context for this life-work of betterment was simultaneously Christian and familial.[10] Exemplars from within the family circle were advanced and recommended. Cousin 'Evan is a pattern of economy which I wish you to coppy, his filling up his time is equally good, he'll make a valluable man, two of his Evenings (after the warehouse is shut up) he devotes to the study of French, two more to reading, to more to learning to play on the German flute, the seventh is allways spent as you know in the servise of his maker'.[11] The lessons were oft repeated: 'In all your time whether in business or otherwise engag'd remember the Eye of God is upon you, and that your most secret thoughts lie open to him, you will then never dare to do amiss'.[12] Watchfulness against the 'inbred corruptions of fallen nature' was ever necessary.[13] But this constantly present vigilance was to be directed both inward and outward: 'I hope my dear John has no need to be reminded of his public or private duties'.[14] Salvation was not to be found in pious retreat. Indeed, John's mother was adamant that 'I have such an opinion of Industry that I think no person of either sex can be good if they are not industrious'.[15] As John's 'dislike of travelling' continued to manifest itself his mother pointedly asked 'What my dear youth do you propose to yourself, sure an inactive life you don't wish for?'[16]

Critically, this sense of the goodness of labour was mixed with a more worldly pride:

> For goodness sake what are you made of; you are no Edwards [his mother's maiden name]; remember upon this your first journey in a 'new way to you', you will stamp your chariskter for a trade's man; I wish I was at your elbow, [I] would endevour to rouse your spirits if you really possess anny.[17]

One can only imagine how the young John, discouraged and alone on the road, received these unsweetened parental injunctions.

Perhaps similar letters from John's father have simply not survived; nonetheless the reader is left with a strong impression that it was Elizabeth Shaw who was the dominant force within this family. She seems sometimes to strain against the constraints and limitations that society placed upon her as a woman born in the mid-eighteenth century. John's mother's understanding of the ways of the world was, in modern terms, explicitly gendered:

> My advice is to be warm in the pursuit of Business, if you meet with repulses follow up and with a chearful countenance and modest resolution you will carry the point – you will say I know nothing abought it, but this much I know, that if nature had form'd me of the other sex I would have made a handsome competency [living] ere now; little rest by day and less slumber by night would I have allow'd myself till I had gain'd (by the Blessing of God) the right path; perseverence perserverence with a steady resolution my dear boy will do wonders.[18]

It must have been at his mother's knee that John learnt the deep respect for women and their capacities that he was to constantly display in his marriage to Elizabeth Wilkinson.

Another vital lesson he learnt was that a man should rely only on himself and his own virtue and hard work. This lesson showed itself throughout his life in his attitudes to the proper conduct of a life in business. Perhaps the deepest lesson was that probity and self-respect were all; thus as he told Elizabeth during their courtship 'there is nothing positively worth having in this life that is to be purchased with the loss of our own esteem'.[19] But the most immediate manifestation of this tenet of self-reliance was revealed in a marked preference for particular forms of business organization. Here were the foundations of a very personal capitalism. John could not have stated more clearly the implications of these foundations when he boldly declared to his future bride that 'I have a very great objection to partnerships unless some very great advantages are held out'.[20] Thus was even this most limited form of reliance on others condemned; it was not an objection he was alone in.[21] In business all burdens – financial, mental and physical – and rewards were to borne alone, if at all possible. The honest business man looked first and foremost to his own resources.

At the same time as John Shaw was imbibing and absorbing these tenets from his mother, Elizabeth Wilkinson was receiving very similar lessons from her own family; themselves deeply involved in personal and familial capitalism as retailers in the Lancashire towns of Colne and Rochdale. Here the role of instructor was taken by brothers as well as parents. Thus in the spring of 1803 Elizabeth's older brother Richard wrote to her from London, telling her that 'It gives me great pleasure in hearing of your Industry and Assiduity in assisting your Parents by alleviating in a Small Degree their Toils and Labours. I hope you will continue it and endeavour still more to excell in Industry, which will be the first and best qualification you can attain'.[22] Here we see the same respect for the dignity of labour and family to which John had been raised. Elizabeth's assiduous toil took the form of helping in the family ironmongery shop in Colne, before moving to Rochdale to live with her brother Thomas, no doubt both to keep house and work in his grocery shop as required. And when crisis struck a part of the family business interests then Elizabeth's aid was essential: 'My Bror [John] could not do without someone to superintend the house and assist in managing his concerns – either my Mother or [I] must go. Therefore without deliberating a moment I propos'd to do for him what I could'.[23] The centrality of female work to the family enterprise is undeniable. Similarly, when John condemned partnerships she concurred: 'Partnerships are as you justly observe dangerous things but I hope in this instance it will prove advantageous to both parties' – being in this instance, Elizabeth's brother John and their cousin John Spencer. The advantage was held to lie in the classic family business strategy of pooled resources:

> My bror ... will require a much larger sum to begin business with than my father offers me – especially were he to begin alone and my Cousin has no money of his own – but then my Uncle John kindly offer'd to lend John Spencer 500 – My father will give John 300 and lend him two more ... They will then have a thousand to stock their shop with.[24]

If John sought a wife well versed in the values and realities of small family business then he chose well.

But, also as in John's family, aspiration was permitted and betterment sought. Elizabeth's eldest brother Richard had already left Lancashire for London in order to pursue a career in banking, and brother John soon followed, seeking a 'berth' in a 'respectal house ... either in ... Wholesale or Retail ... I shall take the first that turns up in either line. I have not been spending my time idly since I came up. I have been improving myself in Accounts and other branches of Learning, besides getting a knowledge of the town which is requisite for every one who goes into a retail house'.[25] Critically, these aspirations were explicitly extended to Elizabeth as well, who had been afforded a good education at a Mrs Chapman's establishment at Gomersall, close to Leeds. Certainly, given their own occupations, the family must have considered shop-keeping a respectable living but when (false) rumours reached brothers Richard and John that Elizabeth was to be married to a Mr Laycock the two were quite 'discomposed' and their mutual acquaintance, Mr Lomax, reacted with near horror: he 'lifted up his hands and said Good God it surely can't be true, and what a pity it was that a Girl of your education should be cag'd to a back of a Grocery counter'.[26]

But ambition had always to be balanced with prudence and modesty.[27] Moreover, Elizabeth well understood that the conduct of a business could impact on a family both materially and in terms of its reputation. John Shaw had for some time had dealings with both Elizabeth's father and her brother Thomas, indeed it was through these connections that they had met, and she felt it acutely when her brother was unable to speedily pay his debts to John:

> I feel asham'd that my bror has not been able to send you your money yet. The truth is he is very poor and every time he gets a little someone fetches it away directly – I hope it will not be long ere he remit you ... [he] is taking stock ... He is sadly afraid lest he should be behind hand.[28]

The exigencies and perils of independent business life were ever present and all too obvious.

These then were the foundations, familial, religious, moral, on which John, first alone and then in partnership Elizabeth, was to begin building his and their life in business. Business was something to be done for and by oneself and one's loved ones and dependents. If rewards were expected then responsibilities and risks were also to be shouldered. The prize was as much self-esteem and independence as it was wealth and comfort. Both wealth and comfort were to be slow in coming. John had many very hard years of work ahead of him as he contemplated the future in 1805, by which year he was in business on his own account.

Early Years, *c.* 1805–15

As already stressed a factor's economic role is to bring together buyer and seller. In the early nineteenth-century this could only be effectively accomplished face-to-face, for it was only in this way that relationships could be built and the system function efficiently. The factor's business life thus revolved around the routine of long selling journeys. Some of the most important early records of John Shaw's firm are a series of seventeen 'Journey Books' covering the period 1810–15 (in which year, despite his stated aversion to them, Shaw entered a long-lived partnership with employee and salesman Henry Crane).

These 'Journey Books,' which are in fact relatively simple logs rather than diaries or journals, allow us to reconstruct the firm's pattern of activities over a number of years, particularly with regard to relations with customers. Specifically, they reveal the planned, systematic, routine and seasonal nature of the factor's business in the early nineteenth-century. The books demonstrate how the firm undertook four selling journeys per annum, each following one of two alternative routes: the 'Kendal Journey' took place each year in late winter/early spring and late summer and the 'Salop [Shropshire] Journey' in early summer and early winter. In the period covered by this section of the archive the 'Salop

Journey' evolved to become known as the 'Liverpool Journey', a change in title that reflected a very real change in strategy and orientation as that great port city quickly emerged to become one of Shaw's most important and valuable destinations. Between them the two journeys, though showing some overlap in routes and coverage, took in considerable portions of North and North-west England. The 'Kendal' journey, covering North Staffordshire (the Potteries in particular), parts of North-east Cheshire (such as the so-called Silk Triangle centred on Macclesfield), much of Lancashire, Cumbria, West and South Yorkshire and Derbyshire, was certainly the most extensive. In contrast the 'Salop Journey' wound its way through South Staffordshire, Shropshire, Cheshire, South-East Lancashire, returning to the Black Country via another trip through North Staffordshire. In time Liverpool was added to this circuit. Scattered references in later records suggest that in time the North-east of England was added to the firm's destinations, but there is no indication of the firm looking South or East from its Midlands location.

The principal purpose of the journeys was twofold: first, the solicitation of new orders and, second, the settling of existing accounts. A third, perhaps equally important purpose must have been the bilateral exchange of information between traveller and customer with regard to demand, taste, general economic conditions and the standing and status of specific customers, existing and potential.

We will examine in detail what these records can tell us of relationships with customers in Chapter 6, which focuses on the totality of the firm's connections in order to illuminate the embeddedness of business within the socio-economic fabric of early nineteenth-century life. Here we concentrate on giving a sense of the overall 'shape' and scale of its trade. These journeys were lengthy and demanding affairs. When the traveller (very possibly John himself) set off from Wolverhampton on the morning of 12 February 1810 (the earliest journey covered by the extant records) he had ahead of him 34 days of travel, during which time a total of 73 customers, running accounts to the value of £1,079 15s. 8d. and located in 34 cities, towns and villages would be visited. If anything the work-rate only increased over the period covered by the records. Journeys in the period 1810–12 lasted on average for slightly less than 35 days, but in the period 1813–14 they had been extended to an average duration of 47 days. As a result the average value of accounts running at the time of a journey grew, in the same periods, from £3,247 to £5,223, an increase in the order of 60 per cent.

As already noted, the geographic coverage achieved was impressive. Equally striking is the diversity of the places visited; from the largest cities to small villages, from those rooted in agriculture to the most advanced manufacturing centres of the day. Shaw's work illustrates perfectly Neil McKendrick's claim that 'the prosperity of Lancashire cotton manufacturers, London brewers, Sheffield cutlers, Staffordshire potters, the toy makers of Birmingham, were based on sales to a mass market'.[29] And this mass market was to be found not only in the great modern metropoli of Manchester, Liverpool, or Leeds, those beacons of the dawning industrial age, but were also to be found in ancient country towns, either those according to Stobart performing a 'gentry' function, such as Nantwich, or a 'servicing' function, such as Middlewich.[30] Here we see how Shaw's work meshed with, depended on, and contributed to an ongoing urban revolution. Indeed, of the thirty towns and cities showing the fastest growth in the urban hierarchy of North-west England during the late eighteenth century, Shaw visited twenty-seven (90 per cent). The three not visited, Malpas, Frodsham and Clitheroe, were amongst those that had shown the lowest levels of percentage growth across the preceding period.[31]

Moreover, examining the data from two sample years (1812 and 1814) suggests that smaller, older, less industrial, or simply more far-flung locations could be just as valuable to Shaw as newer, high-growth urban centres.[32] Ranking locations by value of accounts (with Manchester as the most important destination valued at 100) reveals that the top ten included not only Manchester, as already indicated, and other essentially industrial towns such as Sheffield, Blackburn and Rochdale (where we know John did business with Elizabeth's brother Thomas) but also, ranked fifth and sixth respectively, Ulverston and Kendal. Extending the analysis shows the top twenty locations by value of account in 1812 to also include Oswestry, Wrexham and Ellesmere. Just as these inclusions may seem surprising then it is worth noting some omissions from this list, including Chester, Liverpool and Warrington, all then thriving centres occupying a significant place in the urban and retail landscape of the North-west. The provincial was, in this sense, far from peripheral.

This story largely holds true for 1814 as well, with the significant exception of the rapid rise of Liverpool to become Shaw's most important destination by total value of accounts. It is interesting to see from the full run of Journey Books how slow, patient work in cultivating new customers in the burgeoning port, which John knew to offer rich pickings from intelligence gleaned from his brother's earlier apprenticeship there, had eventually paid rich dividends. Potential customers had been gradually converted in to actual customers, their overall numbers growing, as did the value of the accounts that many of them were running. The growing centrality of Liverpool to Shaw's trade portrays him as fully capable of deliberate, targeted strategy rather than mere reactivity or plodding routine.

Customers in all locations were overwhelmingly comprised of small businesses, largely organized as sole proprietors, operating either a primary or secondary retail function. In the period 1810–15 Shaw and his traveller(s) visited a total of 525 customers. Of these occupations have been identified for 338 (74 per cent).[33] 244 (46.5 per cent of all customers and 63 per cent of those identified) operated retail shops – fully 231 (44 per cent and 59.5 per cent) were ironmongers and the remainder either grocers (7) or toy shops (6). Given his trade in Black Country metal wares this profile is hardly surprising. A number of trades also formed a significant part of the customer base though: braziers and glazers (29), white and tinsmiths (10), builders (8), clock and gun-makers (7), saddlers (4), coopers and trunk-makers (4), and cabinetmakers (3) – all of whom required locks, tacks, nails, handles, brass fittings and the like. Most of these trades-people probably operated a secondary retail function. Manufacturers visited included iron-founders, machine-makers and cutlers. A final but significant set of customers included wholesale ironmongers and other factors and merchants.

Thus, the vast majority of customers were operating 'petty' businesses – but this does not mean that they conducted a petty trade with John; many ran very considerable accounts over long periods of time. Nor were customers in smaller or more rural locations any less valuable to the firm. In fact customer type and behaviour show no meaningful variation from place to place – again we see how prosperity was derived from the complex interlocking of the English economy as a system-like whole.[34]

The constant work – and tedium – of life of on the road was complemented by the daily bustle of activity at the warehouse in Wolverhampton.[35] As orders from customers were constantly fed back by letter suppliers had to be found amongst the near numberless small producers spread across Wolverhampton, the Black Country and the wider West Midlands.[36] Buying the right product at the right price was probably as much a core competence.[37] Dissatisfaction with goods supplied could lead to returns, rebates and, potentially, a loss of future business. Equally important to customer satisfaction was prompt and secure delivery. Shaw and Crane didn't sell particularly fashion-oriented products but, nonetheless, orders were often placed with a particular selling 'window' in mind, a seasonal fair perhaps, when a town might be thronged with potential purchasers. Late or damaged goods were no good to anyone.[38] When travelling John clearly had the smooth functioning of the warehouse on his mind and frequently sought assurance that all was well at home.[39]

Little direct evidence of work at the warehouse remains. However, a warehouse account book covering the first half of 1815 gives some sense of the scale and nature of the operation. Of central importance is the number of employees. The account book details wages paid to four individuals in a period of just over six months and these include Henry Crane, who was made to be made a partner in the business in August of the same year (see the following section). E. Laws was paid a wage on a near weekly basis, typically with a sum of eighteen shillings (occasionally he was paid either less or also received larger payments not fitting the weekly schedule). Laws was perhaps the physical backbone of the warehouse

One P. Dodds was paid just once in this period (£1 in early February) suggesting he provided more casual labour. In contrast to Laws Jos Latham, though a regular employee was paid both less frequently but also considerably larger sums; £14 in late April and £6 in early May. Crane too received relatively large periodic payments; £8 in April and £10 in July.[40] Besides wages the regular costs incurred at the warehouse were quite limited in number; hay, nails and coals all appeared often, more occasional were requisites such as ink or bill stamps, but dominating all was postage, testament to the dependence of the business on a constant flow of information. This was a business focused on coordination.

During these early years then, through the tedium, isolation, hard work and discomfort of commercial travelling, at the constant risk of loss, physical as well as financial, John Shaw built a network that penetrated far and wide across northern England, putting Midlands hardware manufacturers in touch with Staffordshire potters and Cheshire gentry, Mancunian spinners and weavers, Cumbrian hill farmers and cutlers in Sheffield – and in doing so he laid a foundation for future growth, for future prosperity and for a secure life that he could share with his bride and, in time, his children. His entrepreneurship to date had formed an unexceptional but very necessary prelude to later comforts. Two years after he married in 1813, however, John took a determined step to expand the scope and organization of his business.[41]

In Partnership: Shaw and Crane, 1815–49

On 1 August 1815 John Shaw and Henry Crane, who had worked for Shaw for an unknown number of years, entered into a partnership together. We have already seen how John held a distinct aversion to partnerships 'unless some very great advantages are held out'. He must have seen great promise in the young Crane, and it was a confidence that proved well placed. The two men were to make their way in the world, side by side, as both partners and friends for more than thirty years. Together they grew John's modest factoring trade into a business of international scope, creating a pattern of expansion and diversification that was to lead after their deaths to the emergence of an impressive multifaceted and multinational company.

The agreement between them boldly declares that they entered into partnership 'in consideration of the special trust and confidence they repose in each other and in order to augment their fortunes'.[42] They promised to continue together as co-partners in the 'buying, manufacturing and selling of all sorts of Goods Wares and Merchandizes incident to the said trade' for a period, in the first instance of ten years. The document then goes on to set how the financial structure of partnership, which had been 'mutually agreed' with the aim and intention of 'more effectually carrying on the said joint trade'.[43] They were to 'bring in and put together a Capital joint stock' of seven thousand pounds in the following proportions; John to bring in four thousand pounds and Henry the remaining three. Moreover, John was to pay in the whole of his investment within eighteen months, whereas Henry's initial contribution was to be limited to the first one thousand pounds (the remaining outstanding capital to be brought in in two further payments of one thousand pounds). Both profits and expenses were to be shared in proportion to investment. John Shaw was clearly the senior partner in the concern.

Relatively few documents survive from the early years of the partnership and, for the most part, those that do suggest a business continuing with known patterns, routines and activities. We see some evidence of an extension to the routes travelled by the firm's representatives,[44] and the hiring of some new employees, but no *transformation* in the nature and character of the firm's operations or strategy. Similarly, John and Elizabeth's private letters attest to periodic perils and threats but not to crises. Partnership had bolstered reserves and resources, perhaps placed each man's prospects on a sounder, more secure basis, and rewarded Henry Crane for his prior diligence, application and aptitudes as an employee – but it had led, at best, to evolution not revolution. The pair exhibited a quiet and steady entrepreneurialism. But one remarkable survival amongst the firm's records demonstrates that this approach was no barrier to success.

The articles of partnership stipulated the books and accounts be scrupulously kept and checked – but this condition seems to have been largely honoured in the breach for in 1823 one Joseph Morton had to be employed to carry out a reckoning of the profits made since 1815. Some books must have been kept for he arrived at a figure of considerable specificity and yet was also forced to note that 'because the accounts have never been taken in 8 years it cannot be said what amount of interest is due to each partner nor in what precise years the interest has arisen'. Further, it was also clear that 'Undoubtedly Mr Shaw sustains some disadvantage from this'; perhaps such entanglements lay behind John's dislike of partnerships. Still, Morton was sanguine: 'I think [Mr Shaw disadvantaged] not to such an extent as to make it an object of much consideration'.[45] Perhaps this relaxed attitude was only made possible by the fact that total profits from the commencement of the partnership in August 1815 to March 1823 (when the calculation was performed) stood at £14,172 – 10 – 6 (£1,070,000 in 2009 using the retail price index, £11,700,00 using average earnings).[46]

It might seem from these results that rich pickings where there for the taking by young men such as John and Henry. In fact, the immediate environment in which this success was achieved was a complex and potentially perilous one. Relationships with multiple small customers had to be maintained across long distances, moreover these customers – as we have seen, overwhelmingly petty shopkeepers - were themselves often in fragile positions, enmeshed in complex, customary credit relations with many of their own customers and prey to unexpected failure.[47] When almost all of John and Henry's trades involved some element of credit constant vigilance was required and fear of losses a constant presence. John's letters home were often full of complaints as to the flatness of business and, in particular, the shortness of money: 'I have been ... very flat in spirits – things are so dreadfully flat and bad'; 'this journey will prove a most sad one both in money and orders in fact it will be neither productive of one or the other or worth going out for ... If something does not turn up for the better it will not be worth carrying on in business'; 'nothing at all to do nor any money to be laid hold of'; 'not one [letter from Henry Crane] I have had from him but what announces some heavy bad debts' (the last written during a journey so productive of orders that John was a week behind in copying them up).[48] However, these laments and complaints were tempered by a practical, non-judgemental reasoning. Striking is John's sense that bad fortune might befall anyone, even the most careful and prudent:

> [e]very now and then I am written to say this person can't pay or [is] calling his creditors together ... and then I am startled by seeing a name this well-known in the Gazette – of the former sort and named I have had two the last week whose debts amount to upwards of one hundred and twenty pounds and am fearful unless things speedily alter – and of which there appears but little prospect – I shall have more for how is it possible people can pay when they have their money locked up abroad or have it in a dead unsaleable stock.[49]

The modern reader may well expect two such rigorously, unbendingly religious people as John and Elizabeth, people for whom heaven and hell were very real places, to have exercised rigid and formidable judgement on issues of morality in the market place; but, as above, they both demonstrated nuanced and deeply compassionate views on the actions of others, even when they stood to lose personally. In the spring of 1816, for example, Elizabeth wrote to John from Wolverhampton to warn him of a local failure:

> I am truly sorry that you will sustain this loss and much more so because you lay it so much to heart. I am at a loss what to say to you respecting it. It is very very trying to toil and fag for another to run with [it] – which is but too commonly the curse at this present time and if it is asked why it is so – I am sorry because men made or speculate beyond their own capital – which is the case with Wilsons – their losses are estimated at twenty thousand pounds everybody is sorry for them and think them very worthy, honest men and yet perhaps they will be the ruin of many an honest man ... if they had not traded beyond their capital they would have lost only their own.[50]

Certainly speculation is seen as suspect – but not inherently incompatible with honesty and worthiness. Exercising the virtues of justice and compassion, Elizabeth and John showed a quiet, subtle faith in the essential honesty and faithfulness of their fellows in the marketplace. The market is acknowledged to be a complex as well as dangerous space – one that might overwhelm even the virtuous and honourable.[51] Such generosity of spirit has to be understood as located in a local culture of credit that did more than merely calculate.[52]

If chains of credit could sometimes seem no more robust than a house of cards then the situation was compounded by the competition. John indeed complained 'exceeding flat' trade was being was being made worse because we 'have got our new and strong opponents here and many others also [so] that we are continually in each other's way'.[53] It is a compelling image of the jostling one expects in an overcrowded arena. Factoring was a relatively easy trade to enter; it required neither arcane craft skills nor any great start-up capital – as a result rival travellers were often found to be crowding roads, inns and customers.

Letters from the travellers working for the firm of Goodall and Alston, Scotch Warehousemen (haberdashers) of Watling Street, London, present a vivid picture of competitive conditions on the ground.[54] In May 1830 John Alston had to report that 'Hansen has just been before me, a few days so that is rather against me' and that, later the same year, 'Cullen ... would have given me a good order but he had just given it to Henderson and McKinley the day before'. A company's own travellers presented another danger, too often tempted to abscond with both cash and lists of customers. In early 1830 Michael Goodall used £100 of his partners' money to start trading on his own account – 'This of Goodals is what always distressed me. I was afraid of it ... depend on it Mr G will do all he can against you'.[55] Thereafter, Goodall always seemed to be one step ahead; 'Goodall has been round in this direction about a week ago, he has been to Leicester, Loughbro and is gone on by Nottingham'. Just two days later, in exasperation, Alston had to report again, from yet another town, that 'Goodall was here last Saturday'.[56] Desperation could push houses to cut corners, take risks, or accept orders that they would struggle to fulfil: 'there are some of the Glasgow houses getting themselves sadly into disgrace by their not executing their orders to patterns and being so long of sending them'.[57] Worcester pin factor John English experienced similar problems and Shaw was himself regularly approached by travellers looking for a berth; many must have been tempted to try their hand at trade when employment could not be found.[58]

Compared to their counterparts in many countries then English entrepreneurs probably operated within a relatively robust institutional environment, with defined property rights, a transparent and reasonably accessible legal system and an advanced and sophisticated financial system. But malfeasance – and plain misfortune – remained common experiences.

Debate continues amongst historians as to how entrepreneurs dealt with these competitive conditions. Did ease of entry and a subsequent proliferation of many small producers and sellers approximate to the economist's ideal of

perfect competition, with many buyers and sellers leading to effective match-
ing of supply to demand via transparent pricing mechanisms readily discernible
to anyone interested in discovering them – or was it instead an environment
with many imperfections and barriers to optimal efficiency. The concept of the
network is central to both sides of this debate; one the one hand, in a world of
hyper-competitive conditions networks between and within entrepreneurs and
other institutions smoothed flows and adjustments to shocks for small atom-
istic firms without large internal reserves, financial or other, in which to base
their resilience; on the other, networks provided the possibility for collusion
and favouritism. In short, do networks work to further or to impede economic
and industrial development?[59] Moreover, how did networks arise, were they 'an
"organic" component of the environment or a creative and purposive entrepreneurial response to its constraints and opportunities? Did "association create ...
networks" or did "the shared experience of business risk [lend] momentum to
efforts to reduce it through combination"?'[60]

Part of the answer to these questions demands attention to family, friendship
and sociability, for it was in part through these mechanisms that many small
businesses met and attempted to control some of the most capricious and vexa-
tious features of the marketplace (we will examine these issues in greater depth
in Chapter 6). But in terms of how traders faced and dealt with others in the
marketplace, the dichotomy between competition and collusion is probably a
false one, instead pragmatic policies ruled the day and small-scale entrepreneurs
did what they needed to to get by; 'The environment of the late eighteenth and
early nineteenth centuries was risky, but also dynamic and rich in opportunity,
creating space for the co-existence of competition and cooperation and for
experimentation with institutional forms'.[61]

John was an individualist, averse to partnerships and shy of social intercourse
and overt attempts to form useful connections and networks, not a 'clubbable'
man at all – but he was also perfectly happy to engross another's trade if the
opportunity presented itself. One such opportunity is captured in a document
of 1820, an agreement between Shaw and Crane and Messrs John and William
Perry, two Wolverhampton based brothers who had 'for several years carried on
the trade and business of factors ... and as such traded to the North of England
and divers other places and also to North America'. The agreement laid out how
John and William Perry were to 'relinquish such trade or business to' Shaw and
Crane in return for a single payment of £300. The agreement was most comprehensive; for the single payment the brothers promised to refrain throughout their
'natural lives' from 'directly or indirectly' trading with any of their then present
customers (any breach to be punished by a payment of £50 to Shaw and Crane
for every instance). Moreover, John and William Perry promised to recommend
that all existing customers transfer their custom to Shaw and Crane, a stricture

reinforced by the transfer of the right to collect their existing trade debts to Shaw and Crane. At one fell swoop a competitor was removed from the field and a new list of potential customers gained.[62] The move was simultaneously defensive and offensive, collusive and competitive. Strategy, unsurprisingly, was pragmatic not principled. The environment demanded that the entrepreneur makeshift however he might, not least because his competitors, customers and suppliers would certainly do the same if the opportunity arose. Thus, John's warehouseman, Jos Latham, reported in 1815 that the 'coffin furniture makes have entered into an agreement not to supply any factor who allows more than 25 P.cen on that article to country ironmonger'.[63]

Conclusions

This was then a busy bustling world, demanding an admixture of diligent hard work, honesty and plain-dealing, a willingness to compromise and be flexible, alertness and canniness, perhaps even cunning on occasion, and above all else the desire and ability to turn very situation that might present itself to the best possible advantage. John, Elizabeth and Henry, as partners, and friends, might be said to have engaged in business and entrepreneurship as a sort of practical coping.

Shouldering risk and responsibility from a young age (he was twenty at most when he began to trade on his own account) John worked long and hard to establish his business on the firmest possible foundations; rooted in self-discipline, esteem and independence. Along the way, he acquired first a wife and then a family and a partner. His duties expanded as he and the firm aged, but so did the support, emotional as well as physical, that he was able to draw from the world as he constructed it. The firm became far more than a vehicle for the making of mere profit (though it did that to very good effect), instead it carried forward a set of loving, sociable relationships as we shall see in Chapter 3.

Nonetheless, the firm itself and the activities if performed remained, relatively unchanged; employees came and went, routes extended and new markets tapped, but there was no dramatic growth in scale, no step-change in what we have today learnt to call the 'business model'. By the early 1830s the firm appeared to be stuck forever in a comfortable and lucrative but ultimately confining rut. However, the events of the next few years were to dramatically reshape both the firm and the fortunes of the families of which it was an outgrowth. Those events will form the subject of Chapter 4. First though we need to understand the true foundation and purpose of this enterprise; the marriage of John Shaw and Elizabeth Wilkinson.

3 JOHN AND ELIZABETH IN LOVE

'I sigh not for grandeur – love in a cottage would suit my wishes better than a splendid mansion devoid of it'[1]

Introduction

When John Shaw and Elizabeth Wilkinson met, perhaps across the counter of her mother and father's shop in Colne in late 1810, they found a love match that was sustain them in their lives together, public and domestic, for nearly fifty years. It was this deeply personal partnership that provided the framework and the reason for their partnership in enterprise. At times passionate and at others comfortable and companionable, or contentious and awkward; and at yet others bereft and sad, it was always a relationship they had chosen. This thing that they had made was theirs in its entirety and every dimension. They showed to it and each other great commitment and, ultimately, love – even if that love was framed within an intense religiosity such that, shortly before her marriage, Elizabeth could write of her hope that 'May we strive to help each other on in the Heavenly road and by bearing each other's burdens fulfil one of the highest duties of our intended union'.[2] They embodied and lived out what historians have come to term the companionate marriage.[3]

Throughout, though, each remained absolutely distinct and unique, with a voice that rings out sharp and clear; Elizabeth fiercely independent, thoughtful, didactic, strong-willed and determined; John perhaps quieter, less confident and more anxious, but ultimately enduring, fond and sentimental. Between them marriage was a living thing that demanded giving, adapting, acceptance, and trust. It came alive in their hands. They gave themselves to it and to them it gave a central purpose in their lives. It was the pole around which hung everything else, business especially.

Marriage à la Mode

In forging their relationship John and Elizabeth inhabited what might be thought of as a marital milieu – a landscape of marriages around them on which they could draw for models and an intellectual and spiritual environment that gave instruction to young adults on the proper purposes and conduct of a marriage.[4] Crucially, when they first met, John's mother and both of Elizabeth's parents were alive; both could draw on examples of long lasting parental marriages – a relatively rare and fortunate position for, even as mortality rates improved from the later eighteenth-century, many marriages were still cut-short by death.[5]

We have little direct evidence of these parental marriages. However, ten letters from John's mother, Elizabeth Shaw (née Edwards), written around the turn of the nineteenth-century, survive, and these contain a few bleak clues. In particular, in an undated letter almost certainly from the period 1800–2, John's mother laments of her husband: 'Poor unhappy man he is, laying up a sourse [*for* source] of endless remorse. He destroys my life by inches, to say nothing of all domestic happiness'.[6] This was clearly by this stage, however it had begun, a desperately unhappy marriage. A further letter, dated 9th September 1802, perhaps gives a clue as to the origins of this unhappiness, for it alludes to a member of the household as 'A certain person of no great respectability [who] drinks so immoderately'.[7] Nonetheless, it is clear that even in these unfortunate circumstances 'domestic happiness' was held up as the ideal end and perfection of marriage, home, and family life.

In response to her unhappiness at home, John's mother poured affection, hope, and anxiety into her relationships with her children, particularly brothers John and William, who had both left home in order to forge careers; William to Liverpool, John closer to home in Wolverhampton but constantly on the road as a commercial traveller. Her letters to John as he travelled northern England are simultaneously declamatory, urgent, didactic and spiritual, austere even at times, but often also affectionate and sentimental. They close with unabashed terms of endearment for 'my much lov'd child', 'thou belov'd of my heart'.[8] Her emotional investment in John is palpable and tender, tempered only by an ever present need to impart a severe religious instruction. Abroad as they were in a wicked world she worried that without her guiding hand 'at your elbow' John and brother William might be too easily led astray from a godly, righteous path – in one piece of doggerel she envisioned John as being left not 'guarded by [her] parental arm'.[9] The child-centred approach to family that was of a piece with the companionate marriage is clearly expressed here. Similarly a small number of surviving letters from John's siblings, two apiece from brother William and sister Elizabeth, evince a warm and loving, if relatively closed, family unit.[10] Terms of endearment are simple, sincere, and freely given and the letters they circulated show care and concern for each other's health and welfare. For example William thanked John for the long tramp he had taken to ensure that a too rare meeting between the separated brothers could take place.[11]

John's mother's letters speak directly of marriage only once, noting that a 'Miss H is tomorrow to have her likeness taken. It will be then be ready my dear John if you please to solisit [*sic*], with an appendage of 2 or 3 thousand and a valluable [*sic*] companion into the bargain'.[12] Here is marriage explicitly reckoned as a bargain. Disappointed in her own desire for domestic happiness Elizabeth reverts to an older and more instrumental, pecuniary model of marriage, even if she does acknowledge that Miss H. should form a good companion. We must wonder at the impact of these experiences on John's view of marriage, in particular whether his mother's almost cloying attachment to her children, her constant urging to hard work and spiritual resolve, her anxiety and her own unhappy, unfulfilled life and marriage left John both desirous of what she had not been able to attain and fearful too of the traps – and misery – that awaited those who married carelessly.

Elizabeth's parents seem to have had a much happier marriage, though it was beset at times by mental illnesses (Elizabeth's father, in particular, may have suffered a series of breakdowns.)[13] Thus, though they had long been married, her father, Thomas, sent his wife Eliza a very doting Valentine in February 1810; 'believe me my Dear that my Heart acknowledges none but you and that my bosom owns an Ardent and Sincere Affection for you and you alone'.[14] This devotion no doubt impressed itself on the young Elizabeth, who wrote a moving note to her father on the 23rd February 1832, almost one year on from her mother's death. In it she acknowledged that 'You have been much on my mind lately. I was with you this time last year witnessing the sufferings and then the last triumphant scene of my dear mother's departure from this world of grief and sin. On Saturday ... she will have twelve months in glory – If we were favor'd with one glimpse of her happiness how should we long to be with her'.[15] This was a family bound with chains of affection and thoughtful consideration as much as by its fervent faith.

Unlike those circulating in John's family, the letters between Elizabeth and her siblings are full of excitable gossip about marriage, particularly about potential partners, either for themselves or for others amongst what seems to have been a large and highly sociable network of friends in Lancashire. It could almost be said to be a preoccupation with the Wilkinson siblings. Almost every letter is full of questions seeking confirmation of fresh rumours of impending marriage between members of their circle: in 1808 brother Thomas demands of Elizabeth 'Tell me in your next of all the Weddings and Buryings there are ab't you'.[16] Brother Richard, making his life in London, reflects often upon his own and other's prospects and as he does so he also tries to dispense brotherly advice to

Elizabeth. A letter of November 1803 cryptically suggests 'I have some thoughts of marriage next Summer, should fortune will it so, though my father seemes [*sic*] averse to the plan'.[17] In early 1806 he was boasting of a London friend who 'is going to marry a young Lady with 7000£, a very handsome you Lady indeed, and she has got a sister whom he wishes me to encounter, but I feel no inclination, being half inclined to make certain proposals elsewhere'.[18] Clearly, money could not always trump attraction. Later the same year he wanted to know 'Does my Brother John say any thing to any female, or does he intend to live a batchelor? Don't let him see this question'.[19] Again, in a letter from later in the same year, he outlined his views and expectations with startling candour:

> I have been violently attached of late with a disposition for Matrimony, but I have searched and have as yet found none that I could conceive fair enough to be the spouse of your humble servant, if the Cocknies had the Economy of the country Ladies, they would far surpass the latter, but if the former had the politeness and etiquette of these, they would far surpass the other. At all Events, I have brought my mind to this, that when I can marry a lovely Girl, with a sufficient fortune to keep herself and family comfortable, that I may then be induced to marry such a one.
>
> London is a place where a young Man may marry plenty of Money without everything else, but I am searching both. I may be sometime before I can meet with one adorned with both those golden Charms, ... I am sometimes half inclined to come and fetch Miss (W) hither, or I fear she will not meet a hero bold enough to encounter her.[20]

Richard seems trapped by the conflicts and tension of his standards and expectations and the reality of the London marriage market – in confusion his motives switch back and forth between money and making a good match, between base interests and a chivalric vision of the suitor as hero. 1807 found him equally preoccupied with the subject, jesting about competition between himself and his brother John for the affections of a Miss Walton and in the same breath seriously expressing the 'fear I shall not be able to meet with a wife in or ab't Colne if I wait much longer, the only seeming Chance for me appears to a certain Lady who has often been solicited to change her name but has never consented'. Increasing desperation seemed to be leading to increasing cynicism, for he noted that 'For where needs must they say the devil drives, I almost in my second whelpage, being this day at the advanced age of twenty four years'. In fact he was still below the average age of males at their first marriage. He concluded these meditations with the words, 'Let me advice you not to let love get the whip hand of you for if it does, you will find it a hard task Master'.[21] Behind the damage done by rebuffs, a love match remained the ideal.

Richard's next surviving letter to Elizabeth, dated 7 June 1807, concerns itself almost entirely with marriage talk; of his prospects, of his brother's, and for the first time, of Elizabeth's: 'I am ... informed that Cupid has insensibly stole upon your repose, tho' you seemed to consider yourself quite secure, you will recollect my kind caution, and for which you thanked me, tho' I suppose you had forgot it, when he found you off Guard, from what I learn he is a nice young man, but consider well before you cast the die, when once done, not be undone'.[22] How Elizabeth reacted to this advice from her, as yet unmarried, elder brother is not known.[23]

Some of Elizabeth's brothers did marry though. In a wry aside, Elizabeth's father, Thomas Wilkinson, observed in 1815, two years after her own marriage, how her brother William 'is quite taken with his wife, a famous domestick [*sic*] I assure you – very careful – he thinks none like his wife'.[24] William was no doubt taken with his new bride but 'Domestick' might also be read as code for termagant. Clearly where choice of marriage partner was left to the child to make on the basis of love or compatibility then there emerged also a source of potential tension with other, perhaps disapproving, family members. And death could still steal in to wreck conjugal hopes – Elizabeth's brother Thomas, father to two young boys, being widowed in January 1816. Thomas too had married for love, his father noting in a letter to Elizabeth that Thomas's wife 'had left a sweet savour behind her – perhaps there was never a more loving couple in Rochdale'.[25]

Both John and Elizabeth moved then in worlds intensely alive to marriage and its possibilities. Elizabeth comments often on marriages familiar to her, such as when she tells John 'I paid Mrs Midgeley the brides visit ... and was much pleased with her manners and conversation – There is something so soft and pleasing about her – Mr M put his eyes in the right place when he went a courting her'.[26] Much of the gossip suggests that this was a world ruled first and foremost by the rules of attraction rather than by the laws of economics – or the imperatives of clan and lineage. These were the middling sorts, shopkeepers, farmers, aspirant bankers and merchants, and money is far from absent from their discussions, but their young people seem to have been given relatively free rein to form attachments on the basis of mutual affection.[27] Both John and Elizabeth also knew though, through the example of the parents' and siblings' marriages, that wedlock could bring sorrow as well as solace, pain as well as passion. Marriage was the great aspiration, the most fulfilling end here on earth and the surest route to happiness, but it was also the greatest and most momentous decision, not to be taken lightly at all. Virtue (and law) dictated that it was not a step that could be reversed. Frivolous gossip amongst the young aside this was a subject of the utmost seriousness. Elizabeth herself explained to John how she thought marriage 'of so great importance that it requires the utmost circumspection and deliberation imaginable – It seems to me as if, both my present, and eternal happiness depended upon it'.[28] And yet, despite its religiosity, its industrious, middling respectability, this was still a milieu within which the idea of a companionable love match was seen as not only possible but perhaps even most desirable.

The Path to Marriage

> I confess I think the married state the happiest where congenial minds meet, because
> they bear each other's burdens, but, such an understanding is of so great an impor-
> tance that it requires the utmost circumspection and deliberation.[29]
>
> How needful ... if possible to get a companion who means to go the same way
> as yourself – then, if one should stumble they will be a ready help in times of need.[30]

As the above quotations from her letters suggest, Elizabeth Wilkinson was very
clear in her view of the nature and purpose of marriage and of the conditions
under which it would best flourish. It took John, despite the attraction for one
another that he and Elizabeth evidently felt, many months and many letters to
persuade her that it was to him that she should attach herself.[31] She warned him
early in their 'connection' both that 'you must patiently persevere ... if you mean
to obtain [my affection] for it is by that only that you can convince me of your
affectionate regard' and, simultaneously, that 'I hope you could not suppose me
capable of being married to you without affection ... I consider it one of the most
miserable states to be united to a person and feel indifference for that person – a
blessed singleness is much superior to it'.[32] If this was to be a love match then it
was also one that was hard won; as Elizabeth argued in letter of late 1811, 'Your
esteem is next to my own and if I were to lose that, I should be a pitiable object
indeed. Esteem precedes love and when that is dead the latter will not long survive'.[33] Love was no mere name for hormonal reactions but a deeply laid store
of sympathy, attachment, and fellow feeling. Moreover, marriage was not the
only destiny she could imagine for herself in life; she would rather accept spin-
sterhood, a much derided state, than a marriage without love, mutual respect,
or compatibility. Such were her feelings that she resisted even beginning a connection with John: 'I felt very backward to give you any encouragement – the
very idea of what I had suffer'd sometime before, almost made me resolve to live
single rather than run any hazard'.[34]

Separated by geography, as they were to be throughout so much of their
married life, John and Elizabeth were forced to establish and negotiate their
relationship through a correspondence. As Dena Goodman has argued, a simplistic distinction between older instrumental models of marriage and the new
companionate mode do not 'adequately take account of either the complexities
posed for young women by the prospect of marriage or the intellectual work
they did in contributing to marriage decisions'.[35] Elizabeth exemplifies this claim.
This contribution was made especially through letter-writing, which 'created a
space for women to lay out the issues, options, and dilemma ... on which their
future happiness depended'.[36] Letters then were means by which women could
position themselves as thinking as well as feeling subjects. Writing and receiving letters was important to Elizabeth. She wrote not only to John but also to

many family members and to friends, other women in particular.[37] These letters provided an opportunity to reason out her views on marriage, and on particular suitors. Letters Elizabeth received from her friend Miss Lomax in mid-1811 reveal this dialogue. Miss Lomax, thanking Elizabeth for 'placing the confidence in me you have' whilst also acknowledging that 'as the subject [marriage] is such a delicate one and as I both love and esteem you dearly I scarcely know how to write for fear I might hurt your feelings unintentionally', also steeled herself for honesty: 'I now intend my dear Friend to tell you exactly what I know of my Br[other]s sentiments because you wish me to do so'.[38] Clearly, specific advice had been sought as Miss Lomax adds 'With regard to Mr Shawe [*sic*] I would have you act as you think best for you can determine that best for yourself ... so I have told you all I know – I wish you well from my heart – and so what may you do I hope it will be for your happiness'.[39] Letters were central to friendship and sociability; Miss Lomax thanked Elizabeth for 'your dear letter' and for sending 'the box w[ith] all my old letters in it'.[40] Writing could give women, as it did for Elizabeth, a place where self-determination became possible.[41]

But if we are to allow this then we must also acknowledge that for 'women who took up their pens to write about marriage choices, there was never a clear path from the heart to happiness'.[42] Separation was a circumstance that led to much doubt, misunderstanding, and anxiety. The most immediate problem centred on the precise nature of John's religious affiliation. Elizabeth, devoutly Methodist, could not countenance marriage to a man with whom she had serious theological differences and, almost fatally for their attachment, she suspected John of Calvinistic tendencies. John, a Presbyterian by upbringing, failed time and again to convince Elizabeth that there were no serious doctrinal differences between them – particularly acceptance of Christ as Saviour.[43] Equally serious were disputes, the word is not too strong, about where they should worship, and whether together or apart, after marriage. No soon as did these vexing, crucial questions seem settled then one or the other would detect fresh doubts or nuances in a newly received letter. The issue dogged the courtship almost throughout its entire two year course. But even as these problems were talked through the young lovers too easily fell into a pattern in which John pushed hard for a promise, or appeared to doubt her affections or sincerity, threatening to provoke wounded revolt on Elizabeth's part. Proudly independent, Elizabeth valued mutual respect and felt sorely tested by John's apparent insecurities.[44]

And thus initially Elizabeth resisted John's advances, refusing to enter into a correspondence with him and then, once she had relented on that point, repeatedly warning him off.[45] Though her heart felt something, her head thought the match deeply compromised by their doctrinal differences: 'Having [your letter] before me the first thing which fixes my attention is the happiness you are anticipating in holding a correspondence with me; how frequently do we find anticipation greater than enjoyment'.[46]

Throughout, Elizabeth seems to lead a negotiated path to mutual understanding; testing John's doctrine, views, and emotions, stating her principles, recommending readings, and exhorting remembrance of the divine – even upbraiding him for his spelling and suggesting he carry a dictionary on his travels. As she was to throughout their married life, Elizabeth to some extent positioned herself as John's conscience – and as a foundational support on which he could lean when weak or tempted. She was without doubt fully justified when she asked: 'You will, at least, give me credit for candour I hope'.[47] John could have no complaint that he had been misled as to the character of his bride.

In marked contrast to the example of Isaac Holden and Sarah Sugden, a near contemporaneous Yorkshire couple who were also Methodist, middling and separated by the demands of business, and whose case was explored by John Tosh, parental or family involvement in this courtship was very limited and John notes in one letter that 'I recollect you saying you were your own mistress in this affair, as your father told me'.[48] Elizabeth's understanding of this same point is subtly different: 'When you were here you bid me remember that I was my own mistress but you did not consider that we are dependent on God and that we ought to ask counsel of him, as well as an earthly parent'.[49] Still, it is counsel not permission that is stressed. Similarly, there appears to be no discussion of money until all else is fully settled – indeed Elizabeth, confessing her anxieties, tells John 'I feel conscious that I have nothing to bring you but affection – sincere, – fervent affection'.[50] For Isaac Holden marriage, whatever it eventually became, was akin to a business deal that he negotiated with his bride's brothers. Her views, despite the fact that she was both middle-aged and married some forty years later than Elizabeth and John, seem to have been largely incidental.[51] In John and Elizabeth's case parental approval was welcome, but permission was not necessary. Elizabeth acts in starting a correspondence with this relative stranger as an independent adult: 'I just mentioned our correspondence to my Father whereat he seemed surprised – And said "were you not a perfect stranger to me?" I said I knew nothing of you but from your calling here and that I had consented to a correspondence with you in order that we might become better acquainted with each other's sentiments. You will believe me, when I say, he seem'd very anxious for the welfare of his child'.[52] The problem that Elizabeth and her family faced in assessing the suitability of this suitor is that he was almost entirely unknown to them and their social networks. Most young people, especially those in the provinces, still selected mates from within relatively restricted social and geographical circles. John Shaw was an outsider, living many miles away.[53] Certainly, he was known to Elizabeth's father Thomas as the energetic young factor who visited periodically to take orders and collects payments, a man seemingly determined to make his way in the world; but how much could this tell them of his true character, or of that of his family? As Elizabeth herself noted; 'Wolverhampton is so far from here that I know nothing of the people in the Methodist connexion' there. Across these distances even religious networks were little help. In response letters of reference were sought, even if third-parties had to be relied upon.[54]

But over the year of 1811, despite her initial grave reservations and reluctance, through letters and visits, her feelings for John grew to have great depth – charted in a relaxation in the forms of address Elizabeth and John used with one another; from 'Dear Sir' to 'My Dear and much lov'd Friend'.[55] And even when his doubts put her through the greatest anguish, her letters could still ring out with plangent sense of commitment to him:

> Suffice it to say that your assiduous and kind behaviour to me together with what I have heard and seen of you – (I am not asham'd to say) has won the affections which were once, in part, given to another ... but, if it is my lot to have you for a companion through this waste howling wilderness you never need to fear a rival in my affections – I think you have had sufficient proof of this ... I need not say what it would cost me to give up this attachment.[56]

And in quieter, less troubled periods Elizabeth could write with pleasure – and a remarkable candour and honesty – about her expectations of marriage. Sometimes too she could even tease John a little:

> If I were to take your advice and encourage this tame red robin (as his father terms him) I should not be the first that ever took a husband to mould and govern. – But if you suppose I want a husband for the sake of governing him, I must tell you that you form wrong ideas of me – I assure you I find it as much as ever I can do ... to govern myself ... – Nevertheless, I do sometimes like people to give up their wills to me when it would not injure themselves – merely for the sake of common civility – I hope you have not so much of the old Bachelor about you that you have made up your mind to have your own will in every trifle – merely because it is your will – I cannot think this of you tho'.[57]

As if he might forget the point, she on another occasion reminded him that 'Scolding has always had a bad effect upon me – inclining me to rebel – so I beg you will remember in future never to mention the word scold'.[58]

Beneath the resistance, the entreaties, the teasing there grew what Elizabeth was increasingly willing to admit; that she loved John. As she noted 'It is an old adage but not the less just that love blinds people. So if I am blinded you have nothing to do but tell me and I believe it would open my eyes'.[59] Elizabeth seemed at times almost at a loss to understand the emotions she was feeling; 'my good thoughts respecting you increase every day and I feel quite astonish'd that upon so short an acquaintance you have gain'd so much upon my affections – do you now call me reserved – or too open?'[60] It was the combination of John's persistence and the depth of her belief in the concept of Providence that had wrought this change in her; 'I should certainly have given you a flat denial and kept to it had you not continued to solicit and I began to think I might be running counter to Providence'.[61] For once, religion was on John's side. Checks were still experienced ('How is that you cannot bring yourself to think that I shall share of that happiness in you, which you hope to do in me'. If John appeared sometimes doubt Elizabeth's affection then perhaps he also doubted that he was worthy to win them. She struggled with his reserve and his obvious fits of jealousy),[62] but throughout Elizabeth strives to remain clear-sighted, conscious of the power of attraction to lead the godly astray: 'my senses were not bewildered in the mazes of love 'ere my judgment was informed of your worth ... This is my opinion of love founded upon esteem'.[63] Gradually the focus of their correspondence shifted to more practical issues; where their new home should be, how it should be furnished, how she might deal with his long absences as a commercial traveller. And yet John continued to imperil the engagement through his letters. As late as October 1812 Elizabeth was provoked to ask: 'From where did your uneasy fears, doubts and conjectures arise – Am I less in your esteem than I used to be? If not you must want that confidence in me which you are so desirous that I should place in you'.[64] John, who admitted that he had not previously formed an attachment to any other woman, constantly betrayed his inexperience as a lover.

Thus, though fewer of John's courtship letters survive than do Elizabeth's, we are struck, reading those we have, and reading the silences between Elizabeth's offerings, by a wilder, more mercurial passion in John. Even in his very first letter, though already denied her consent for a correspondence, he presses her hard: 'let me be a[llowe]d ... to renew my request for a correspondence. Do not, pray do not, deny me'.[65] His second letter, unabashed by her continued resistance, displays the same urgent passion; 'I have waited in conformity with your request until my stock of patience is quite exhausted and that is the case I trust I shall stand acquitted of not acting as you wishes'.[66] By only his fourth extant letter John is looking forward to married bliss with 'my dear girl':

> But however happy I am in seeing or hearing from you, it bears little proportion to that pleasure I anticipate in of ere long I hope being permitted to call you mine, of the happiness of transplanting you into the bosom of a family where you will be received with that love and affection which will be due to one whose happiness and welfare will be closely interwoven with their own.[67]

As Elizabeth, perhaps flustered and vexed by the ardency of his claims upon her, suggests the correspondence be broken, John's letters became only more impassioned. Soon he was driven to admit 'of feeling so strong and feverish an attachment to you'.[68] The contrast with Elizabeth's slowly-growing affection, rooted in a strengthening esteem, could hardly be more pronounced. Elizabeth

herself admitted 'My strongest friendships have been of the growing kind –
indeed, I can not suddenly form an acquaintance, much more such a connexion
as I am now forming but when once formed nothing save dire necessity can compel me to give up those I have consider'd as my friends'.[69] She was to prove the
truth of her words throughout their marriage.

With time John's effusions did become both more measured and, perhaps,
more convincing, for the most part at least. Typical is a passage from a letter of
November 1812:

> One thing I must and will assure you of – that is my sincere and unaltered affection
> – will this do any good – could you my Dear Girl look into my heart and read my
> every thought and feeling then it would not – it could not fail of doing you good
> – you could then be fully convinced how closely your happiness, welfare and com-
> fort is connected with my own. What a relief it is to the mind to have a sincere and
> faithful friend to whom we can at all times communicate our thoughts and unbosom
> ourselves – one who will share in all our joys and be a source of comfort to us in all
> our trials.[70]

When Elizabeth at lasts consents to name the day on which they will be married,
John becomes rhapsodic: 'I shall ... look forward to it as the happiest day of my life
... [it will have] wafted me into the presence of my best and dearest friend and companion – my better half ... united in inseparable bonds of love and affection ... Oh
happy, happy state to be united with such congeniality of mind and soul'.[71] John
had learned to tame his sometimes unrestrained passions so as to win his bride.

The question remains as to how we might understand Elizabeth and John's
courtship and marriage historically; the modernity – if that is the appropriate
term – of the way in which these two people forged their relationship. Did their
marriage represent the epitome of the eighteenth-century affective, companionate marriage in those last decades before it was to be closed off as a possibility
by a Victorian resurgence of patriarchy? In what way did these two people relate
to each other not simply as individuals in love, but as men and women? How,
indeed, did the shift to companionate and affective marriage impact men and
women's relationships? Here there are important disputes. Stone states clearly
his belief that greater freedom of choice, and thus greater emotional commitment to spouses, had 'its effect in equalizing relationships between husband and
wife'.[72] For Goodman, however, companionate marriage, at least in its French
Enlightenment guise, represented just a subtler version of an ancient device that
offered freedom to men and servitude to women. In the ideal Roussean marriage
'the husband was supposed to be the master and the wife his dutiful second'.[73] As
ever, a wife's happiness depended not on her freedom of choice in marriage partner but instead on 'how the man she married exercised the power he now held
over her, and her own willingness to accept that power as legitimate'.[74] Going
further, Vickery and others have seriously undermined the whole chronology

laid down by Stone. As a result we need to pay much closer attention to practices on the ground as lived out by the men and women of the past. The example of Elizabeth and John allows us to that for one case.[75] In fact they provide us with a glimpse of those intermingling forces and traditions that make Stone's thesis increasingly difficult to accept.

On the surface, Elizabeth would appear to have admitted absolute acceptance of the power – legal, social, and cultural – that marriage accorded John as her husband. She says most clearly: 'I will never be inclined to dispute the mastership with you (it will be put out of my power in the Church)'.[76] However, we have already seen how letter-writing could allow women to constitute themselves as active subjects with agency and Elizabeth's treatment of the relationship between men and women in marriage, their dispositions, needs, and respective roles, is both more complex and subtler than her apparent accession to John's power would suggest. Her attitudes undoubtedly reflected both currents of thought and concrete practices around her – but also her own character and interpretations. First, she clearly believed and repeatedly affirmed, the tenet that love, rooted in esteem, was the only sound basis for marriage – and that love must precede rather than grow out of matrimony: her sister-in-law had asserted the belief that "a woman should not be in love till she is married – or at least keep it secret both from herself and her lover" – are you of her opinion, mine is quite the reverse'.[77] Her views seem to chime perfectly with those of Daniel Defoe who had, earlier in the eighteenth-century, succinctly stated that 'matrimony without love is the cart before the horse'.[78] It was her belief that 'particularly women ... have need of both loving and being loved fervently'. It is hardly surprising that her views were thus gendered, and this comment on the particular nature of women hints at some conventionalities in her thought.

This disposition can in part be attributed to the milieu in which she moved; respectable, aspirant, and deeply religious. These views were reinforced by available literature. Elizabeth was a practiced reader who often mentioned in her letters the lessons she had derived from particular authors.[79] One book she acknowledged as having read was Thomas Gisborne's *An Enquiry into the Duties of the Female Sex* (1797), though only 'some years since ... [and] I do not recall anything in it more than I lik'd it ... well'.[80] For Gisborne, an Anglican divine and abolitionist, the 'effect of the female character is most important. First, In contributing daily and hourly to the comfort of husbands, of parents, of brothers and sisters, and of other relations, connections and friends, in the intercourse of domestic life, under every vicissitude of sickness and health, of joy and affliction'.[81] This was a very conventionally drawn role for women based on clearly delineated differences in character, temperament, and aptitudes between the sexes.

At times Elizabeth, as we have already seen, seemed to accept this dispensation: 'I think it a woman's duty to obey her husband's reasonable requests (because God commands it)'. But she also frequently, subtly undercut her apparent docility. In this respect, it is significant that as well Thomas Gisborne she also read Hester Chapone, whom Stone quotes as arguing that:

> I believe it ... absolutely necessary to conjugal happiness that the husband have such an opinion of his wife's understanding, principles and integrity of heart as would induce him to exalt her to the rank of his *first and dearest friend*.[82]

Chapone presents a very different perspective on gender relations in comparison to the conservative and conventional Gisborne. The accomplishments Chapone recommends as suitable to a young woman included: the natural sciences, household management and book-keeping (significantly, shortly before their marriage, Elizabeth, who already had extensive experience working in the family's shops and was helping run her bachelor brother Thomas' household, tells John she has been studying household accounting). Sentimental novels are to be eschewed – and much as we may detect passion in Elizabeth's correspondence the merely sentimental is entirely absent.[83] It is a testament to Chapone's radicalism that her advice manuals for young girls, particularly *Letters on the Improvement of the Mind, Addressed to a Young Lady* (first published 1773 but republished multiple times across succeeding decades) was favoured by Mary Wollstonecraft.[84] Elizabeth tells John that Chapone's book 'appears to be excellent, but not upon so large a scale as Gisborne'.[85] Nonetheless, she takes the time to quote a passage that seems of particular significance to her:

> In speaking upon friendship – she says "The highest kind of friendship is indeed confin'd to one: I mean the conjugal, which in its perfection is so intire and absolute a union of interest, will, and affection as no other connexion can stand in competition with" – I feel a hope we shall enjoy it in its perfection.[86]

The whole of the courtship, from Elizabeth's perspective, may be read as having been conducted according to the principles set out by Chapone; of establishing with John such an understanding of Elizabeth's qualities. Elizabeth carefully elucidated for John her views and principles and, perhaps most importantly, what she saw as the fundamental, almost ineluctable features of her character and John in turn acknowledged 'that degree of frankness and candour that I cannot but admire'.[87] That is, she wished to set out those elements of *her* with which John would have to come to terms if they were to live together happily. For example, if she thought it right to respect John's 'reasonable requests' then that was also because she 'would not consent to marry a man I did not consider reasonable. I considered this over before I promis'd to become your wife'.[88] It was not to *any* man that she would submit. Almost on the eve of marriage John was gently reminded that command would rarely work with her:

See how submissive I am to intreaty – When you are invested with authority you
will find (if you should ever wish to try) that a command will not go half so far with
a woman as an intreaty – but I hope your curiosity will not lead you so far out of the
beaten path.[89]

And when his curiosity did lead him out of that path then she resisted. When,
in an early letter, John complains at her delay in writing and tells her that 'I feel
almost inclined to scold' she replies with great directness: 'Scolding has always
had a bad effect upon me – inclining me to rebel – so I beg you will remember
in future never to mention the word scold'.[90] At times she could so far as to reject
the conventional, refusing for example to take part in the custom of bride visiting or to bring with her to Wolverhampton a female friend from Lancashire.[91]
In this independence she had an ally in a Miss Chafer, who was to marry her
brother Thomas in late 1812. Miss Chafer, who did 'not think men ought always
to have their own way', would not, when it came to her wedding day, 'say obey
– she only said bay and never said I will'.[92] Elizabeth was comfortable enough
to tease John that 'I suppose you intend to give attention when I ought to pro-
nounce the word 'Obey'.[93] Conventions and customs were never going to mask
entirely an independence of mind that Elizabeth herself sometimes saw as stub-
bornness. Elizabeth thus went to great lengths to carefully set out the degree of
freedom and equality she expected to enjoy within the matrimonial state. Her
apparent accession to John's nominal power was, at best, partial.

Married Love

With pleasure and satisfaction I look forward to the time when we can sit under
our own vine and fig tree none daring to make us afraid.[94]

If time continues to have the same effect that it has had, shall I not love too
much?[95]

Lawrence Stone has argued that across the eighteenth-century 'more and
more [potential spouses] began to put the prospects of emotional satisfaction
before the ambition of increased income or status. This is turn also had its effect
in equalizing relationships between husband and wife'.[96] Of course, Stone's
arguments have been significantly qualified, or even rejected, but even Amanda
Vickery, one of his most effective critics, has concluded that 'The eighteenth
century saw a sustained, secular celebration of romantic marriage and loving
domesticity'.[97] The marriage of John and Elizabeth Shaw exemplified such virtues and values as they flowered in the final decades of the Georgian period.
The difficult and sometimes very painful work Elizabeth and John had done in
preparing the ground for marriage reaped a rich harvest. As Elizabeth herself
noted, 'I don't think our courtship at all too long – Time serves to shew upon
what foundation love is built'.[98] It is remarkable how quickly and completely the

doubts, slights, and insecurities that characterized their courtship disappeared once they were married. Moreover, marriage itself seems to have wrought an immediate transformation in Elizabeth and John's emotions and relationships. Elizabeth had always feared the absences that would be involved in marriage to a commercial traveller and within just a few months of marriage she found herself reflecting on how:

> Well it will be the case with us married folks now – I thought I knew what absence was before I was married but I believe I never knew rightly what it was till now – I feel as if part of [my]self was torn from me – was not about to be speedily recovered – I cannot look forward three weeks – it looks as long as three months used to.[99]

John's first extant post-marriage letter is dated 1816, three afters they were married, yet it is still rapt with love and devotion. Elizabeth had been aggrieved and pained by a longer than expected silence from John, who, in turn, is mortified and spills out his emotions in a barely controlled stream:

> Had I had the most distant idea that the time would have had such an effect upon your mind be assured my dear love it could not have happened – you should have had a dozen letters in the time ... I pray do not my dearest love entertain a thought that is has come from want of affection, from neglect, from any disrespect ... but believe me – and what language shall I make use of – I hope, sincerely hope – never will be wanting to convince you that you are as dear – ah still dearer – than ever to the man who has given you all – all his love and affection and would give you twice as much was it in his power to give more.[100]

The elapse of nearly twenty years found a little of this initial passion perhaps spent, but if anything the mutual fondness had only deepened:

> I got your of this day week on Monday last at the top of which I find a calculation of years we have been married which appears quite correct altho' I was not aware it was nineteen years past – how quickly as the time flown and should we be spared for another such a period I suppose it will not appear to have been much longer. I much fear we are neither of us sufficiently grateful and thankful for the protection and success we have so abundantly enjoyed during so long a period and hope and trust we may be more so for the future.[101]

Their marriage had become an object of reverence and thanks.

Animal Spirits

> My animal spirits got above par at Buxton and when that is the case I am generally condemn'd in my mind for it afterwards.[102]

Elizabeth seemed acutely aware that she was possessed of a passionate nature and 'have my fears lest my passions should not all times be subject to reason and religion'.[103] As Tosh has shown, we should be wary of seeing even the most religious and bourgeois of nineteenth-century marriages as sexually repressed and unfulfilling. Scattered evidence suggests that the example of John and Elizabeth reinforces this argument.

Just as Tosh has shown how sex could be enjoyed and even celebrated within the bourgeois nineteenth-century marriage so other researchers have shown levels of sexual activity among young unmarried adults of the middling classes to have been higher than might perhaps be expected for the period in which Elizabeth and John came to sexual maturity.[104] Nonetheless, virginity at marriage was probably the norm amongst the most respectable and religious sections of society. For example, the potter Josiah Wedgwood wrote to partner Thomas Bentley on 23 January 1764 to announce that 'I yesterday prevailed upon my dear Girl to name the day, the blissful day! when she will reward all my faithful services, & take me to her Arms! to her Nuptial bed! to – Pleasures which I am yet ignorant of'.[105] Yet, as Rothman observes, 'young middle class men and women possessed a degree of autonomy and privacy that allowed them to develop genuine closeness in their relationships with one another'. This is true of Elizabeth and John, who even before marriage visited one another, took country walks together, and slept under the same roof.[106] Most telling is a passage in one of Elizabeth's last letters before marriage: 'I have many things to tell you when you come [to visit] – I have a very snugg little room to put you in – it is over the shop and my bedroom upon the same floor to the front – What an indulgence – only one step into it – I used to grumble sadly at having to go so far at Br Thos'.[107] At the very least there is a flirtatious anticipation of sexual pleasure and very possibly a suggestion that they had been used to visiting one another's bedrooms. As Nelson has shown, though again for America, even the most evangelical of the unmarried young found it difficult to resist a degree of sexual contact before marriage, even if it often stopped short of full intercourse.[108]

The evidence seems to suggest that this anticipation was not misplaced and that John and Elizabeth enjoyed a satisfying sexual relationship after marriage. In contrast to the case explored by Tosh, it was Elizabeth who was both frankest and warmest in her appreciation of this aspect of their married life. Within months of being married she was telling John that in his absence 'I have been so starved in bed that last night I had an extra blanket'.[109] Frequent prolonged separation led to an unmistakeable yearning:

> Oh my dear John, I lay in bed thinking how I shall enjoy clasping you to my bosom calling you by all those names my affection can invent. I think of it till I almost imagine it a reality ... I feel as if I never should be satisfied with kissing and embracing you so you must prepare yourself for it. Nay I even talk of eating you – but at this rate I shall frighten you so I had better hold my tongue till I have you safe here.[110]

And again, 'One night I dream'd that you were locked in my embrace. The pleasure I felt awoke me [and] I was disappointed to find it nothing but a dream'.[111] Yet John also missed and hankered after her warm presence in the marital bed. In 1825, after twelve years of marriage, out on a sales journey, he found he 'would give whatever I have to find you in my chamber as if at home – a sigh is heard involuntarily as I write this last line and I must say and think no more about it as a thing impossible'.[112] Just as the long and sometimes difficult courtship, based in free choice of mate on the basis of love and affection, had laid the foundations for a strong and enduring companionate marriage so had it also laid the foundations for a mutually satisfying physical relationship.[113] The evident transparency, compatibility and equality of John and Elizabeth's marriage gave it great and enduring strengths.

Conclusion

'Your esteem and love I value – I prize more than any – more than even worldly goods'[114]

In one of his earliest letters to Elizabeth, John saw fit to quote a piece of verse, on 'the happy state of matrimony', that had been brought to his mind while 'thus contemplating scenes of future bliss':

If the stock of our bliss is in strangers' hands rested
The fund insecured oft in bankruptcy ends
But the heart issues bills which are never protested
When drawn on the firm of Wife, Children and Friends.
Tho' spice breathing gales on his caravan hover
And Arabia's whole fragrance around him descends
The merchant still thinks of the used bonds that cover
The bower he sat with Wife, Children and Friends.[115]

The conjoining of commercial, financial, and familial imagery is striking and remarkable. But it is, I believe, easily misread as comparing or even conflating family with firm. Business history would often have us place the firm before the family, subordinating the family to a subsidiary role, a supplier of important resources – trust and personnel for example – to be used by the firm. The 'familiness' of the family firm, such as John's was, becomes an important economic asset and a strategic competitive advantage.[116] A confused reading of this verse is easy, given the imagery of bankruptcy and bills. Instead, the verse is better read as a testimony to the immense superiority of the family over firm, of the superiority of loving bonds over fickle relations in the anonymous market place; of the greater depth, stability, endurance, meaning, and value of family; of the entirely different claims on the soul and on the body made by family and firm. It is family that is primary and foundational, the firm that is, at best, a resource for the family. Both John and Elizabeth, herself deeply rooted in a complex of family enterprises amongst her parents, siblings, aunts and uncles, knew this absolutely and instinctively:

> If, when you get this, you should be poreing [*sic*] over Compositions of Debtors and Bankrupt Stocks – Do you think all my nonsense will have any tendency to make you forget a few moments – forget all your cares and sorrow and think that as you love, so you are belov'd – but shall I call this nonsense? No, rather let me term it the greatest earthly bliss that can be enjoy'd where minds in unison are mutually disclos'd.[117]

It is the transient world of commerce, money, and wealth that is ethereal and 'nonsense' when set against the solidities and certainties of love. True, it is the case, as John observed, that making a living, getting on the world, cannot be ignored; he recognizes this with great and penetrating force when he asks 'for in neglecting my business should I have your best interest at heart?'[118] And yet, though the answer is, of course, no, there is also a realization that the business is a mean and hollow thing without the love that it exists to serve. This, not any functional, instrumental notion of enhanced trust and competitive advantage, is the true meaning of being in business as a family. It was a meaning and a purpose that Elizabeth and John found through the courtship, love, and marriage explored in this chapter. And in time, becoming a family in the fullest sense changed the meaning and the experience of being in business. Eventually those changes led to both the adventures and the losses we turn to next.

4 'OUR PRESENT ADVENTURE': INDIA AND BEYOND.

Introduction

By 1830 John and Elizabeth seemed to have secured a contented and fulfilling life for themselves. John might, with some justice, have claimed to have at last become that 'virtuous and active tradesman' that his mother had wished to see him be. The business of Shaw and Crane was soundly founded on the twin pillars of steady, cautious finances and the warm, sociable amity of the partnership with Henry. Both men had burgeoning families and John in particular, by now in his mid-forties, might have been forgiven for relaxing into the role of presiding paterfamilias, at work as at home. Indeed, it is easy to detect signs of a sort of quiescence in the letters he and Elizabeth exchange in this period. As early as the summer of 1826 John was encouraging Elizabeth to small indulgences: rides out 'in a chaise. I beg you will think nothing of the expense – maybe a caring physic costs more than a chaise so let me beg you will do as I request and go as often as you feel able'.[1] They probably did not think of themselves as by any means 'rich', as yet, but the tone speaks of a financial confidence markedly in contrast to the often harassed, harried and insecure figure John cut in the 1810s and early 1820s. Moreover they we were aware and appreciative of their steadily improving condition. In the summer of 1829 Elizabeth reminded John 'Don't let your spirits down to much with the badness of the times. Let us be thankful we are not so much dependent upon them as they who have to get their daily bread – We have much to be thankful for if we only reflect upon the goodness of God in our temporal prosperity'.[2] Elizabeth in effect acknowledges that they are now capitalists and thus relatively privileged. As all business people of the early nineteenth century were very aware, failure was an ever present threat.[3] For John and Elizabeth with reserves and assets carefully harvested that threat seemed both less immediate and less material now.

Besides this sense of greater material comfort though, John's letters increasingly hint of a life shifting inexorably into its later stages.[4] The letters become shot through with a nostalgia for a youth that in retrospect (and ironically, given its grinding hard work and long months of separation) appears light-hearted and carefree, when love was young and life was yet to be fully faced. This nostalgia is necessarily tinged with a certain sadness, as all nostalgia is, but also speaks of a quiet contentment, and a pride perhaps, in what had been achieved; the very prototype of the mid-Victorian ideal, an active, honourable man abroad in the world and ruling with dignity and magnanimity at home; a wife loving, dutiful and supportive, devoted to the begetting and raising of delightful children.

And yet into this stable world, so painstakingly achieved over many years, so uncertain in its attainment for so long, the partners deliberately chose to introduce an influence that had the potential to entirely overturn their lives, one with the power to wreck fortunes, one that was in fact to claim the life of a child. In the context of all their foregrounding experiences and achievements to that date, the decision taken by the partners to establish the business of T.E. Thomson and Co. in Calcutta in 1834 seems obscure and hard to fathom. The move was undoubtedly risky. Failure might have meant total ruin and failure was a very real possibility – international trade was at this time fraught with dangers both financial and physical. In fact the very opportunity that the partners in part exploited and in part created when they took this move had its roots in the crises and failures of others. This chapter will explore how that decision came about and how it unfolded, it will place the move in relation to the partnership's capabilities and strategies, and try to make sense of it in terms of wider familial and emotional dynamics.

The Road to Calcutta

The road leading to the opening of the Calcutta business was a long and circuitous one. It was never a path that suggested that this or any other particular outcome was inevitable. From 1820 or 1825 or even 1830 it would have been impossible to read forward to what the firm was shortly to become. Indeed, even with hindsight, the actions eventually taken in 1834 remain surprising and to some extent counter-intuitive. Instead, it can be characterized as an entirely emergent strategy in which intent and purpose are, at best, weak or soft presences. Holt and Chia name this form of relatively undirected or design-less strategizing as 'wayfaring', a perhaps apt metaphor for an extension of business so dependent on the vagaries of nineteenth-century ocean voyages. We may think of it as of a part with the notion of 'practical coping' that was used in the Introduction to capture the essence of the story of the original domestic business and its growth and development.

At the same time, and helping us to better understand the emergent nature of the India story, the firm was almost wholly reliant for initiative and success on its ability to draw on resources and capabilities firmly located outside the conventional boundaries of the firm or partnership. This is not say that Shaw and Crane and then T.E Thomson and Co.,[5] do not stand out as distinct and capable entities – they do – but is instead to gesture towards the way in which they stood out against a rich field of other enterprises and resources to which they were intimately tied via a variety of connections. To use the parlance of economists and economic sociologists, this was a networked enterprise. Appreciation of this characteristic of Shaw and Crane's developing Indian 'adventure' provides insight into its emergent quality because it forces us to recognize the extent to which their ability to act was, at the same time, both enabled and constrained by a much wider set of circumstances, conditions, actions and structures. Firm and context – and lives indeed – necessarily unfolded together.

Thus, the emergent and networked nature of this enterprise together demand that we complicate or add nuance to two core concepts from economics: agency and the vital concept of entrepreneurial opportunity. For the mainstream of economic theorists and scholars of entrepreneurship, opportunity is a discrete, containable concept. Opportunities exist in a set of possibilities stable for all time and entirely independent of those that exploit them or are, strictly, the discoverers rather than the creators. The principal role of the entrepreneur is to discover, evaluate and exploit those autonomous, pre-existing opportunities. The concept has little common sense appeal – and, it can be argued, it does a violence to our historical subjects. It strips away from them the ability to act, to create, and, in particular, because it insists on the fixed timelessness of opportunity, it denies to them the reality of acting in the flow of time. Here I want to argue for an approach that gives back to the entrepreneur an active, creative, imaginative ability – one of almost 'poetic power', in the words of heterodox English economist G.L.S. Shackle. This is the ability to envision a future that does not yet exist. Here we return to the impossibility of predicting of Shaw and Crane's actions of 1834 from their lives in 1830. They made their future, actively, energetically and imaginatively.[6]

But this approach might seem to give John and Henry an almost unlimited power to recreate the world anew. It lends to them a very great deal of what economists call agency; the ability to exert themselves upon the world. This too runs up against commonsense understandings of our relative powerlessness in a world that can seem implacable, unyielding, or even hostile. The counterweight to this impossible degree of agency is found in the embeddedness of the actors and firms in webs of resources, capabilities and structures; an embeddedness that demands they thread their way through to emerging possibilities, taking what they can along the way, turning to advantage the blocks, constraints and accidents thrown up as life unfolds.

The question remains; where to start? No single starting point can be truly settled on but we start with a solitary letter, uninvited and unexpected, that arrived at the Wolverhampton warehouse of Shaw and Crane in the late summer of 1827. The letter, from Sheffield merchants Joseph Rogers and Sons, was simple and direct, announcing that they had the:

> [p]leasure to introduce our friends Mr Rawson and Mr Holdsworth who have an establishment in Calcutta and are visiting Wolverhampton for the purpose of obtaining consignments to be sent out there. We have done some business through their hands and have always found them exceedingly punctual and attentive to our interests.[7]

The tone is interesting. Rogers and Sons, old and well-established correspondents of Shaw and Crane, seem anxious to appear disinterested in the matter and yet willing to lend some of their own reputation and standing to their 'highly reputable' 'friends' Rawson and Holdsworth; this is classic networking behaviour – even if business efficiency and acumen seem to weigh at least as heavily as probity, trust and friendship. Rogers further urged their recommendation by noting that Rawson and Holdsworth not only had a house in London but that Mr Rawson had 'joined the house only lately he was a Banker in Rochdale and no doubt you will recollect him'. As Rogers and Sons clearly knew, John had through both trade and his marriage to Elizabeth, long-standing connections to the business community of Rochdale.[8] Rogers continued, by offering further advice:

> [s]hould you be inclined to make a treat in that Quarter we have no doubt you would find it a very profitable business if proper selections are sent out and we should be very glad to give you the advantage of our knowledge and experience in the trade as we find the amount of Sheffield manufacturers is as much as we can attend to and there is now a probability of a great increase in the demand for Wolverhampton goods.[9]

It is important to note that the Sheffield firm's apparently disinterested stance was contingent on how they were currently placed; if their capacities had allowed then competitive instincts might have pushed them into pursuing the opening offered by Rawson and Holdsworth themselves. Thus we must be cautious in how we characterize this network behaviour; despite the various intersecting connections, and for all the talk of reputable friends, this was a network rooted overwhelmingly in ongoing business relationships and driven primarily by the diktats and qualities of punctuality, attentiveness and the prospect of profitability. Certainly interpersonal relationships were useful to establishing the connexions – but also essentially ancillary or complementary rather than absolutely central.

We know from Rogers and Sons next extant letter, dated 4 October 1827, that Shaw and Crane replied on 31 August 1827 (though that reply is now lost). The apparent delay in correspondence occurred because Rogers and Sons had been awaiting from Rawson and Holdsworth:

> [i]nformation ... whether they made any other engagements during their visit to Wolverhampton as we gave them a letter ... to be used in case you did not wish to extend your trade to that quarter. We have this day received a letter from them stating that they did not make any arrangements for similar good to what you supply with any house in Birmingham or Wolverhampton. We therefore feel pleasure in recommending you to make treat and if you pursue the same plan that we have done we hope you will be equally successful.10

First, it should be noted that, for the time being, the correspondence between Shaw and Crane and Rawson and Holdsworth remained brokered by Rogers and Sons, though they do not seem to have had any immediate pecuniary interest in acting so. It is also clear Shaw and Crane, for now at least, had to act in competition with other *potential* correspondents in Wolverhampton and the wider Black Country industrial district. All in all, though intriguing, the way forward remained obscure or opague and only slowly was a more concrete picture of the possibilities emerging. Still, if Shaw and Crane remained diffident, Rogers continued to urge that they 'make treat'.

As if to allay Shaw and Crane's fears and uncertainties, the more experienced Sheffield firm moved on to the provision of detailed practical advice on how an Indian trade might be best conducted. This advice covered such issues as the suggested value of any initial consignments ('£300 to £400 by any one ship'), how goods be packed, the paper work that should accompany any shipment, levels of sensible insurance ('to always insure to the full amount'), and how to make and present an appealing and saleable selection of goods. Particularly pertinent was how to charge; Rogers admitting that in their own export trade that they 'always reduce every article to nett cost price (as Discounts are unknown there) and we then put on an advance of fifty per cent'.11 But, they warned, nothing was certain in such a trade: Rawson and Holdsworth sometimes managed to sell in advance of this invoice price, sometimes at it and sometimes below it 'but we put the good against the bad on this trade and take the average for the whole of the year'.12 And if Shaw and Crane were experienced in and adept at managing chains of credit and delayed payment in their domestic business then they still needed to be prepared – psychologically as well as financially – for the 'the great length of time which you will be out your money and the ... expenses which you incur ... as well as by the exchange'.13 There is a strong sense of the more experienced Rogers and Sons instructing the novice Shaw and Crane in that world of 'simple merchant practice' that was coming to characterize an increasingly impersonalized, even formalized, world of international commerce.14

The first extant correspondence from Rawson and Holdsworth to Shaw and Crane is dated 8th November 1827 and is an intensely practical affair, largely concerned with advice on where and when it is best to pay freight and shipping charges ('as the ship owners in this case ... draw at a very low rate of exchange we think it more to your advantage to pay it here'); the goods to be sent ('It is particularly desirable that this first shipment should be made as general as possible'); and the paperwork, both that to be sent with the goods and to be retained by Shaw and Crane. Rawson and Holdsworth also offered to arrange insurance if Shaw and Crane had no correspondents in London able to carry out this service for them. The only note of what we might term commercial sentiment came in a short concluding paragraph in which the language of mutuality and exploration are co-mingled with that advantage and profit:

> We hope the present adventure may lead to a lasting and mutually advantageous correspondence, at all events we beg to assure you that no exertion on our part shall be wanting in India to make the trade a profitable one for you.[15]

An adventure it was certainly to be – but for now practicalities remained to be dealt with. Still, with help, these were clearly surmountable, for Rawson and Holdsworth wrote again from London on 17 November 1827 enclosing an insurance policy for Shaw and Crane's first shipment (to the value of £800) along with a cover note that again expressed a desire to see their mutual interests prosper: 'It will give us much pleasure to find that this first shipment to our Calcutta house [succeeds] ... so as to encourage you to continue your correspondence ... we can at all events promise you that no exertion will be spared to render the correspondence active and mutually interesting'.[16] This language of action and engagement is stirring, and deliberately so no doubt. It also provides a ghostly echo of John's mother's words of more than twenty years earlier. It seems likely she would have approved of such vigorous sentiments. All in all, these first steps had proved relatively quick and easy to take; a shipment was on its way within three months of first receiving the approach from Rogers and Sons.

At this point, the archive falls almost completely silent on the Indian trade, for the time being at least. But from 1831 onwards, there is a flowering of correspondence with other merchants and shipping agents about trade to even more remote and then exotic destinations, including Batavia (Jakarta, Indonesia, but then part of the Dutch East Indies) and Singapore. Much, if not all, of this far-Eastern trade was handled by the interconnected firms of Anderson, Wise and Company of Liverpool and Robert Wise and Company of Batavia and Singapore.[17] Given the multiple risks involved in such long-distance trade even these relatively small steps cannot be regarded as either haphazard or lightly taken.[18] Rogers and Sons' first approach had reopened in Shaw and Crane an adventurous entrepreneurialism that had begun to slip into dormancy. In time it was to lead to a remarkable re-flowering that was, over coming generations, to transform the firm.

This rediscovered dynamism unfolded thus. Though we cannot now know for certain it seems likely that Shaw and Crane continued to send consignments of goods to India through Rawson and Holdsworth between 1827 and 1834. The next significant piece of evidence about trade with India is a letter from Rawson and Holdsworth to Shaw and Crane dated 8 October 1834. The letter opened by noting that:

> Our house in London Messrs. Rawson, Norton and Co., advise having received a letter from Messrs. Rodgers and Sons, stating that it was your wish to extend your business to India ... We can only assure you that should you confide your interests to our establishments either here or in India, the greatest attention shall be paid to them and nothing will be wanting on their part to make the trade a lucrative one to you.[19]

This certainly suggests, even if it cannot confirm, that Shaw and Crane's had continued to trade with India, and probably through Rawson and Holdsworth, between 1827 and 1834 – it hardly seems likely that they would speak of revisiting a one-off shipment from some seven years earlier as an 'extension' of trade. What is certain is that at some point during 1834, Shaw and Crane had taken the deliberate decision to 'extend' this line of business – we might cast this as a moment of entrepreneurial action. The rest of what was only a brief note detailed (three) ships sailing from Liverpool to Calcutta during October 1834 and offered to engage freight on behalf of Shaw and Crane. A further note from Rawson and Holdsworth on the 25th of the same month, in response to a lost letter from Shaw and Crane, was again largely concerned with sailings and which, in particular, would be best 'should Mr Thomson be ready [to sail] at the time you state'.[20] Clearly the decision had been taken not merely to extend the trade with India, but also to locate personnel in Calcutta itself.

But in sending Thomson (and others) to Calcutta Shaw and Crane meant that he should be far more than a superintendent overseeing the handling of their interests by third parties.[21] Instead, that Shaw and Crane had far more ambitious intentions are made clear in the agreement between Shaw and Crane and one Joseph Anderson on the 7th November of that year, which opened by boldly declaring that:

> [W]hereas the said John Shaw and Henry Crane have lately determined to open an Establishment at Calcutta in the East Indies for the sale of Ironmongery, Hardware and other goods wares and merchandise and have agreed with their late traveller Thomas Edward Thomson to manage and conduct the same as their agent who will forthwith embark with a cargo of goods for that purpose.[22]

There can be no mistake as to Shaw and Crane's intentions to invest directly in their overseas business. As early as 11 November 1834, Thomson was writing from Liverpool to his employers in Wolverhampton to tell them that he had received instructions to be ready to board ship at seven o'clock the next morning, having, seemingly for the first time, met Mr Rawson, whom he had found to be 'a very active man of business and also a very pleasant man'.[23] The adventure had entered upon a new chapter.

A Context of Crisis

Of course, these events did not take place outside of a wider history and context. These were tumultuous years for British trade and traders in India. Historians of British merchant enterprise, such as Chapman, Jones and Matheson Connell have all stressed how moments of crisis and the 'vacuums' that they created were crucial to the emergence and evolution of British merchant enterprise in Asia.[24] Chapman, for example, traces the development of the managing agency system that dominated British merchant enterprise in the East Indies through to the final quarter of the nineteenth-century to the experiences of the 'five great agency houses that were founded towards the end of the eighteenth century and became insolvent in 1830–5'.[25] But if this volatility could prove wildly destructive if could also, as Jones notes, be the very source of a 'literally a world of opportunities'.[26] Nowhere was this truer than in India, where the demise of the East India Company's monopoly of trade to India in 1813 opened up an environment comprising both rich potential and considerable risk in a world of under-developed supporting institutions.[27]

In 1830, the prestigious Anglo-Indian merchant house of Palmer and Company, based in Calcutta and considered a 'prince' amongst merchants, collapsed into ignominious bankruptcy. Profligate, generous, keenly aware of status and standing, but poorly-controlled, and riven by conflict, the fall of Palmer and Company sent out shock waves that, one-by-one, felled the remaining British merchant houses in Calcutta. As historian Tony Webster notes, 'access to capital' was key to 'growth and success' and that Palmer deployed 'social intimacy, paternalistic concern and patronage ... to secure funds'.[28] But once confidence had collapsed these guarantees proved illusory and worthless. Weighed down by chains of credit and prey to the animal spirits of the market they were annihilated. The ground was swept clean. But this was not in itself 'opportunity' but only the field on which possibility of opportunity might be explored and conjured with. There was no inevitably to Shaw and Crane's reactions, either broadly or in detail, as is highlighted by the reactions of others to the same events. Thus, as early as 1831 for example, James Matheson agreed to establish his nephew in Calcutta 'on the express understanding that the house is one of mere agency, and that above all you must abstain from speculating'.[29] Shaw and Crane were then not the only new entrants to the field, but their specific choices were idiosyncratic and personal.

Shaw and Crane, as did others, had to find what we would now call a business model that matched and made the best of their own strengths and weaknesses. As James Matheson's cautionary advice suggested, a greater modesty of purpose and intent was to be watchword, and one heeded by Shaw and Crane. Thus 'the new generation houses were investing even before the ... crisis [of the early 1830s] was over'.[30] With many of these small new firms, Shaw and Crane shared a commitment to trading on their own account rather than consignment. Thus, though meeting fresh competition on the ground in India the partners needed to find a way to differentiate themselves by drawing on their own prior business experience. They did this primarily through a decision to combine, in a highly novel twist, merchanting and retail functions within a single enterprise. In doing so they, first, corrected a major omission of Palmer and the other merchant princes of an earlier generation, who had largely neglected the potential for a trade in British manufactures to India. Second, this new combination of activities gave them the possibility of far greater control over the sale of the wealth of goods they could import. Here they drew on decades of past experience in interpreting and satisfying consumer demand and taste combined with an intimate knowledge of and links to the dense networks of supply in their home region of the Black Country industrial district.

One particular example, an agreement reached in June 1844 to act as sole agent in Calcutta for renowned Wolverhampton lock manufacturers Chubb and Co, demonstrates how these Black Country connections functioned and how they underpinned Shaw and Crane's capabilities and advantages. Strikingly, this valuable trade emerged from physical proximity within Wolverhampton, from an almost chance:

> [c]onversation I had some weeks ago at Wolverhampton with Mr Crane. I mentioned to him that I was sorry that Messrs Shaw and Crane sold so few of our Patent Locks at Calcutta whilst we were selling so many at the other two presidencies in Ceylon in each of which we have several agents ... I felt quite sure that if proper means were taken we might sell at Calcutta as many or more than we do in all other parts of India and that we had made up our minds to have some efficient agents there. [31]

Chubb's proposal was straight and clear: 'provided ... you will take up the thing with spirit we will make you sole agent in Calcutta and as the merit of our locks are now becoming more generally known and duly appreciated in India I think such an arrangement would be mutually beneficial'.[32]

But Shaw, Crane and Thomson, as well as relying on these long developed strengths, also did something entirely new, both in terms of their own business practices and those of other British houses operating in India, they opened a shop in Calcutta. By 1841 this new enterprise was publishing a neatly printed catalogue that ran to nearly forty closely-printed pages. This catalogue listed a seemingly unending variety of household good, all and more that could be imagined as necessary. Indeed, with a single purchase the lucky consumer, perhaps newly arrived in India from Britain, could even equip a whole household – whether for a single person or an entire family – simply by selecting one the various complete and dizzingly comprehensive 'packages' offered, with terms and conditions set out in clear and simple printed form at a time when bargaining and haggle were still the norm.[33] Of course, they had never themselves run a shop, but they had been inside perhaps hundreds over the preceding decades and, moreover, Elizabeth was born of a family of shop-keepers. They knew how shops worked. They had watched them succeed and watched them fail.

Far from simply conforming mimetically to the gap left by the collapse of Palmer and the other merchant houses, or isomorphically to the forms being adopted by other new entrants, Shaw and Crane rethought what trade with India might be. They conjured, imagined and cast forward, expectant and hesitant, into a future as yet undecided. They were released to create.

Being in Business in India

However, if, as John and Henry had already realized, long distance trade through third parties came with risks and uncertainty – from the seizure of vessels by hostile and competitive foreign powers to shipments that would not sell – then managing such trade within the firm itself provided its own challenges. First, coordination of the relatively simple activities between Britain and India was complicated ferociously by the extremely delayed nature of communication via seaborne letter. Moreover, though Thomson was clearly a deeply trusted lieutenant, aligning the priorities and interests of home and foreign branches was still by no means guaranteed. Nominally independent, the Indian house was very much a subsidiary and relationships with 'headquarters' became at times strained or even fractious. Perhaps the slight ambiguity of this relationship was an additional factor. We see both conflicting instructions from the two principals at home and Thomson being treated variously as both servant and master. Second, some of these same problems, particularly the very long lags in shipments, sales and remittances produced serious tensions with suppliers that needed careful management if supplies were to be maintained. This was another source of tension within the organization as it was often Shaw and Crane, on the ground in the Black Country where most suppliers were located, who bore the immediate brunt of Thomson's failure to remit in a timely fashion. Despite the long apprenticeship as exporters the three Midlanders found they had much to learn about life as multinational traders.

There can be little doubt though as to Thomson's loyalty and fidelity to his principals. In total, he was employed by Shaw and Crane for at least 21 years, twelve of them in Calcutta and he was eventually to die in service in India in 1846. Letters to him from home are full of business concerns, naturally, but they are also solicitous of his well-being and happiness. Crane, for example, relates a Sunday evening gathering at home in Wolverhampton and supposes 'you some-times think of us. How soon have half a dozen years past away' and elsewhere regrets that 'I have not had an opportunity of seeing your young ones'.[34] Interna-tional business imposed most painful separations on servants, friends and family. The firm provided a supportive framework, it was a family firm of course but also exercised a kind of broadened famialism that extended to a care for non-kin members. In some senses the firm was a synonym for the contemporary house-hold which made space for both kin and non-kin, such as friends, lodgers and servants as part of a single affective unit.[35] Though terribly, almost irrevocably separated the members of this unit remained tied by bonds far stronger than those of pecuniary self-interest or collective profit-maximization.

Nonetheless, as suggested, neither these sentiments nor the trust clearly placed in Thomson as friend, long-term employee and head of the firm in Calcutta were able to guarantee always smooth and easy relations between England and India. Amidst much routine discussion, Thomson was, for example, reminded from Wolverhampton against laying out too money ready money on purchasing cheap goods in Calcutta (although it be 'true that you at times buy some goods very cheap'), to follow instructions more accurately ('do not send anymore of them, they will not sell. My old advice to you was Sugar to Liverpool Indigo to London. If you had stuck to that we should have made a deal more money'), to make his remittances back to England in a full and timely fashion, and generally to pursue the business more vigorously ('I would like to see your remittances reach £2000 per month over and above any amount you may draw upon us'). Thompson had necessarily been given great discretion to trade on the firm's behalf, both in order-ing manufactures from England and in purchasing commodities in India for the return journey, the great slowness of communication making micro-management from home an impossibility. At the same time, however, this discretion was clearly also not entirely unlimited and was closely monitored.[36]

Relationships with English suppliers similarly mixed elements of familiar-ity, sociability and obligation with tension and competing interests. A detailed example is presented by the case of Ben Walton, a Wolverhampton-based manu-facturer of tin, iron and japanned wares. Seriously pressed for money following the dissolution of an earlier partnership, Walton's many letters of the early 1840s were frequently filled with complaints over slow or incomplete payments from India, as was the case in a typically long letter of November 1840:

> I have been daily expecting to hear from you with a remittance and assure you I am
> seriously inconvenienced for want of money ... I have Mr Ryton's capital to pay out of
> the trade and of course every hundred pounds is an object to me – I do most earnestly
> entreat that upon receipt of this letter you will draw upon Messrs Shaw and Crane
> for the balance ... If you will look at the dates you will find profit on part of this
> transaction quite out of the question add to two years and half credit at six months
> bill and judge of the loss we have to sustain ... From my present situation with regard
> to money it will be impossible for me to give the credit that you have taken from
> the last firm and I shall want your remittance and reply to this before I put the new
> [order] in hand.[37]

However, having continued to set out the terms and conditions he expected if
the trade was to continue, particularly with regard to the length of credit, Walton proceeded in the same letter to promise that 'you shall upon these terms
have any new articles that may be produced reserved exclusively for you as
regards the East Indies'.[38] Clearly, despite seriously delayed payments from India,
Walton was prepared to continue allowing Thomson a favoured status amongst
his customers. Walton struggled to be dispassionately business-like.

Further letters, mixing business matters with personal news and reflections
on the Shaw and Crane families, demonstrate the reasons for this struggle; this
was not and could not be a purely commercial relationship. Never was this
clearer than in a letter Walton wrote in April 1840, in which were combined a
glowing pride in the manufacturing prowess of the firm, and the Black Country
as a whole, with touching family details:

> With this you will receive an Invoice of paper tables and ... patent coffee pots. The
> tables were very much admired by everyone who saw them before they left here. We
> had visits from some of the principal ladies of the town and neighbourhood and sev-
> eral tables ordered. With the rest of the visitors we had Mr and Mrs Shaw who very
> much admired them, little did they think at the time that their son would never see
> them. Mr Shaw spoke with the greatest delight upon the pleasure it would be to his
> son to see so good a specimen of the manufactures of his native town.[39]

Delight, pride, love, loss, pathos are here inseparable. Walton was touching most
poignantly and delicately on the tragic events that had befallen the Shaw family in late 1839, when John and Elizabeth's eldest son, also John, visiting the
business in India, succumbed quickly to tropical disease and died many thousands of miles away from home and family. Walton's words point up the central
importance of the emotional dynamics of doing family business across such great
distances – the importance of doing one's duty and the pain that that duty might
bring in train – and those dynamics might in turn point both to an explanation
for the whole 'adventure' and to a lens for understanding how it was experienced
as more than mere money-making.

Making Sense of Adventure: Emotional Dynamics

Walton's words are not the only clues to the ways in which emotion was entangled in this story; ways that could, like the pull of the moon, tug at motives, wants, decisions and reactions. In the autumn of 1835, one year after the launch of the Indian venture, John sat down to write, as was his custom, to his Elizabeth, then absent on a visit to a resort in the north of England. His mood was unsettled, mingling excitement and anxiety, hopes and fears, and his feelings complex:

> It is rather uncanny one of the ministers we have with us also has been a missionary at Calcutta very lately and has given me a great deal of information respecting that place. Bye the bye we have this week had despatches from Thompson for the first time and am happy to say both he and Anderson are quite well he writes in most excellent spirits seems most sanguine as to what his adventure has done and as to future prospect has already sold two thirds of his cargo and sends us very considerable order which he begs me to send forward without delay as he shall have nothing to sell by the time they arrive. Desires we will send them out two more young men similar to the ones he has got with whom he is well pleased. He has got one of the best positions for a shop and store in all Calcutta directly opposite the Government House for which he pays 100 rupees a month in other words about one hundred and thirty pounds a year. A new field for trade is there open and [he is] quite elated with success. Hope he may not be too sanguine. He has sent us orders which will amount to I should think six to eight thousand but as this is such an unexpected sum I think it will be well to send about half for present. I do believe we have let open the finest field for commercial pursuits that we could have thought of as such a concern is not known in that place and altogether new as to its character and operation. Says he and Anderson board and lodge together in a very respectable family.[40]

He is cautious, concerned perhaps by Thomson's almost giddy enthusiasm, and worrying still, as he did as younger man, about the possibility of over-reaching oneself and hubristically inviting in ruin by challenging providence; yet, still, he is also quietly satisfied with the location of the premises and with the respectability of the lodgings Thomson has found and, ultimately, he is not quite able fully to contain his own feelings of pride at what they have done so far and what they might yet achieve. One tone runs underneath it at all, best captured in a word John uses himself: 'uncanny'. How strange and unexpected to find himself engaged upon this enterprise. India is *terra incognita* for these stolid and ageing Englishmen. We glimpse John's avid desire to learn all he can of this very foreign land from the missionaries who lodge with them. The distances and differences must have seemed hard to grasp.

What pitched John, Elizabeth, Henry and his wife into this strange world, expanded and made anew by their business decisions? Simple want cannot explain it, the domestic business was well established and stable, affording the Shaw and Crane families comfortable lives if we are to judge from the general tone of letters in this period.[41] Of course they were also acting as part of something much bigger than themselves; the making of empire in India. Perhaps these forces – the gathering, dizzying onrush of global flows of commodities, finance and people – explain their actions? These will have played their part. Still, we need to understand the particular decisions they took at concrete points in time if we are not to reduce them to mere ciphers for larger structures and forces. Margot Finn has argued that whilst imperial history has typically dealt in grand, depersonalized narratives a renewed interest in family biography might bring new understandings. These new understandings promise to go in at least two directions; towards an understanding of empire made on the ground and of lives lived in the quotidian interstices of the unfolding imperial project – a 'rooting of British imperial history firmly within the history of the family'.[42] At the heart of Finn's arguments is the contention that 'kin relations were both a central socio-economic cause of imperial endeavour ... and a vital socio-political mechanism for managing expansion'.[43]

Of necessity, the demographies of individual families often mandated 'sustained familial investment to establish them securely within the middle class through marriage, trade or the professions'.[44] In essence, imperial endeavour and expansion was driven as much by familial needs as by as high politics or ideology. Critically, given the methods and sources used in this study, Finn concludes that 'private correspondence cries out for an alternative genealogy of empire ... [comprising] poverty, demography and social aspiration'.[45]

How did the demographies of the Shaw and Crane families stand at this point in time? John and Elizabeth's first child, John, had been born in 1815, in the second year of their marriage, by which date John was aged 33 And Elizabeth 27. Thereafter, following a brief pause, a number of pregnancies followed in quick succession; Thomas in 1818, Elizabeth in 1819, Edward Dethick in 1821, Mary in 1823, and, finally, Richard in 1827, by which time Elizabeth was herself thirty-nine. John and Elizabeth were unusually fortunate that all six of their live-born children survived into adulthood.[46] Thus, at the time of the launch of Thomson and Co. in 1834 John Jnr had already reached maturity and another three boys were pressing close on his heels (though Edward had suffered badly with lameness, and possibly other ailments, since early childhood and was, it seems, never intended by his parents for a strenuous working life). Moreover, Henry Crane had started his own family by the early 1820s.[47] These children needed both support through childhood and meaningful roles in adulthood; the domestic business was unlikely to supply enough of either and especially perhaps of the latter.

And maybe Crane, the younger of the two partners and someone who had always seemed to treat being in business as his 'hobbyhorse', a plaything as much as a serious pursuit, was simply bored with the humdrum routine of running the very well-established domestic business? Certainly a letter written by Elizabeth

in the summer of 1834, at which time the investment in India must have already
been under consideration, suggests his faltering engagement with the day-to-day
details of the business: 'Mr Crane will never kill himself with business – he has
left John [John and Elizabeth's eldest son] to take care these two days – yesterday he gave him a long invoice to write that has taken him till today at noon
... he [John] was by himself most of the time yesterday and this morning [the
warehouse] was quite deserted – He found Mr Crane's keys left in his drawers'.[48]
Certainly the next generation had to be trained up to the business, but this also
speaks of a certain dilatoriness on Crane's part.[49] Read this way, the launch of
the Indian business is much more than simply an attempt to tap into the profit
opportunities presented by the collapse of Palmer and Company and the other
Anglo houses in Calcutta. Instead it was also a vehicle for renewal at the level
of both individuals and families. It provided John and Henry with a redoubled
stimulus to enterprise and exertion, a recalibration of an entrepreneurial spirit
that had been slipping into dormancy. At some risk it also sought to guarantee
family fortunes, a risk that proved well-taken as the Calcutta enterprise survived,
flourished and then became a foundation for further expansion towards the east
and, eventually, many years later, to Australasia, Africa and beyond.

Instead, the real risk proved all too bodily and was to family not finances,
the very family that was to be have been enriched in its fields of expression and
potential by the move. The story of the death in India of the eldest born son
John, fragmentary though it is, is heartbreaking in its simplicity and universal-
ity. He was just twenty-four years old. The news of John's death was conveyed
in a now lost letter from Thomson dated 10th of November 1839, a letter not
received in England until late January 1840 – the first extant response being a
letter from Crane dated the last day of that month. The force of the blow still
resonates through Crane's words today:

> Your [letter] has spread gloom around. I scarcely know what to write to you, espe-
> cially [as] Mr Shaw having by this mail addressed you[50] ... it is the worst blow that
> ever the Calcutta concern met with and when Mr Shaw will get over it I do not know.
> Since the receipt of the letter from you on 31st October last [and] also one from poor
> John of the same date[51] he has done everything in his power for the Calcutta concern
> what he will do the months I cannot tell he is at present so unnerv'd that he scarce
> knows what to do, it is a most unfortunate affair, he was worth to you almost a piece
> of Gold of his own weight and had he been able to stand the climate it would I doubt
> not have been a capital thing for the concern.[52]

Crane next goes on to touch on the circumstances of John's death, which remain
obscure in detail but clear enough in outline. John, having presumably begun to
show signs of illness and fever had it seems quit the notoriously fetid conditions
found on the coast at Calcutta for inland Meerut, in the state of Uttar Pradesh,
where cooler, cleaner airs might have been expected at that time of the year. But

these passages also touch on inevitable under-currents of guilt. What, all must have been asking themselves, if he had not been sent?

> I do not blame anybody for the part they took in getting him out nor do I see any blame that can be laid for his going to Meerut it having decidedly a better climate than Calcutta. The arrival of the next mail is look[ed] for with anxiety however he is gone and cannot be restored. I do not know what effect this may have.[53]

These last comments seem remarkably prosaic, almost callous, but as he continues it is clear that Crane is grappling with a realization that no matter how terrible these events decisions with regard to the business needed to be taken if the disaster was not to be further exacerbated:

> One thing is quite clear that we must try to keep the concern all right during the [duration of] Mr Shaw's feelings on the late event, do not act in a hurry respecting the information he may have written you under excited feelings, but I know nothing of what he has said ... send home all the money you can, you see Mr Shaw now says suppose Mr Thompsons life should sigh [expire?] what will become of us. I think you should make your will if you have not done so yet and also hand us a copy ... and try to place us in the most [secure] position on this point for you must see it will be to the advantage of the concern for us to know in case of need what is likely to be done so we should not be thrown into confusion.[54]

Crane ends at last on the simplest, most human note: 'be sure [to] take care of yourself for that is of all the greatest importance'.[55]

It is almost unbearably sad: Crane scrabbling around to keep the concern afloat; John, always a kind and doting father, almost entirely unmanned by the loss of his dear boy. If Crane was able absolve Thomson of any sense of guilt or blame then perhaps Shaw was unable to do the same for himself. The effects lingered long and painfully and evidence from following years paint John's involvement with the Indian concern as languishing and half-hearted. Thus, Crane wrote to Thompson in March 1843 to urge him on:

> Your letter received last month though pretty stiff is scarcely stiff enough for Shaw has only put part [of an order received] in hand and at present none of Griffin's hoes, Elwell's part he has put in hand you must continually keep pushing him on ... I am very much vexed Shaw does not continue supplying as he ought to do but I cannot persuade him.[56]

Adventure had brought a catastrophe that laid waste to family, ambition and energy.[57] A final most poignant note was supplied by Crane with the simple observation to Thomson that 'Mr Shaw still continues [to be] trouble[d] about not getting John's things'.[58] The physical gulf, thwarting the return of simple tokens of remembrance, speaks of a far greater emotional gulf.

Thus the vast distance between Staffordshire and Calcutta that had once seemed simultaneously uncanny and exciting became a terrible mechanism for compounding grief and the lags and delays that merely inconvenienced the doing of business stretched loss unbearably. Absence in life was continued, achingly, into an absence in death. A son's grave never to be seen or visited with the promise of reunion in the hereafter the only balm.

Conclusion

Shaw and Crane's Indian adventure proved to be a bittersweet experience. Together as partners, for both firm and families, they ventured at considerable risk and won. Probably more than any other act since the formation of the partnership in 1815, at the uncertain climax of the Napoleonic wars, the formation of T.E. Thomson in Calcutta in 1834 laid the foundations of firm as a multigenerational and multinational company that was to eventually encompass near global operations. A superficial glance might paint the moves of 1834 as a classic case of two alert, evaluative, calculative entrepreneurial agents identifying and seizing an opportunity opened up by shifts in markets and institutions. A more careful, longer-run perspective paints Shaw and Crane's actions in subtly different light; adaptive, emergent, gradual and even cautious; the making present of possibilities that remained vague and opaque and whose resolution and fulfilment was to be found in a future that did not yet exist and could not be predicted, a future that they had to actively bring about.

Effecting a strategy of bricolage that took skills, knowledge and capabilities from an eclectic range of sources they forged something new that enabled people, particularly expatriate customers in India, to do things differently (setting up their new homes as a simple, single purchase package at a clearly advertised price for example). They took from their own experiences of dealing with supply and credit, of managing business at a distance, from their own intimate if second-hand knowledge of shop-keeping, supplemented with Elizabeth's own first-hand experience behind the counter in the shops of parents and brothers, and from the merchants who introduced them to trade to the Indies. Even once the initial perilous transition had been made to operating from Calcutta the way forward remained often frustrating and unrewarding. Efforts to push East into the so-called 'Country trade' were frequently disappointingly unrewarding.[59] However, stability and success eventually followed and T.E. Thomson and Co. remained a presence in Asia for many more decades.

But success had first to extract a terrible price. Family demography and dynamics were advanced as one way of understanding a move to India that is hard to explain on purely rational grounds. The Indian adventure promised an (admittedly uncertain) route to greater profits as the families of both partners grew, but more importantly it might have provided an greater range of outlets for the energies and talents of a maturing and somewhat crowded second-generation, an inference backed-up by the younger John's posting to Calcutta. The outcome was tragic though and only heightened by the great distances this business expansion had necessarily involved. If the dynamics of international family business were never purely economic or pecuniary then the results were far from only so. It was impossible to disentangle emotion from any facet of this venture. John and Elizabeth would surely have exchanged every material gain to have been spared their loss and grief. Some calculations are always easy.

5 'TO WORK HARD FOR A LARGER FAMILY': MANAGING WORK AND FAMILY.

'To Work Hard for a Larger Family'[1]

Introduction

'Betsey says we will go a journey when Mamma and the boy come home – She says you are gone a journey to get orders'.[2]

Betsey [John and Elizabeth's eldest daughter, also Elizabeth] was wrong; her mother had not gone a journey to get orders. Instead, she was visiting her family in Lancashire. But the child's innocent words spoke to a very powerful truth about the deep impression made by business on every aspect of life for the Shaws, unwittingly revealing the complex skeins binding together working life and family life, husband and wife, man and woman, public and private, worldly and domestic. These threads were as tightly woven together as any Gordian Knot. In their everyday practices, at home and at work, the lines between John and Elizabeth, and what each of them did, what they were and what they might be, were blurred to a remarkable degree, sometimes almost to the point where they were completely dissolved.

In this chapter I will explore the demands made upon John and Elizabeth, and in time, the wider family, by an enterprising life. Naturally, the business required long hours, whether John was at the home or on the road. This took a toll that was both physical and emotional and was experienced by all alike. John, in particular, also seems to have experienced being in business as a considerable psychological burden, at least at times, and even from a young age he periodically wished himself out of trade altogether. The anxiety it bred in him might have been too much if his mother had not raised him to an ethic of virtue through industry. Family life too placed its own pressures on the couple in ways that were complex yet still all too familiar to many families today. It was not simply an issue of bearing and raising children, difficult enough though that was. Elizabeth remained deeply attached to her own family after her marriage to John and made, as we have seen, frequent prolonged visits to Lancashire, during which John was left home, often with one or more of the children.

Being an enterprising couple and family demanded then considerable adjustments and accommodations, it meant that a pattern of living had to be worked out and followed, roles tried out and negotiated, settlements reached – sometimes that also undoubtedly meant compromises made. The chapter will explore those negotiations and the arrangements and accommodations they resulted in. This is the stuff of everyday life in most families – and therein lays its beauty and profundity. The material touches upon several important historical themes: what was the relationship between the private domestic sphere and its public counterpart during this critical period of modernization; what behaviours and qualities were proper to each of these so-called spheres; where did they sit in relation to work and the economy; and, above all else, how did men and women relate to each of these questions and to each other. Elizabeth and John's story is an often confounding, unsettling one as they upend our expectations and assumptions. Ultimately it is also a story that underlines the complete inseparability from all of the other domains of life of what we persist in delineating and naming as 'entrepreneurship'.

Work and Life, Men and Women

As we saw in the chapter on their courtship and marriage, both Elizabeth and John were raised in deeply affectionate, tightly bound and largely contented families. Home held good memories. These foundations undoubtedly coloured their beliefs and they themselves moved into adulthood and responsibility. They knew at first hand both the rewards and the strains of an enterprising life. In particular, Elizabeth, coming from a singularly warm domestic environment, began to fear the life of a traveller's wife even before she and John were married. In part this sprang from her recognition of the unavoidable separation that they would have to endure. Thus, she admitted that 'The greatest evil I fear (next to your being jealous) is your having to leave me so often – I shall have to be nearly half my time alone thinking about what ills may befall you while away'.[3] But, much more powerfully, she also looked with anxiety towards the emotional, psychological and moral effect of this way of life. These threats were, she perceived, far more dangerous to happiness than mere time apart. Elizabeth's musings were prompted by several days she had herself spent away from home in Rochdale:

> I believe I was three or four days before I got perfectly settled after coming home – Altho' I was much gratified, and I believe benefitted by my Buxton journey yet I was glad to get home. I should not like to be obliged to travel like you, it would unsettle me, and a cause a dissipation of the mind which would unfit me for reflecting, or meditating upon serious things – a little solitude is useful and necessary, to become acquainted with ourselves – My animal spirits got above par at Buxton.[4]

Several important and long-lasting themes are evident in this early letter. Dominant is a view of the world-at-large as a place of perilous temptation. Both John and Elizabeth would recur to this perception from time to time over the years. Of a part with this view is Elizabeth's belief in an essential, inherently 'animal' or fallen dimension to her character; a dimension that she both acknowledges and, to an extent, even accepts, whilst still recognizing the need to wrestle with and quell it. Corresponding with both of these stances, and yet much more striking in such an energetic and enterprising couple, is the validation given to a life of retreat. There would be an undeniable tension between this emphasis on 'reflecting' and the action and engagement with the hurly burly of the world essential to the entrepreneur – especially one such as John thrown into the immediacy of buying and selling, of bargaining and cutting – if she was recommending the contemplative life to him as well. Instead, she sees him as 'obliged' to travel. Elizabeth seems to posit that she and John are in some essential way equipped to perform quite distinct roles in life and that hers was not to be found abroad in the world. Thus, that tension identified by Elizabeth prompts reflection on the concept of 'separate spheres'. Critically, we will see how Elizabeth and John and worked to resolve these forces pulling at them through their everyday practices rather than by adherence to ideological precepts or prescriptions as to proper male and female roles.

The separate spheres thesis has been the most prominent organizing concept in women's history over recent decades and despite the thorough critique published by Amanda Vickery in the early 1990s it continues to exert a considerable pull – even if only as a construct against which to react.[5] The separate spheres thesis argues that from the late eighteenth-century, if not before, far reaching structural and qualitative changes in the economy (industrialization in particular) forced women to retreat from public view (and thus also power, influence and significance) to the private realm of the home; in Vickery's pithy summation the 'assumption [was] that capitalist man needed a hostage in the house'.[6] Once confined to the home she was not only stripped of her former role in public life but subordinated to a suffocating patriarchy and corseted into a narrow confining view of what was 'true' womanhood. The result was the simpering, fragile and sexless Victorian woman of popular imagination, a pale shadow of earlier sisters who had, in an idealization, been 'true partners to their husbands, demonstrated a capacity for business and [whose] engagement in commercial life aroused no comment'.[7] And, of course, as a corollary, if women were constrained by this ideology then so were men restricted to an increasingly narrow version of what constituted a proper 'manliness'. That this model is driven by economic forces is clearly important in the context of a study of early nineteenth-century entrepreneurship.

Similarly it is important not miss the role of home as a place of physical separation, an isolating, insulating space that kept women apart from the public (and

male) world of work; for, again in the idealized version, 'Once production left
the home, the wife was divorced from her husband's trade and lost the informal opportunity to learn his skills'.[8] Women were reduced to busying themselves
with the fripperies of home-making and socializing (and child-bearing and rearing). The separation is multi-layered then; of the public from the private in terms
of roles and institutions, of men from women, of the economically productive
from economically unproductive, of the home from the world.

However, as well as Vickery's withering conceptual critique, the separate
spheres thesis has also been subject to extensive empirical revision. As brief
examples, John Tosh's extensive work on masculinity[9] has led to a far more varied picture of how men understood themselves and behaved whilst the work of
Gordon and Nair has unpicked how households were constructed and how men
and women acted within them. Their conclusions are deceptively simple but no
less important for that; first that the 'public and private spheres were permeable
and interconnected'.[10] And second, in relation to men and women, and particularly, those key roles of motherhood and fatherhood; 'there were many different
ways of being a mother' and, equally, that there 'were many acceptable ways of
being a father'.[11] Certainly Gordon and Nair are focused on a slightly later period
in the nineteenth-century, so it is also worth noting their assertion that 'there
was always a complexity to the constitution of fatherhood'.[12] Similarly, it is useful to stress their claim that the formation of the domestic ideology supposedly
underpinning these separate spheres is 'usually associated with the industrial
revolution and the rising middles classes, particularly those of an evangelical
persuasion'.[13] It would be hard to find better exemplars of these attributes than
enterprising John and Elizabeth Shaw.

At the same time, Vickery also highlights Keith Wrightson's fundamental
question; 'did "theoretical adherence to the doctrine of male authority and *public* female subordination" mask "the *private* existence of a strong complementary
and companionate ethos'. We certainly know the latter was true of Elizabeth
and John.[14] Did that complementarity translate into other aspects of their lives?
Answering these questions, which will require insights into values, ideology and
mentalities, as well as behaviours, is not easy. Not only does the separate spheres
construct not 'capture the texture of female subordination and the complex
interplay of emotion and power in family life' at a conceptual level, but attempts
to explore it also repeatedly expose the 'deficiencies in our knowledge of the distinctions between public and private in language, *never mind as social practice*'.[15]
As Gordon and Nair argue 'Competing models of motherhood, the mobility
of meaning within the term and the disjuncture between the ideal and the lived
experience all point to the varied experiences of motherhood even within the
middle classes'.[16] All of these arguments are readily transposed to the wider concept of separate spheres of which motherhood was an important component.

Elizabeth and John's correspondence, rich, dense and descriptive, gives us a relatively rare and thus valuable portal on to the texture of their social practices around work and home, public and private, the male and female. We will be concerned to try and discern not only what each of them *did*, but also how they *thought* and *felt* about it individually and as a couple.

Critically, because the correspondence is two-handed, back and forth between them, it begs us to consider not simply the historical construction and reconstruction of women or the feminine but instead the historical construction and reconstruction of gender – of men and women together. What it was to be a man was no more given than what it was to be a woman.[17]

'The Worries and Anxietys of Business'[18]

> You know not from what variety of causes women can draw fear, at least, if I may judge from my own mind and be allow'd to make a comparison I should say that men in general know nothing of it. It is an old adage that 'the most safety lies in fear'. – What do you think of it?[19]

Elizabeth's words were prompted by a loss in trade John had suffered, for which she was 'truly sorry'.[20] In doing so she appears to present a clearly and explicitly gendered reading of male and female dispositions – and one that conforms to convention in assigning valour to men and timidity to women.[21] Similarly, a few months before marriage she doubtingly hoped that 'you will not be disappointed in looking for happiness at your own fire side', as though a man will naturally yearn for a wider stage, one that will be cramped by her proper domesticity.[22] But, as we saw very clearly in Chapter 3, Elizabeth was far from timid in much of her life, such as in the negotiation of her developing relationship with John. And besides, as we shall see in this chapter, John was never happier than when shut away from the world, by his own fireside. Was Elizabeth, in these exchanges, engaged in something more nuanced and sophisticated than merely parroting the dominant ideology? Here, perhaps, is a first clue to that 'texture of female subordination and the complex interplay of emotion and power in family life', one that is cast in a quite different light in a letter Elizabeth wrote just over one month later than that just quoted. She observes how:

> In one part of your letter you say females cannot be too cautious [undoubtedly in response to her own comments on female timidity] – If I were to take your advice and begin to act cautiously – should you like it or not? Hitherto I have acted without reserve and I shall continue it without you deny me the privilege.[23]

But had she not, just a few weeks earlier, confessed her own fearfulness? Instead, her rhetoric comes into view; John is not to be allowed his easy confining of the female sex – or her. This becomes even more apparent if we let the sentence run on from where we stop it in the quotation above: 'and if I may judge I think you will not tho' you deny it to another – How do you account for such partiality – It is self interest, what a long way it will carry a person'. John's socially validated male authority is in reality constrained within the terms of their relationship. In this second letter, Elizabeth's earlier words about gender are revealed as showing playful subversion and switching. One senses her subtly establishing certain rules and limits, including a refusal to conform to expectations, certainly not his and perhaps not society's. At root some might discern an assertion of her sexual power. This switching or transference was to characterize much about the way in which they worked and lived.

If he sometimes had to give ground at home then, in addition, far from being the heroic entrepreneur of (largely discredited) legend, John very often experienced being in business as a series of trials. In addition he was far from comfortable on the public stage. As we saw in Chapter 2, John found his immersion into the life of an apprentice traveller for Mr Sparrow a shock. His letters from that early period do not survive but we hardly need to read between the lines of his mother's letters to feel his reluctance, even dislike, for the life he had embarked on. Loving tenderness is mixed with stern admonitions to pluck up his courage, show his real character, be active and virtuous – she all but tells him to be a proper man. This is not too far-fetched; her rhetoric is acutely gendered as she laments that she was not born of a different sex. Later evidence hardly suggests that John ever fully overcame or reconciled himself too these feelings towards the public life of commerce.

His strong emotions around being business had two origins. The first was physical. Such extensive and continuous travelling under the conditions John faced was gruelling and exhausting. It was also often miserable; cold, wet and comfortless. It took a very real toll on his constitution and his spirits at times. The second was psychological. John was rarely free of anxiety about the state of trade. Most pressing, an almost constant pressure, was the shortage of money. If orders sometimes dried up then ready money seemed to be constantly in short supply. Of course, much of this trade, both with suppliers and customers, was conducted with credit, whether via bills of exchange or delayed payment. This imposed its own demands, a constant juggling of multiple transactions that probably felt as though they were never quite settled – and never would be. Still, accounts had to be reckoned up from time to time and that meant cash and there never seemed to be enough. On top of these constant, almost mundane pressures there came the more occasional threat of calamity and collapse, which might originate from almost any point in the complex system in which John was enmeshed as just one very small cog. This was no mere spectre; more than once these dangers came perilously close to touching John's own enterprise. He issued a particularly clear statement of these fears and pressures in December 1816:

This journey will prove a most sad one both in money and orders in fact it will be neither productive of one or the other or worth going out for. It makes me most truly uncomfortable and unhappy I never could have supposed it possible such a reverse of things could have taken place. If something does turn up for the better it will not be worth carrying on business.[24]

It is striking how John couches his reactions in a language of emotions; the journey is a 'sad' one, his response is one of discomfort and unhappiness.[25] It is hardly surprising that he contemplated ways in which he might travel less.[26] Moreover, on the same journey he had to face considerable physical hardships:

I have not been very well since last I wrote you by some means or other took cold in my Bowells [sic] which has given me most violent purging for three or four days and made me sadly out of sorts but am now much better – indeed I have quite lost it – I think I got it travelling all night upon the top of the coach, but for the time it made me very unwell indeed.[27]

Better times brought their own challenges – a case of feast or famine as a more buoyant market stretched John's (and the firm's) capacities to the maximum. Summer 1817 found him able to offer Elizabeth only a short letter: 'I have so much entering to do that I really cannot write so much as I would wish ... I am most sadly behind in copying my orders. I cannot get it up do all I will. I have more orders taken – a week not yet copied'.[28] Bountiful orders meant more than long nights recording them properly, it also meant debts to collect. A fat order book could still mean lean accounts. It is remarkable how quickly John's tenor can change in a single letter. One minute he is scrambling to keep up with paperwork, the next complaining that:

I have a letter from Mr Crane today and write you in low spirits not one I have had from him but what announces some heavy bad debts. I am much pleased I did not purchase the house for if bad debts go on in this kind of way it will find employment for all my money and more if things do not alter. I know not what things will come to but they are in a most alarming state at present. I heartily wish I was out of trade instead of going more into it.[29]

John shows an acute understanding of the need to keep money working for him through its unceasing circulation but still remains oppressed by deep uncertainties ('I know not what things will come to') about the future.[30] Still, he seems helpless to resist the pull of ever deeper involvement. We know, of course, that his involvement with trade both continued to deepen and carried on for many more years and growing success but security did not necessarily mean that the burden could be shifted on to others, and so in autumn 1831 John found himself unable to write a long letter 'As I am really as full of business as an egg is full of meat'.[31]

Yet, the troubles, woes, and bad times seemed almost ever present:

I have been well in health since I saw you but very flat in spirits – things are so dreadfully flat and bad that it is almost impossible to keep in good spirits – travelling these
times is certainly one of the most irksome and disagreeable callings I think a man can
follow. I sent Mr Crane a sheet of orders yesterday for the first time and shall write
him again tomorrow but please tell him he must not expect any great doings from
this journey or he will be surely disappointed.[32]

Still, a full eleven years later, though now surely well-established in business,
John still had cause to complain that 'I find things exceeding flat and dull here
and money scarce indeed, all say I am too soon after Christmas to get any'.[33]

Unsurprisingly, it was not merely these immediate trials under which John
struggled – but, in addition, the sense of what he was missing, or sacrificing,
whilst on the road. Thus he was prompted to reflect on how the 'pleasures and
enjoyments of home acquire much more might and influence upon ones mind
every time I go from home and if it goes on thus progressively shall but be
obliged to remain at home altogether'.[34] It was a terrible dilemma; the very thing
that enabled John to provide for, nourish and sustain his beloved family was at
the same thing that time and time again removed him from them. He was very
slow to become reconciled to these absences, if, indeed, he ever was. December
1821 saw him admitting that 'I feel exceeding low – indeed I always do on leaving home and perhaps more at this time of year than at other times, the dull dark
days and heavy weather damps [my mood]'.[35] Moreover, as often seemed to be
case, his reluctance to travel was compounded by the torpid condition of the
market: 'my spirits added to the exceeding dull and bad business for have experienced such heavy complaints as past my memory – no orders, nothing doing'.[36]
His lament has a despairing, almost existential quality.

It is hardly a surprise that from time to time John found himself wondering
whether to go on a journey when 'I know Mr Crane will have too much upon
his hands having a good many orders and its being Quarter Week also will be
hardly able to get through and again your mother being with you, you will not
perhaps feel an inclination to leave her'.[37] Naturally, John was also concerned
with Elizabeth's feelings: 'I can assure you I shall be as reluctant to take again so
long a journey as you will be for me so to do, I am quite confident, with so long
an absence'.[38] Similarly, absence and leave taking only became more difficult as
John and Elizabeth started their own family.[39] There was to be little relief from
this routine of parting for many years to come however, as late as 1831 (that is
after eighteen years of marriage), John could not help but notice that 'we shall
then ... [have had] as long a separation as we have had before – namely all January, February and March'.[40] Elizabeth too continued to feel these absences; in
1832 she told her father in tones of weary resignation how John 'has been out
from seven to eight weeks and I do not expect him home till the latter end of
next ... It is a trial to me but what must we expect'.[41]

Moreover the pain of separation was far from straightforward but had sub-tle inflections and shades depending upon the precise circumstances. Thus John wrote to Elizabeth from home whilst she was away, struck by the thought that:

It appears now my Dear Girl a long time since I saw you. I do assure you being at home when you are away is very different to being on a journey – one has much to occupy ones mind and time and attention but coming into one meals and all other parts of the days without seeing you does appear so strange and uncomfortable that I could not live alone again for a trifle. Its true I have got our little lad to play with but ...'[42]

Suddenly the demands and distractions of life on the road seem like a blessing.

These attitudes towards and emotions about business were neither iso-lated nor fleeting but suffused John's feelings about the commercial life. They are reflected for example in his frequently repeated suggestion that Elizabeth's ageing parents give up their own hardware shop. In one very strong passage he makes it very clear that he does not believe business, industry and exertion to be in all cases worth the toll that it could take:

I would advise you to persuade your Mother to give up Business to William [one of Elizabeth's brothers] if she can do it for she under present circumstances be kill-ing herself in being such a slave and for doing which one half of her children will not thank her for it and if in endeavouring to do as she thinks something better for them she would kill herself, the prosperity she may have accumulated will be knocked down in all probability twice as fast as she has got it.[43]

This is a complex stew of feelings: wealth is fleeting, insubstantial and easily lost; toil is not always a virtue; family are not always grateful or even deserving.[44] But as he develops his argument he continues to draw on familial resources, but in ways that differentiate between the qualities and characteristics of various mem-bers. Family might be more important than business at any cost but, crudely, not all family is equal:

I think you had better get Thomas over and Mrs S and try to persuade her into it – it is high time she had done with business and have no doubt but your Uncle Thomas Wilkinson would see it in this way and do all in his power to persuade her into it – don't you think it would be quite the best plan – I [doubt] she will be much benefitted in carrying it on with John [another of Elizabeth's brothers] there for his expenses I have no doubt are much more than she is aware of and which must of course come out of the business and added to which [if] he does not now he certainly will when she declines, make a demand for a handsome salary and which he will get – so that having him to keep in this extravagant way ... I don't think she will be much in pocket and better if she has [previously] give it up to William [yet another of Elizabeth's brothers][45]

Several aspects of this discourse deserve comment, including the way in which John calls upon wider family authority, such as Elizabeth's uncle Thomas Wilkinson (her father's brother), equally striking is the forthright manner in which John condemns brother John, whom he clearly views as both profligate but indulged – family emotions sometimes lead to decisions that are far from optimal in a commercial sense.[46] This is potentially very delicate ground, involving loyalties that are deep and instinctual but John has enough confidence in the strength of his relationship with Elizabeth to speak his mind freely on what he believes to be a vital issue. Still, he knew they were in accord, for before they were even married Elizabeth had expressed her wish that 'I could persuade my father and mother to give up business and live comfortably while they do live – My mother cannot stand it as she used to do and my father is grown tired of it – They are quite old enough to give over'.[47] The experience of watching her parents work themselves into old age and exhaustion cannot but have coloured her view of being business as a married couple and family.[48] Of course, it is also most striking that it is Elizabeth's *mother*, and not her father, who has the responsibility for deciding whether or not to continue in business. With her husband frequently incapacitated for prolonged periods (almost certainly with some form of depression) no-one had any difficulty in recognizing Elizabeth's mother as the *de facto* head of both the family and the business.[49]

Perhaps inspired by this example, and by the frustration at her constrained position so clearly shown by his mother, John and Elizabeth took the same approach to their own working and domestic lives, which bled over into each other until they were almost indistinguishable. This bleeding over happened most obviously in relation to roles but also took in physical spaces and wider sets of relationships. So, for example, on marriage the other's family became their own. All, whether John's birth family at Goldthornhill, on the outskirts of Wolverhampton, or Elizabeth's family at Colne and Rochdale in Lancashire, became universally known as 'our friends'. John referred to Elizabeth's parents and siblings as mother, father, sister and brother, as did Elizabeth with his family. Whilst he was away, she shared social visits with her in-laws and even a bed on many occasions with his sister.[50] John in turn was a solicitous and dutiful son-in-law, always visiting her kith and kin when his journeys allowed. He offered them succour, support and advice and, in turn, reassurance to Elizabeth. Letters from both of them almost invariably contained news about both halves of their extended family. We will explore the nature and importance of these wider connections in more detail in the next chapter, but they are important here in that they indicate the porosity and permeability of the boundaries in John and Elizabeth's lives; qualities that characterized their core relationship – that is the one between themselves.

Another example of this porosity was the organization of the physical space within which their lives were lived, perhaps not surprising in a couple who through the necessities of travel and separation were forced to construct what we would now recognize as a 'virtual' space constituted through and in their letters. Still, they could not live purely in this virtual world and even before they were married Elizabeth realized the importance of ensuring that when they were actually together in Wolverhampton then further separation should be minimized. A central claim of the separate spheres concept is that women became progressively excluded from the public realm and public roles because these were increasingly located or enacted away from the home. Elizabeth was adamant this was not to happen to her. Indeed, even before marriage and her first sight of Wolverhampton, Elizabeth was already measuring the space between home and workplace, imagining 'you, perhaps ... trudging home from the ware-house well-tired for it is betwixt nine and ten at night'.[51] She was very clear that she wanted no slog between home and workplace once they were married. Virtually the only instruction she offered about the marital home John was seeking for them was that 'the nearer you can get one to the ware house the better'. In this, she noted, 'you have anticipated my wishes with respect to the situation of a house'.[52]

Proximity between home and the warehouse allowed Elizabeth to play an active and important role in the conduct of the business, particularly in the early years of their marriage (1813) and before John took Henry Crane as a partner in 1815. This work alongside John in the business had in fact begun before marriage, at least in the sense of Elizabeth offering moral support, commiserating with him in his financial losses,[53] and delivering exhortations to remember his faith – but intensified very significantly thereafter. Elizabeth, who had long assisted both her parents and her brothers in their respective retail businesses, probably both in serving at the counter and in managing such things as accounts and stock, very quickly became a trusted and much needed lieutenant. She had learnt by good example. Her mother was no mere titular head of the Colne business but active principal, abroad in the world. A letter of 1812 recounts how:

> Last Tuesday morning but one I went in [the] coach to Manchester to meet my Mother ... [who] had a great deal of business to do and I wanted a few things that made me go – I was however quite tired before night in walking from one from one warehouse to another – I left M-chester on Wednesday noon – my Mother had not done her business.[54]

Clearly this was a buying trip that Elizabeth's mother had undertaken, evidently unaccompanied by her husband, or any other man, and no doubt necessitating some hard bargaining with Manchester wholesalers. As recent scholarship has begun to reveal, the scope for female entrepreneurship in England in this period was perhaps much greater than previously thought. Elizabeth was not raised to see a woman's life as retiring, sheltered, or unassertive but instead as one were active engagement in commerce was a possibility.[55]

It is not surprising then that Elizabeth's earliest post-marriage letters, which make constant reference to slipping back and forth between home and warehouse (in token of this parcels and letters also constantly shuffled back and forth between the two locations),[56] are crammed with business reports, intelligence and updates. She relays messages about orders that have come in, invoices received from suppliers,[57] both customers and suppliers who have visited in person, payments made and disbursed, including by herself, and pays monies into the bank[58] – moreover she is clearly not simply reporting all of these actions as having been done but as having been done by her personally. She copies up letters received; makes memoranda; relays vital information about the creditworthiness of contacts; of partnerships made and broken; and relays news of general trading conditions,[59] and of banking and other business failures;[60] and surveys the labour market for potential new recruits as travellers – an ever scarce commodity.[61] Only once does she betray any real doubt or uncertainty as to how she should act in an unexpected situation when:

> Rich'd [a hand from the warehouse] just now brought me a note to say I was to give Mr Best of Bolton a cheque upon the bank for his account somewhere about 18–0–0 but having no instructions from you I told you I could not – he said he always has ready money and he had called twice before – he said to send Mr Crane up as he said he must have it. I don't know what I am to do. Oh I shall be so glad to see you at home again ... Crane has been, Best will not go without his money. I see there are no cheques in the book to fill up so have given him the £10 bill of Moores and the remainder in cash. Have I done right?[62]

Having received confirmation from Crane of the propriety of paying Best (clearly a matter of established but particular precedence with this customer, of which she could not be expected to know) Elizabeth takes important decisions about how best to make the payment. Still, the note of anxiety in her final question is unmistakable. Nonetheless, despite these doubts, the workmen must have recognized her as having authority; after all it is to her that Richard has come with Best's request for ready cash. Indeed, in the same letter she notes that 'As to the letters Crane almost always brings them to me'.[63] A little later the same year she offers to speak to an agent about letting a house for the family (for she was then pregnant for the first time). Again this is striking in that she voluntarily offers to perform a role that would normally then (and now by many historians) be considered overtly public and masculine.

At the same time as carrying out these functions, which played an important part in the smooth running of the business in John's absence, Elizabeth also kept a watchful eye over the warehouse and its staff. In March 1815, for example, she was able to report that 'I think they are very attentive at the W'house and get off the orders as fast as they can get them in', even if the workmen were only 'making up for it against quarter' having been 'lazy lately'.[64] Still, in her next she is again able to report that 'they are going on well at the warehouse from what I hear'.[65] This oversight was very important and on another occasion, when Elizabeth had to report she had not been to the warehouse since the previous week, she had to admit that 'I think it was well that Crane came into the Warehouse when he did because Latham was so strange to the workmen – did not know where they lived – consequently mishaps occurred. They seem to go on very well now'.[66] And sometimes, in reverse, John would specifically ask her: 'You say they are busy at the Warehouse – do they seem attentive also?'[67]

The impression is of near constant rather than merely occasional involvement on Elizabeth's part. Indeed, in the mid-1820s John went so far as to ask 'How do you get on with your Treasuryship?'[68] Various hints suggest that they were still living extremely close to the warehouse, in reach of easy communication, in the early 1830s. Nonetheless, quite naturally, as Elizabeth became increasingly pre-occupied and busy with childbearing and rearing, as the business became more established, and Crane matured into his role as a partner, then her immediate, day-to-day involvement did recede somewhat – but never to the point where it ceased entirely.[69] Moreover, her role was not restricted to the relatively confined space of the warehouse and the privacy of correspondence. Just as her mother had undertaken buying trips to Manchester so Elizabeth took advantage of her own journeys home to Lancashire to work at maintaining John's commercial relationships, cementing them with a sociable touch.[70]

The bleeding over of warehouse into home, and vice versa, extended as we have seen in previous chapters to bleeding over from working relationships to those based in a friendly sociability. Crane in particular was a welcome guest at the Shaw's home, even whilst John was away and he was still an employee, and Elizabeth's friendship towards him may well have played an important role in persuading him to settle in business and accept the offer of a partnership.[71]

Critically, John allowed that Elizabeth had skills that fitted her well for this sort of work, telling her that 'It is your province to see and to direct others to work'. Of course, this statement had its complications, for she was in part suited to such work through being ill-fitted 'to do it [the work] yourself – will you keep this in mind – try if you can'. Still, in so directing, John was thinking more of Elizabeth's health and constitution than her sex and in allowing her skills of oversight and direction (which we may think of as equivalent to management) he allowed her much more credit than perhaps many other men would have done with regard to their wives' aptitudes. He must have been cognizant of and grateful for all that she did.

However, no matter how openly acknowledged was Elizabeth's role in the firm, no matter how publicly some of it was performed, she had no formal role in either its management or its ownership. She was never John's partner in the business in a formal sense. She held no shares; indeed as a married woman she had no right to hold any property as her own. Certainly she can have drawn no salary (though it is true that the evidence suggests a porous boundary between firm and family finances, even in such a well-run concern). But none of these facts should lead us to underestimate her role. As Eleanor Hamilton's studies of modern family businesses remind us 'the "invisibility" of women [in such firms] contributes towards, and reinforces, a dominant discourse of entrepreneurship, which has been described as individualistic, gender-biased and discriminatory'.[72] Certainly it would be easy to write the history of the Shaw/Shaw and Crane/John Shaw and Sons businesses as John's history – but it would also be wrong. Instead of focusing on the archetypal (and male) entrepreneur-as-lone-hero, Hamilton suggests, we might ask 'how women maintain their influence given what ... is frequently a position of marginality'.[73] If that marginality remains the case for many women in family businesses today then how much more might it have been so for Elizabeth? One answer to understanding the influence of a woman such as Elizabeth is to see and to explore how a different perspective on the story of a family business can 'bring to light subtle relationships of duty, love, power, and conflict'.[74] Undoubtedly attempting to adopt the kind of perspective we take here can help us to work to undermine entrepreneurship's casual association with a crude masculinity – and in any case, is it not true that different men perform many different types of masculinity – and an assertive individualism. This last point is particularly pertinent to John and Elizabeth's case, for if she could not enter into a formal partnership with her husband then it is surely the case that the partnership she did enjoy with him was far more profound and unlimited.

If Elizabeth willingly, gladly, helped John in shouldering the burdens of his life in business then his stance mirrored hers. As she stepped sometimes into the public, working sphere so he played a very full role in the private sphere of the home and the family. Indeed, he took a conspicuous and very touching delight in domesticity, home and, in particular, the children. He was unabashed and unashamed of his deep sentimental engagement with these worlds, just as he had been unabashed and unashamed in avowing his love and affection for Elizabeth during their courtship. It was in this part of his life that John was happiest and most comfortable, perhaps most himself.[75]

In part, this attraction to home was a reaction against the wider world framed in terms of its temptations. When, in courtship, Elizabeth confessed the fears she attached to a traveller's life abroad in the world John concurred, saying as 'regards travelling I am quite of your opinion respecting ... in any way mingling so much with the world that it certainly has a tendency to withdraw all serious impressions and without particular care watchfulness'.[76] But, in part, he simply did not much enjoy socializing, especially when weighed against the attractions of home. Indeed, he told Elizabeth very bluntly that 'I do very much dislike it [visiting] – I have made but few or no acquaintances in Town – my whole time has been spent in my business'.[77] Even as a bachelor living alone John could take real pleasure in domesticity. On Christmas day 1812, just a few months before his much longed-for marriage to Elizabeth, he wrote to tell her how 'I soon found that I was alone [and] I experienced a pleasure in sitting in my own House and by my own fireside – such as one that I had never before felt and I prized them highly'.[78] Still, he acknowledged, the picture was as yet incomplete: 'but still I found something else wanting. I wanted a sincere, tender and affectionate friend – one to whom I could unbosom myself and speak my inmost thoughts – one who would be feeling alive to all my pleasures and pains'.[79] As he went on to spell out, he meant, of course, her and only her. Once he had secured his companion, and especially after the process of building a family had begun, his satisfaction in the domestic only strengthened and deepened.

Most striking, even to the modern eye, is the way in which John's pleasure is so very far from that of the authoritative paterfamilias, never merely lord and master of all that he surveys. He never appears to see home, or wife and children, as symbolic of or testament to his masculinity or as the proper reward for his success in the world of commerce. Instead, his letters are full of what it is hard to read as anything but an unfeigned delight in the simple routines of life at home looking after the children, the home and the garden.

John had frequent opportunities to exercise and develop this dimension of his character because of Elizabeth's often quite prolonged visits either to her family in Lancashire or such fashionable resorts as Buxton, Skipton, or Harrowgate. John never betrayed any resentment of or irritation with these absences and indeed often encouraged her not to hurry home unnecessarily. Perhaps he knew – and feared – that her return would often mean that the time for his own departure on another sales journey was close at hand. The time at home was precious in a very simple and direct way.

This chapter opened with a quotation describing the infant Betsey's belief her mother had gone on a journey to get orders. The letter continued in the same delightful vein:

> [Betsey] is very cute and well contented – the first word I get from her in the morning and other parts of the day is shall go in the Park with Papa and me. In general we get a good batch of play ere we get out again. Thomas is very well and full of life and sturdy – you will find a wonderful alteration in him on your return for I can – or think I can – see one every day – he is certainly for his age the finest child of the three … he can all but walk at which I expect he will be quite perfect by the time you return.

> If you can make yourself comfortable and your Mother wishes to, remain as long as you think you possibly can – pray don't hurry home for we are doing exceeding well – all very quiet, orderly and steady I can assure you.[80]

He concluded the letter by telling her that 'If Betsey knew I was writing you she would I doubt not send you a kiss'.[81] The details of the letter, particularly its references to playing and trips to the park suggest that as a father John was very far from being a stern or distant figure. Nor did he merely indulge or play with their children but tended them in illness, sat with them at dinner, and made sure that they attended to their lessons, music and other activities.[82] And as with other aspects of their lives that we have looked at in this chapter it is easy to detect very long-run patterns of continuity, to see them as settled into comfortable patterns and routines. And so, a full thirteen years after the letter just quoted, John was still writing from Wolverhampton to Lancashire to reassure his wife that 'We shall all be glad to see you but don't hurry home if you are comfortable [as] we are all doing well and it may be perhaps a long time ere you go again'.[83]

Thus, as he and Elizabeth moved into middle age and the older children spent more time away at school, John's pleasure in both home and parenthood seemed not at all diminished. In the spring of 1831 for example, as Elizabeth was in Lancashire dealing with illness amongst her own family, John could happily assure her that 'As regards home we are I believe doing well. I can see nothing to cause me to think otherwise. We are all very well and very quiet and orderly. Richard is a good boy'.[84] Indeed, if anything his fond doting on and delight in the children only seemed to increase with time:

> I can assure we are doing as well as we can do – all is quiet and still and as regular as the clock and out little Mary gets a great Mary – in other words she gets a bouncer and a funny thing talking – I am desired by Sarah to say she has got two or three more teeth. I am sure you will find a great alteration in her. I think she is as heavy again as when you left and so fond of kissing any time of which opens wide her mouth – so funny you can't think – she gets a sweet little body.[85]

Elizabeth cannot fail to have been both moved and reassured to receive such an endearing portrait of domestic harmony and pleasure from her husband. Likewise she must have been pleased the next year to hear that 'Mary has not forgot you – I ask her where is Mamma – she clearly points to the window and says gone a tatta'.[86]

Conclusions

John and Elizabeth were able to make business and family work and coexist because they themselves worked together. They showed to each other a marked consideration rooted in deep understanding and affection. This understanding and affection had been established, developed, cemented during the long and sometimes difficult courtship that we explored in Chapter 3. But it was only after courtship that this remarkable relationship was really to flourish as it met – and overcame – the trials and contingencies of making a life together in the world through business. It is only through understanding the nature and origins of that marriage, all the influences and experiences that informed and made it, that we can begin to understand the ways in which a life in business as a family was met and experienced as both challenging and worthwhile. Through negotiation, accommodation, and an understanding of each other's characters, strengths, weaknesses and dispositions they crafted a way of living and working that delivered both business and familial success, if we may think in those terms.

They found solutions to the everyday dilemmas and demands of life in a family business that even today wear a remarkably modern quality.[87] Their lives had a degree of fluidity that we often, perhaps mistakenly, see as part of the condition of late modernity. They defy our crude and fixed characterizations of what it was to be a man and a woman in the early nineteenth-century. They each moved constantly between multiple role, identities and relationships, just as they each moved back and forth across the supposed divide between the public and the private, whether constituted either ideologically or as a physical space, the economic and the non-economic, the male and the female. Thus, for example, John came to life and truly flourished not as entrepreneur and businessman but as loving husband and father. Perhaps Elizabeth didn't enter 'his' world with quite such commitment or pleasure – and there were still many barriers against her doing so that we cannot pretend simply did not exist – but nonetheless, when called upon, she did so willingly and ably. Just as John could happily retire to the simple pleasures of home so she could be active, engaged and forthright. It was in thus acting, informed by their own respective upbringings, cultures and influences, that they truly forged their unlimited partnership as a precept by which to live. In the next chapter we will see how that very personal unlimited partnership was set in a wider web of relationships.

6 'THE WHOLE CIRCLE OF OUR ACQUAINTANCE': NETWORKS AND SOCIABILITY.

'The Whole Circle of Our Acquaintance'[1]

Introduction

The Shaw's world, shaped by ties of kinship, friendship and trade, was overwhelmingly oriented to the country north of their Wolverhampton home. Links to London were rare, and to the wider South-east and South-west seemingly nonexistent. When London did figure it was inevitably as a centre of the country's financial and banking systems rather than as a market in itself. It is true that two of Elizabeth's brothers had tried to establish themselves in London but they both, sooner or later, returned to the North. Until the nascent Asian trade began escalating in scale and scope from 1827, culminating in the dramatic events of 1834 and the formation of a direct and very personal bridge to India, traces of international connections are equally rare; little more than a few scattered overseas orders here and there. The letters contain only two references to John himself travelling overseas; once to Dublin and once to Holland – a stormy passage across the North Sea causing Elizabeth great anxiety.[2] Scotland is entirely absent.

The Shaws were, however, far from parochial. Within an area largely defined by the counties of Shropshire, Staffordshire, Derbyshire, Cheshire, Lancashire and the West Riding of Yorkshire they travelled extensively and frequently, and often for reasons other than the imperatives of trade that impelled John's commercial travels. They were very often at Colne and Rochdale in Lancashire but also Manchester and Liverpool, then both also in Lancashire. Their children were in time sent to schools across Shropshire, in such towns as Bridgnorth. They took holidays in a range of resorts including Aberystwyth (Cardiganshire), Leamington Spa (Warwickshire), Buxton (Derbyshire) and Skipton (then in the West Riding of Yorkshire), many of them known for the restorative properties of their waters, whether sea or spring.[3] These travels were almost always about people; they were undertaken to make, maintain and renew a range of relationships and connections. As we have seen, both John and Elizabeth claim to have been happiest in the quiet, private retreat provided by the home. In reality they mixed easily and often as both hosts and guests, spontaneously and with planning, and rarely if ever with any great formality. Relationships between persons of different ages and genders seem to have been marked by a degree of equality and openness. It is true, however, that their circles were both relatively compact, based in an affective sympathy, and, above all else, very stable. The same names recur time and again as either visitors or hosts. Due to Elizabeth marrying out of her locality a number of these relationships were sustained over separation in time and space; visiting (when possible) and corresponding (when not) did the work of maintaining such relationships. And through these processes John and Elizabeth's respective birth families showed a degree of meshing, if not actual merging.

This chapter will explore in more depth a subject already touched on at several points; namely the role of sociability and relationships in Elizabeth and John's world, on how relationships worked to sustain them, individually and together, and any role those relationships may have played in their entrepreneurial career. We can identify three broad categories of relationship based in, respectively; kith and kin, friendship and finally those displaying a greater (economic) instrumentality. These categories overlapped to varying degrees but the final one, that consisting of more instrumental, economically-related connections, was undoubtedly both weakest and the least well integrated with the others. This is important. There is a strong argument, and a significant supporting literature, that suggests first, that more or less informal networking was extremely important to the structure, conduct and performance of most British business during the period of the classic industrial revolution and onward through much of the nineteenth-century and, second, that this networking was often based in and emerged out of ties of family, friendship and locality; the level at which such ties naturally operated with the greatest force and effectiveness. New fledged entrepreneurs in particular, it is argued, were often highly reliant on familial and friendship sources of what we would now call venture capital. In turn, network related business success and wealth was often recycled, being returned to the local and regional economy via investments in other manufacturing or commercial enterprises, especially those begun by family and friends, as well as banks, and utilities, such as gas or railway companies. Such banking and utility enterprise often brought together congeries of local business elites in concerted action to generate semi-public goods.[4]

But, as we have seen, John and Elizabeth prized self-reliance above all else, received little familial financing for their enterprise, tended to keep affect and business as separate as possible, and forged relationships that were emotionally and spiritually sustaining rather than promising of worldly advancement. In turn, though John came to own considerable amounts of property in the Black Country district (consisting largely of domestic properties, so far as it is possible to tell) the archive contains only scattered evidence of investment in the regional economy. Similarly, Elizabeth and he seemed to have done little to court social advancement, instead they remained loyal to the friends with whom they had embarked on adult life even as their own (financial) position improved considerably. They were not the sort to develop the ridiculous parvenu social pretentions so wickedly caricatured by Dickens in the Podsnap family. We should not, though, see their lives as circumscribed or, that dread word, provincial; instead their social world was warm, convivial and supportive. In contrast, their business networks, particularly those associated with credit and finance, were necessarily relatively long-distance or non-local but they were also for the most part much more impersonal.

Ties that bind

Of course, we should be wary of drawing these distinctions too tightly or the separation between the different compartments of their lives too exclusively. After all, John and Elizabeth first met in a commercial context, across the counter of her father's shop in Colne, and that chance meeting led to family ties that stretched across different regions. Indeed, just a few months after marriage Elizabeth recounted to John how 'Father says all the tradesmen know that I was married and it was advertised in a great many papers'. The private was also public and the news was significant amongst not only circles of friends but also those of other traders in the places where Elizabeth was known and where her father and brothers did business. Her change in status had a commercial dimension that piqued the interest of her father's fellow Lancashire retailers. 'Indeed', she concluded, 'I believe we are both pretty well known'.[5] Perhaps the competition wondered whether the Wilkinson family enterprises would now see favoured treatment from the young factor. At the same time, at least one of Elizabeth's brothers remained a customer of John's for some years thereafter. Similarly, there is also evidence of intra-family financing of new business ventures amongst the Wilkinson family and John did receive a dowry from Elizabeth's family on their wedding, money that was seen, at least in part, as contributing towards the young couple's ability to succeed in business, earn a living and achieve independence. It is notable, however, that these specific cases were far from happy and harmonious and perhaps tempered any enthusiasm various family members may have had for entangling bonds of blood with those of credit and debt.

In particular, the issue of how much John was to receive from Elizabeth's father was a source of real pain, especially to Elizabeth. Before exploring the issue in more depth it is important to stress that the issue only arose, in least in writing, once the plans for their marriage were at a very advanced stage and formed no part of a negotiated settlement prior to marriage being agreed upon. Indeed, as we have seen, there was no such negotiation in the sense expected in arranged marriages. Elizabeth and John chose each other freely; any negotiation was of their feelings and hearts.

The first mention of the issue occurs in a letter written by Elizabeth on 19 October 1812, prompted by John's perhaps jealous observation that Elizabeth's father had found cash to establish her brother John in a partnership. Having concurred in his view of partnerships as 'dangerous things', Elizabeth feels forced into offering her betrothed an explanation of the family's finances and priorities. In the background there loomed the question of what sum John Shaw was to receive. Having carefully outlined her dislike of partnerships and her hope that in this case it will 'prove advantageous' she goes on by first acknowledging that:

> My bro' as you say, will require a much larger sum to begin business than my father offers me – especially were he to begin alone and my Cousin [the other partner] has no money of his own ...[6]

before continuing to explain how:

> but then my Uncle John has kindly offer'd to lend John Spencer £500 [the cousin] – My father will give John [Wilkinson, her brother] £300 and lend him two more – but one of the two must be taken in shop goods. They will then have a thousand to stock their shop with – Spencer has got almost what will be wanted in household furniture. He is a very good disposition'd lad – not of great ability except in serving a customer.[7]

Elizabeth has clearly felt it to be of great importance that she explain with precision both the sources of and conditions attached to this financing of the new familial venture. Still, there is more that she feels the need to lay-out before John. In particular that:

> My father could not have found John [Wilkinson] a thousand to begin living with – Nor could he have easily spar'd him what he has now, but that he had [it] in readiness for me not knowing when I should want it – I shall very much pleased when he [her brother] is settled as I know it will greatly lighten their cares (my father and mother) – I do not suppose that my father will give me more or less than he has promised, he has been ask'd more than once and I should be sorry that it should be named to him again.[8]

Elizabeth expressed great admiration and of devotion to her parents throughout her life and perhaps towards her father particularly. Here she shows a depth of consideration to not only his circumstances but even more towards his emotions and sentiments. That these were her primary concerns she goes on to make absolutely explicit in a far-reaching discussion:

> If he could do it without injuring himself, I make no doubt of his compliance but I am convinced he cannot, and I should be sorry in his declining years to rob him of

anything that would add to his comforts – He cannot do less than set his boys up in the world – If he does not who will but as to the Girls there's no necessity for it as he would always be able to keep them – I feel obliged to him for his offer to be me – but at the same time I am convinced and I know that my property in comparison with yours is a mere trifle – and especially at the present – but you have known it from the time of your asking after it – If I had a thousand or two I should be very Glad for your sake – Providence could have given it to me if He had seen fit but as it is I must be content with my small portion.[9]

This was a difficult and complex mix of forces and emotions that Elizabeth (and John) were forced to negotiate. Though not ashamed of her slight monetary worth she was conscious of just how little she was able to bring to the marriage in financial and material terms. But with characteristic forthrightness she reminded John that he had always known this and could have no complaint. At the same time that forthrightness, a refusal to be confined by her sex which we have already seen expressed in many different situations, here confronts head on a differently gendered sense of duty to family. Her father has no choice but to do all he can to establish his sons in life. If needs must, her role will be to not wed and stay at home. For once she is able to accommodate herself to the possibility of that subordinate position, something she was rarely comfortable in doing, because her sense of her familial duty as a daughter became entirely overriding when it concerned her parents and her father especially.

Despite the clarity of her explanation to John she was forced to open her next letter 'lost in gloomy conjectures'; John had, it seems, reopened the subject.[10] Her brother's projected partnership had collapsed ('a circumstance, which I cannot now inform you of … happen'd that entirely frustrated their design'),[11] an unlooked for calamity which had not only required Elizabeth's full participation in the fevered attempts to get John Wilkinson's new shop ready for its opening ('If possible we must open next Saturday as it is the fair – I sadly fear we shall not') but which had also thrown the fledging enterprise's finances into disarray.[12] Again her feelings are undergirded by a sentiment towards of love and devotion towards her father; 'for no person ever shew'd so affection towards me as my father nor was so tender over me in sickness'. But still, between her and John, it came down, for now, 'as to money matters'. She is 'persuaded' that her father cannot be 'conscious of doing me wrong'. Indeed, if he has a favourite then it is her. Nor, she insists, does he actually do her wrong for 'He gives me the same as the other two [her brothers John and Thomas] – what is over and above is only lent and they pay interest for it'.[13] These arrangements betray a (perhaps hopeless) determination to keep money and sentiment separate within the family. Still Elizabeth works away at a worry that John will not be satisfied with his share:

And he spoke nothing but the truth when he said he could not spare me more that what he had promised – altho' it may appear a mystery to you how he come at the money for Bro^r John. I will endeavour to unfold if for you, for I can't bear to hear an indifferent person speak slightly of my father, my blood mounts high when that is the case – then how could I bear you to do it?[14]

Elizabeth, at least, finds it impossible to keep feelings apart from finances. In attempting to resolve both her own and John Shaw's confusion, doubts, perhaps even mistrust, she again lays out precisely how her brother John's business is now to be financed in the wake of the breakdown of his partnership. Her words reveal a web of familial resources that we would expect and think typical of petty enterprises in this period.[15]

However, what concerns her far more than the precise details of these arrangements is the effect the issue has on her emotions and on her relationships, with John especially. Her words are simple and heartfelt:

> I feel a good deal in consequence of what you say respecting money. More than ever I thought I should feel. I never felt a want of it [money] before. But how can I remedy it? I would rather be pennyless than that my father should be distress'd for want of money in his business ... It is a pity to be blamed for kindness. My father was only too kind. How soon will you be here after you commence your journey? I feel as if it would do me good to see and converse with you on these subjects.[16]

Before she leaves the subject she observes how she 'can't describe to you how very much my mind is distress'd ... I feel such an uneasiness such a weight at my heart together with an agitation that disorders my whole frame'.[17]

His one surviving letter from this period paints John showing a remarkably hard-headed, perhaps intransigent attitude to the dispute. There is no doubt he felt slighted as well as disadvantaged. He justified his insistence on the issue with the claim that 'I have no thoughts that I would not wish you to know and I could not have acquitted myself of not acting in that fair open and candid manner I should wish always to appear to you if I had not done it [spoken his mind]'. This principle explained John continued to press his point – and his claim – with words that could not be misunderstood:

> The difference which you Father has and still contrived to make between you and your Brothers I must say I think hard – it hurts me more than ... the loss of money would because I can't see in any point of view why he should do it if he has the same affection for me as another. I have thought of it a great deal and I can't see why I am not entitled to an equal share of what he has now to give or lend as well your Brothers – He perhaps may think I could do better without it but then I must according to my ideas differ from him but independent of this present difference the thought will present itself to me – forgive me if I am wrong – I hope always to be open to correction – that the same cause that operates with him to make this difference now may weigh with him in like manner hereafter when it may not be yourself alone but a family that may have claims upon him.[18]

Here he concludes, one might think slightly disingenuously, by declaring 'But enough upon this unpleasant subject. If anything more is said upon it let it be when we see each other as it makes me unhappy as I have before observed to be in any way a means of distressing your mind upon a subject for which there appears to be remedy'.[19] It is little wonder Elizabeth was hurt as John cast doubt on her father's affection not only for him but also for her and even for any children she might go on to have.[20]

It is hard to believe that Elizabeth was not to some degree scarred by these disputes and though her and John's relationship survived and flourished memories of the incident perhaps coloured their attitudes to money and family for many years to come. But John did, it seems, realise how seriously he had both offended and upset Elizabeth. In the same letter as the one we have just quoted from he prefaces his comments on her father's actions with the following lines on the continuing nature of his affection:

> I hope you will not think different nor will you I hope think so from what has in part formed the subject of my last letter or two for although I could not – not can I now – bring myself to think upon the subject as I could wish it has not in the least my D^r [for Dear] Girl been the cause of [a] lessening of my affections for you – that remains and will I doubt not still remain the same. I am truly sorry [that] what I have said should have been the cause of uneasiness to you and I believe I can truly say it has been full as painful to me'.[21]

For Elizabeth this seems to have sufficed as an apology or justification, for her next letter finds her adopting a much brighter tone, declaring that 'If you have nothing else but your unaltered and sincere affection to offer me, believe me (now that I know your value) it is of more avail than riches, honors, pleasures or all that the world calls great and good'.[22] She was also responding to John's declaration that his affection, 'unaltered and sincere', was 'at present the only thing I have to offer – will this do any good'. To know that there was no great disparity in the wealth between them, even if it meant both had little, seems to have come as a relief to Elizabeth. They were able to enter marriage on more or less equal terms. It was his love, not his wealth, however it might stand, that she wished to have and to hold. Never again in all the years that were to follow did this issue, or anything like, it reappear in their correspondence. A painful lesson had been learnt.

This did not mean that a total disentanglement of family, trade and finance took place. Members of Elizabeth's family continued to do business with John (as they had done before the couple began their relationship) for many years.[23] The majority of John's small retail customers did a relatively petty trade with him.[24] With such customers there was certainly less potential for serious contention. Similarly, whilst his business as a whole was highly reliant on a delicately poised edifice of credit and trust, the failure of any individual customer (or the simple failure to pay on time) was unlikely to threaten collapse. Still non- or late payment was frustrating, worry-inducing and time consuming. It must have been galling then for Elizabeth to have to write to her betrothed in the Spring of 1812 in the following terms: 'I feel asham'd that my bro^r has not been able to send your money yet. The truth is he is very poor and every time he gets a little some one fetches it away directly – I hope it will not be long ere he remit you'.[25] Her words, seeming to betray a strange naivety about the workings of trade and the circulation of money, are curious. Elizabeth, who had spent her whole life in shops, was certainly not so innocent of the mechanisms at work here. Her brother was simply not getting in enough money to meet his obligations. Her words do not try to dissemble but they do try and excuse. Still, behind those excuses hovers the shadow of shame – readily admitted to, one of the key factors that theorists claim motivates the maintenance of trust and social capital.

However, despite that incidence of non-payment, we can still detect some forbearance in John's attitude towards brother Thomas. The various Journey books covering the period 1812 to 1814 show Thomas Wilkinson of Rochdale running a consistently high account: £163–10–3 in November 1812, £85–10–0 in May 1813, a very significant spike to £205–12–7 in June 1814, £126–17–4 in August 1814 (the last two entries showing some attempt to reduce the account), followed by another slight rise to £159–6–3 in November 1814.[26] These figures are very much at the top end in terms of the value of customer accounts. In November 1812 only five out of dozens of customers were running larger accounts (four of those being in Liverpool, a much larger and more prosperous town where shopkeepers were presumably able to do a much larger trade). The only other Rochdale customer running an account at that time, one Meanley, owed John just £3–7–10. Accounts valued at over £200 were extremely rare. Remarkably, by early 1815 Thomas had managed to entirely settle his account and the only entry against his name in the Journey book indicates a remittance of £20. This represented either an heroic effort at retrenchment and repayment or that some other – likely familial – mechanism had come into play. In any case, there is evidence enough that John treated his brother-in-law with some lenience, though whether from genuine sentiment, a sense of obligation, or moral suasion from the family we will never know.[27] These were not to be the end of Thomas' troubles with money and as late as 1828 he seemed to be in serious trouble.[28] There is in addition more scattered evidence of trade with Elizabeth's father, who, for example, noted 'inclosure [sic] of a Bill value £99–1–8 which is passed to your credit' in a letter dated 1815.[29]

But money was not the only route via which trade and business could encroach on family life and relations. As we saw in the previous chapter, the divide between work and life was rarely a clear cut one, especially perhaps for women. This was a fact of life. Nonetheless, as families grow more complex through intermarriage then the potential for conflicts of interest, pulling between conflicting senses of duty and obligation, only grow. For John Elizabeth's birth family maintained a claim on her labour that could seem problematic:

> I have no cause in one respect to complain for I always enjoy your society at Rochdale much more than I can and do at Colne but at the same time I am not without my feats for the result of this your visit to Rochdale which I am fearful will do you no good but harm knowing your anxious disposition and let me beg of you at the same time you are studying your Brother's interest not to lose sight of your own and instead of working and fatiguing yourself only to see that others do so.[30]

It is possible that family, and marriage in particular, has been somewhat idealized at points in this study; here is laid bare a side we have seen less often, one that if not actually coercive could actually compel through a self-imposed burden of obligation.[31]

For the most part though relations between the extended Shaw-Wilkinson family were not merely cordial or harmonious but warm, affectionate and loving. 'Marrying out' and travel imposed separation not only on John and Elizabeth but also on the wider networks of family relationships; as Elizabeth ruefully observed to in a letter to John during the first few months of their marriage (in fact her first extant letter post-marriage): 'if you see Colne will you tell the good folks I often think of the days that are passed and that I should like to lift Colne a little nearer Wolverhampton'.[32] But both worked diligently and with good spirit to build and maintain relationships with their in-laws, each often acting for the other as a bridge back to their birth family. The same very early post-marriage letter just quoted contains a seemingly simple but telling example of this work, in which Elizabeth recounts how 'your mother is better and in pretty good spirits, Bro' and sister pretty well – I drank tea there on Saturday with Miss Mander, her cousin, Mr Steward and Doctor Toulman. The two last came for a walk'.[33] Freshly transplanted to the Midlands, having never met John's family prior to their marriage, Elizabeth willingly commits herself to both John's family and his existing social networks.[34] Elizabeth's family was much larger than John's with many more siblings, aunts and uncles, and eventually sisters-in-law and nieces and nephews (especially beloved Betsey, first born of Richard, her eldest brother).[35] This large but close family fostered an ability to get along with one another, indeed Elizabeth described how she and her brother Thomas 'live very comfortably and have learnt to put up with each others faults, so that we are almost become a proverb in the neighbourhood – and many take us for man and wife yet'.[36] As she went on to reflect in the very next sentence, 'Of all things dissentions in a family are most disagreeable'.[37] Familial harmony was clearly very important to Elizabeth and she worked hard to maintain it. At the same time, a properly ordered and harmonious family was the best of schools in which to prepare children for life. To Elizabeth 'Public schools are almost as bad as the Factories for corrupting the morals of children'. As a result she determined that 'If ever I have children I mean to instruct them myself so far as I am able and tho' I shall not do it as I should wish yet I think I could please myself better than another could please me'.[38]

And of course family linked not only to family but also to friends. So particularly significant at the informal gathering at John's mother's house, just noted, was the presence of Miss Mander. The Shaw and Mander families were to develop a particularly strong and long-lasting relationship as they together emerged as pillars of the Wolverhampton business community.[39] Both John and Elizabeth's letters down through the years, before and after marriage, speaking of both Lancashire and the Black Country, are replete with references to friends, gatherings and visits. For this most part they are marked by both a great informality or spontaneity and distinct lack of aspiration. Most often friends, neighbours and relations seem to have simply called on the off-chance, seeking a chance to share a cup of tea and the opportunity to share news and gossip.[40] Certainly these interactions rarely seem to have had either the stiffness or the social significance (or snobbery) of much of the visiting undertaken by the lesser north country Gentry in the same period, as witnessed in the contemporaneous diaries of Anne Lister of Shibden Hall, West Yorkshire.[41]

It is true that much later, in 1823, that is after ten years of marriage and having established a solid position in trade and thus perhaps also in society, Elizabeth recounts with some evident pleasure how:

> Mrs W[eaver?] I find is quite round and I found it out by seeing her at Mrs Barkers when paying the Brides visit with your sister – met such a party there all the grandees belonging to Queen St and I have got my foot in it by going – having got an invitation to meet a party there next Tuesday and who know how many more [invitations] will follow.[42]

But if there is some enjoyment in at last gaining some standing in Wolverhampton society then we may also detect a slight ironic detachment too – and it should be noted that Elizabeth very quickly concludes 'and I am sure I cannot go' – though whether she feels so from a lack of confidence, availability, or simply desire is not clear. Perhaps it was a lesson she had learnt many years earlier from her Aunt, whom she described as:

> [a] woman in a thousand, she might visit amongst the highest circles in this Town and neighbourhood but she is well convinced that it would spoil their domestic happiness and so she gives denials to all invitations of that nature – She is possess'd of that common sense of which a number of females are destitute and makes her husband comfortable in spight of fashion.[43]

Moreover, if sociability was informal, spontaneous and small in scale then it was also, for the most part, private. The letters contain very few if any references to large public gatherings and certainly no balls, dances, or grand dinners. The few exceptions thus stand out, such as from 1823 when 'we have had an astronomical lecture held in the theatre here [Wolverhampton] the first was last Thursday night and was so well attended that the lecturer ventured upon another on Monday evening – the latter of which your sister and I attended accompanied by Mr B Mander and his sister'.[44] No doubt this event was suitably improving. Equally scant is evidence of membership of societies and associations (beyond chapel of course). One exception is hinted at when Elizabeth informs John how Henry Crane had 'brought me a note from the Harmonic Society stating that their public meeting would be next Monday night and he asked me for ⅜ to pay for your ticket or he said you would lose your entrance money'.[45] A little forlornly she went on to note how 'I feel no desire to go as you are not here to go with me'. Certainly such frequent and prolonged separations as Elizabeth and John had to endure must have made developing a fuller public social life both more difficult and less attractive.[46] Still, John was sure to encourage her to go out and to enjoy herself at those events – sacred and profane – that the locality could furnish. Thus, in the summer of 1825, he supposed that:

> [g]reat preparations are making with you, some on one account and some on another, some for the opening of the chapel and some for the races – I can't see any prospect of my being at home to the one or the other. I hope no accident will happen at either but can't say I am without fears, at all accts I shall not entertain any fears in your going to the Race course – you should take to go into the Grandstand, you will have a full time since so I dare say there is the fair [too] and of course you will be well provided to entertain all the necessary friends that will visit you.[47]

Nor, despite the undoubted depth and sincerity of their Christian faith, do they seem to have been deeply involved in the life of the Chapel or John very actively involved in its organizational life, for example by fulfilling the sorts of roles which David Jeremy has portrayed as playing a significant role in developing the managerial (and accounting) capacities of many non-conformist businessmen. It is apparent that when young John had fulfilled such offices, telling Elizabeth that he could not immediately change his place of worship (to which she had doctrinal objections) because:

> I ought not to give up ever altogether attending my own place. I am one of the younger branches of the society upon whom a serious charge descends. I am a trustee for the property which is somewhat considerable and when I became one I then promised to the utmost of my power and ability to support and watch over the best interests of the place and congregation. The charge was made to me by a late minister whose memory will ever be dear to me and such a promise I cannot well forget.

John evokes a very considerable sense of duty here, but there is little evidence of very deep institutional involvement in his later life.[48] It is true that he remained a prominent member of the largely working-class Queen Street Congregational Chapel, helped found Wolverhampton Library, appended his signature to the petition calling for the town to be awarded Borough status in 1848, and eventually served as a magistrate.[49] Compared to many industrialists of the time, however, this is a relatively modest roll-call of public service.

The Bounds of Commerce

In their domestic lives then the Shaws kept to a relatively sheltered and compact orbit and after those early difficulties over the settlement or portion Elizabeth was to receive from her father (and brother Thomas' difficulties as a customer) they also tried as far as possible not to blur the lines between family and friendship, on the one hand, and trade and finance on the other. We already have seen in an earlier chapter that John could share moments of sociability with customers – the taking of drinks with or from customers was almost an occupational hazard for commercial travellers – but again mention of such activities is scarce.[50] Perhaps at the everyday level social interaction within a commercial setting was so common and mundane as to not warrant any attention – but it is the unusually convivial and pleasant nature of one evening spent at a customer's home that singles it out for detailed description, suggesting it was in fact a rare event.[51] And of course, the relationship with Henry Crane blurred business and pleasure. He may have been first an employee and then a partner but Crane, and in time his wife and their children, became close family friends –despite the entanglements of co-partnership. In other aspects of the concern too it proved hard to keep sentiment out of business. The separation from colleagues and home imposed by the Indian enterprise was countered by a resilient extended familism that took in not only kith and kin but also even quite junior employees. We may think of these relationships as a form of *in loco parentis* that though separate from the family nonetheless drew on it for its strength and character.[52]

All of these though are relatively soft examples of that intense networking that is supposed to have characterized business growth and development during the Industrial Revolution period, especially at the regional level.[53] Family was not a significant source of start-up or working capital, no doubt because at marriage John had already completed an apprenticeship and been in business on his own account for eight years. Crane straddled both the public and private spheres as both partner and welcome guest – but his movement was from commerce into friendship rather than the reverse. Familism to an extent bound employees and employers together and helped them combat the stresses of business life but was hardly central to either the survival or even the flourishing of the enterprise.

Just as the Shaw family itself represents a relatively hermetic unit, foreshadowing the deeply domestic nuclear family of the high-Victorian bourgeoisie so the firm remained relatively independent of the surrounding economic landscape.

The one area in which the firm had little or no chance of such independence was with regard to credit and the wider working of the trading system of which it was a part. As has been shown several times, Shaw and Crane, like all comparable firms, were extremely reliant on credit in order to conduct their business; credit from suppliers, and credit to customers. This wide-reaching use of credit has been understood as reflecting both underlying institutional weaknesses or absences and the ready availability of high-trust relationships in highly localized regional economies where personal reputation still meant something. In other words, trust, based in mutual knowledge, substituted for the highly efficient, impersonal and essentially mechanistic methods of transacting we are all familiar with today. The most common mechanism in this system of credit was the bill of exchange, itself an instrument inseparable from notions of trust and creditworthiness; after all, as one character observes in Arnold Bennett's *Anna of the Five Towns*, the bill of exchange was 'but a promise'[54]. The survival of at least one 'Bill Book' amongst the Shaw archives gives us a glimpse into the ubiquity and the scope of this credit system.[55]

This 'Bill Book', which interestingly came ready printed up by Shelmerdine and Co. and sold by Bloxham and Fourdriniers of Lombard Street in the heart of the City of London, dates from the late eighteen-teens (most of the bills are dated 1817, a few 1818) and across its thirty-eight double pages (each demarcated by fifteen blank rows across, from left to right, columns for 'Of whom received', 'No.', 'Where and when dated', 'Date', 'To whom payable', 'Value', 'By whom drawn', 'On whom drawn', and 'To whom paid and when') records the passage through the firm's hands in just a few months of some 570 bills of exchange ranging in value from just a few pounds to well over one hundred. The extent of the system, of the reliance of all upon it, is vividly conveyed. The readily commercial availability of such blank bill books is a further indicator of this. But it perhaps also conveys that this had become even by this date as much a system, with all the impersonality that implies, as it was a set of relationships mediated by personal knowledge and regular close trading. Moreover, though Shaw and Crane will, naturally, have had knowledge of – and presumably some degree of trust in – the person from whom they received bills much of the rest of the system that lay behind any one bill must have been at best opaque. In particular, the vast majority of bills were drawn on individuals, partnerships and firms based in London, a part of the country with which Shaw and Crane had no meaningful links and, so far as we can discern, no trade whatsoever at this time. At the heart of this web then lay the London acceptance houses, distant and aloof. This was a 'network' then but one barely overlaid at all with any of those connotations of social embeddedness normally implied by that term.[56]

Ultimately, experience also taught that appearances and standing might well be concealing a multitude of sins. The summer of 1815 brought distressed times with 'no work for the lower classes and no money for the middling'. Crucially, 'we have [bad bills] return'd ... daily but most not complain ... We hear of the Bailiffs being in this and the other respectable house every day – people that one would have thought had a mint of money but nothing seems to resist the tides of the times'.[57] These lessons were reinforced with great harshness when a similar calamity visited the Wilkinson family itself. The precise circumstances are now lost but in 1822 Elizabeth's mother wrote to her thus:

> You want to know what resource R[ichard] hath for beginning housekeeping – he hath none at all but what must come from us all as his debts must be given up to the court and if he be freed from his creditors and I shall be very thankful if they leave him in possession of his satificate [certificate, though to practice which profession is not certain]. Can assure you he is in a bad situation ... Most of their [clothes] is in the P'Broker's hand.[58]

Unsurprisingly, Elizabeth's mother was desperate to find an explanation that excused her son responsibility for this disaster, which she ascribed not 'for any injustice on his part but for want of being upon his guard against a set of vilinous [villainous] jews who if it were possible w[ould] swear his life away'.[59] The Wilkinson family felt the blow as a public shame, and one that threatened to divide them for she also had to report that Richard and Elizabeth's brother William 'is very unkind – says I am a town's talk for taking them in to keep and sometimes uses [language] not becoming a child to a parent but this will not make me add to the affliction to the afflict'd'.[60] This seeming digression may have led us away from our focus, but it nonetheless makes an important point. John's relative lack of strong social embeddedness may not have been the great disadvantage theorists paint it as; character and the credit that flowed from it were sometimes fragile attributes easily washed away by the tides of time.[61]

The other principal way in which early nineteenth-century businessmen and enterprises are thought to have been networked into the economy, and again the local economy in particular, was via their investments and involvement in further enterprises, especially those dedicated to providing utilities and infrastructure with public good like characteristics.[62] Such local investments, for example in financial services in joint stock banks or in utilities such as gas or improved transportation such as turnpikes, canals and railways, are thought to have generated not only income streams but also 'spillover' effects vital to regional economic development. Hence erstwhile competitors might well choose to co-operate when all would benefit from a generalized increase in economic activity.

At the same time, because such investments might often be accompanied by direct involvement via directorships and other public or quasi-public roles they could also function as paths to power, status and prestige. Local business leaders were often also significant in local religion, politics, philanthropy and wider economic development.[63]

John Shaw was, by his own admission, not a 'clubbable' man though and none of these possible spheres of public action and standing exerted any great pull on him. At best there are scattered references to share ownership. In August 1825, for example, John sent Elizabeth ten pounds with respect to a call of two pounds a share on a total of ten shares – in what is not specified.[64] The next surviving mention of share ownership dates from 1831 and is much more substantial:

> I sent you a paper by this days post and you will see the two Banking concerns are gone – one [of] which I think a good job. We had the most respectable meeting ... yesterday I think upwards of 6000 shares were taken and a committee appointed to [treat] with miss Hordern as to giving up their banking concern which they had done and purchased it and the Company which takes the title 'The Wolverhampton and Staffordshire Banking Company' starts the 1st of January. I have got one hundred shares which is the greatest number anyone is allowed to hold – this will cost me five hundred pounds and do you know I am sanguine enough to believe that in three months there will be another Thousand pounds. I have also got my Liverpool purchase complete where I hold fifty share with have cost me £500.[65]

These were clearly dramatic events, the rescue of a failing local bank once famed for its role in financing the Shropshire iron industry and John certainly paints himself as a substantial, perhaps important shareholder. But he does not position himself as an activist, he notes only that a meeting was called and a committee appointed without in anyway indicating his own involvement. In particular it seems unlikely he would have neglected to mention his own appointment to the steering committee. Instead he seems much more interested in the possibility for further investments in the future. Equally, he seems very comfortable making extra-regional investments, though given the nature of his own work and personal experiences his horizons and opportunities were necessarily more expansive than those of many other businessmen, such as manufacturers, rooted more to fixed locations.[66] And as ever, it seemed natural for him to look north, not south.

Conclusions

John and Elizabeth's approach to building relationships was essentially one of modesty and restraint; they were more interested in affect than effect. Though far more widely travelled than the majority of their contemporaries they remained largely content within quite narrow social horizons; family came first, long-established friends a close second. Despite acquiring the wealth necessary to lever themselves up through the ranks social aspiration seems to have had little attraction for them. Socializing was frequent, informal and relaxed but it was essentially a private affair conducted at home and away from the public gaze. Friendships were carefully maintained and family nurtured. Though there were trials and tribulations[67] and even dispute, rancour and bad blood,[68] for the most part wider family remained a source of strength and a sanctuary away from the hurly burly of the public world, especially the regular storms that swept through economic life. John's birth family remained very tranquil and small, neither his brother nor his sister ever married, and despite the great strains placed on it by failure, death and the behaviour of brother even Elizabeth's family held together and kept an important place at the centre of her world. John and Elizabeth's own family, they and their children, was content and mercifully untouched by tragedy, such as infant mortality, until the death of John junior in India in 1839. The wider networks of friendship and sociability showed similar levels of cohesion and persistence.

Family, friends and sociability, on the one hand, could never be entirely divorced from business and finance on the other but they were not so deeply enmeshed as some of the literature on social embeddedness and social capital has led us to expect. Trade sustained rather than supplanted life. Family and friends were not there to be leveraged for advantage. All of these connections, affective or more instrumental, unfolded across a defined geographical area that delimited the physical scope of their lives. Their world had a twin, interdependent rootedness in people and places. But compared to many contemporaries they probably travelled both widely and frequently. Relatively private and domestic they were both still out and about and engaged with a much wider world. In the next chapter we will pursue a similar theme and explore the material world they built, their homes and their things, and how they thought and felt about them.

7 'HAPPINESS (IN EARTHLY THINGS)': GETTING AND HAVING.

'I sigh not for grandeur – love in a cottage would suit my wishes better than a splendid mansion devoid of it'.[1]

Introduction: Becoming Wealthy

The Shaw's endeavours helped to create a world of things and possessions, pleasures and comforts, for themselves as for others. John's working life was devoted to selling things that would make people's lives better and more convenient, if not actually more beautiful or elevated. He sold, for the most, the useful, practical things that the Black Country was so adept in producing. The nails and tacks that secured joints and fixtures, the pans and kettles with which to cook, the door furniture that allowed elegant egress, the japanned ware such as trays that served at sociable teas, even the mills that ground coffee for those soirees, the locks and keys that secured a burgeoning world of private goods, the coffin plates and handles that added a dignified gloss to a customer's journey to the final bourne.

Today we expect a successful entrepreneur to show an uncomplicated enjoyment of the material benefits that their work has brought them. John and Elizabeth, though, had a decidedly ambiguous relationship to this realm of 'earthly things' and the wealth that it generated. Elizabeth often feared that to turn her back on her conscience 'in order to gratify the senses momentarily' might lead in return to 'days, weeks, and months of sorrow'.[2] The corporeal world of things and pleasures was a dangerous one, strewn with tares and traps. She continued her paean to the modest virtues of a humble yet loving life with which I began this chapter by asserting that:

> Therefore – if Providence should seem to frown upon our feeble endeavours in the beginning of life, let us not murmur but be thankful for the blessings which we do enjoy and all things will work together for good to them that love God – We did not come into this world merely to get a little food and raiment for these our perishing bodies but that we might watch a moment to secure a lot amongst the Blest.[3]

Clearly, these attitudes towards gratification of the senses were driven by an intense religiosity. Elizabeth saw the world as one of distracting temptations. She frequently recurred to assertions of her weak and fallen nature and her lack of proper gratitude for or use of her opportunities for leading a godly life.

What were attitudes to wealth and acquisition amongst the non-conformists groups to which John and Elizabeth belonged? W.R. Ward appears to offer an unambiguous judgment in claiming that for Methodists 'Luxury was unspeakable'.[4] But his reading actually suggests a subtler, more nuanced set of attitudes, and little in the way of outright prescription and censure. Indeed, Ward maintains that Wesley himself had a relatively defined 'economic ethic' that can be 'pungently summed up in the threefold formulary "gain all you can, save all you can, and give all you can."'[5] In other words, it was not wealth per se that mattered but rather the ends to which it was put. Indeed, he contends that nowhere did Wesley condemn the holding of private property. Critically, Ward historicizes Wesley's attitudes to wealth, so that we can see how they derived not only from scriptural readings but also from the conditions of the age in which he (and his followers) were to live, in ways that are highly relevant to economic and business history and histories of entrepreneurship. Namely, that Wesley did not:

> [re]quire even the Methodist wealthy to divest themselves of their possessions, and he was sufficiently alive to the needs of his age to allow that money was not required not only to purchase the necessities of life, but also for commercial and industrial investment.[6]

Still, this much admitted, he cites studies that seem to show that Methodist businessmen rarely became 'fabulously' wealthy and were, moreover, typically more generous than other entrepreneurs, even during the start-up phases of their entrepreneurial careers when pressures on funds available for investment were probably most acute. Indeed, echoing this relative modesty, Elizabeth very consciously identified with lower classes in society, at least in her youth. In one of her earliest letters to John she explained how 'the Methodist societies in general consist of middle and poorest classes of the people – very few of the rich and great have cast in their lost amongst them'.[7] As the daughter and sister of successful, established shopkeepers Elizabeth clearly felt comfortable accepting this identification or marker as something of societal outsider. Still if the rich had not cast in their lot, then some insiders were in time to become very wealthy indeed.

Before touching on that issue however it is worth pausing with Elizabeth's words on class, for as well speaking truth to the existence of the rich and the poor they also touch silently on another issue quite as thorny: aspiration. Far from being immutable, class actually offered only the softest ground on which to build a social identity. Just one year after her acceptance of a form of community with the poor, dramatic events flung Elizabeth in entirely another direction, into the arms of capital. 1812 was a year of near insurrection in the manufacturing districts of the North and Midlands as Luddism crackled like fire through towns and valleys. These conflagrations touched down frighteningly close to Elizabeth, especially at Middleton, Lancashire, where on the 20th April a violent assault on Burton's Mill led to considerable bloodshed. Elizabeth's account is alarmed and breathless, yet her ultimate sympathies are clear, despite the evident dislike of factories that she expressed at other times:

> I hope by the time you commence your journey, these riots will have an end – We had one on the day on which I receiv'd your letter – and I make no doubt but we should have been in a deplorable condition now – had it not been for the Military – who exerted themselves very much. We have about a hundred in all – with recruiting parties who are all made useful – some of them are constantly on duty both night and day. There was sad work at Middleton and many lives were lost ... The Country at present is quieter than it has been – strong measures are taking to keep it [so] ... I understand a letter is posted to this effect – that the mob intend being in this town to regulate the market – if so we are well prepared as a fresh troop of horse arrived yesterday and we have 6 cannon in different parts of the town ready for their reception. Am sorry to hear that a great number of the mob are composed of the Local Militia – It will hard with them if caught. Have you any Military in W[olverhampton] to protect you – perhaps the populace don't molest the Factors.[8]

Concern for the friend to whom she was growing steadily closer is natural but it is striking how readily she falls in to the language of reaction. The poorer sorts she identified with the year before are now simply the mob, the soldiery admirable in their exertions. She gives little or no credence to customary notions of a moral economy with rights to regulate the market (though perhaps a little sympathy for some of those asserting such rights). There is it seems an implicit recognition that she and her family could now never make common-cause with labour. They had through their petty capitalism crossed to the other side. The hope that the mob would somehow overlook the Factors' complicity with industrial capitalism was surely forlorn. Radicals of all persuasions, such as William Cobbett, had long singled out the middle man's parasitical position for particular scorn.

As capitalists, however small in scale, the Wilkinsons and the Shaws were then aspirers, achievers and accumulators. It is evident that individuals, families and groups could make significant transitions across their lives. Thus, these religious and personal attitudes to wealth and acquisition were, of course, far from fixed but instead displayed evolution and change, not least as society and circumstances changed. Methodists were not immune from such pressures. As Deborah Cohen has argued, it would be tempting to see the Victorian 'embrace of materials goods', the exuberant abundance typical of Middle Class homes in the second-half of the nineteenth-century, as 'a renunciation of evangelical asceticism'.[9] Such an asceticism certainly possessed some, such as the Mrs Grant, quoted by Cohen as proclaiming that 'It is a fearful thing in this fluctuating state to possess much ... [for] in proportion to what we enjoy we must suffer under the privation of these enjoyments'.[10] But, Cohen argues, such a reductive explanation would be simplistic. Instead, furnishings became infused with moral content and the 'locomotive of Victorian acquisitiveness was an engine that ran on the unlikely fuel of spiritual striving'.[11] Many thousands in the rapidly expanding middle-class faced the same dilemma as the Shaws as growing wealth enabled ever more consumption; in response 'emphasizing the moral virtues of possessions served to reconcile spiritual good with material abundance. Affluence did not mean that moral concerns were left behind'.[12] The issue became not whether you consumed and owned, but how and what. It was a gradual accommodation that can be traced across the course of John and Elizabeth's lives. Most tellingly, in the autumn of 1831 John playfully chided Elizabeth over her unwillingness to spend money during a pleasure visit to the Midlands spa town of Leamington. 'I am sorry to hear you get no rides', he teased, 'is it because you afraid of the expense ... I would not let it hinder me – you should learn to act liberally you know – these are days [of] liberality in everything'.[13] Whether or not Elizabeth took his advice and indulged herself with a hired coach and horses, these words would most surely have been deeply shocking, perhaps even blasphemous, to her younger self. Still a strong streak of piety continued to run through their world view. The year after light-heartedly exhorting Elizabeth to greater liberality John adopted a much altered tone in reflecting on their nineteen years of marriage: 'I much fear we are neither of us sufficiently grateful and thankful for the protection and success we have so abundantly enjoyed during so long a period'.[14] It is striking that he pairs success with abundance.[15] Religion and earthly reward were now comingled in their lives.[16]

Last Will and Testament

Despite the undoubted depth and sincerity of their faith, the strength of their belief that the only true treasures were to be found in heaven, John and Elizabeth worked assiduously for many years at making money, and when John died in 1858 he did so a rich man, living a life of material comfort at Oxley House, in the parish of Bushbury, Staffordshire (then a rural location but now effectively absorbed into Wolverhampton), having moved there during the 1830s from George Street, in central Wolverhampton, itself a fine street of handsome Georgian townhouses.[17] Indeed, their material ascent had been relatively rapid and by 1823 they had attained one of the greater markers of social distinction – the ability to maintain their own equipage, Elizabeth writing to John that 'the new gig is not come. He has written to say it is ready and that he has put either a ramping or rampant lion upon it (instead of a bunch of arrows – He will alter it if you wish – it is varnish'd – so if you wish it to be alter'd you must say so in your next'.[18]

Together, John's final residence and his will spelt out the worldly position that had been attained. Oxley House was an elegant and undoubtedly substantial mansion – villa is inadequate – in the Palladian style. Though now converted into flats it remains a dignified residence entirely befitting to the epitome of a successful provincial merchant. In the strict sense excessively large for his family, the house can nonetheless be said to possess a simplicity of line and ornament in keeping with his and Elizabeth's former views on the ideal domestic environment – which, as we shall see, was emphatically not to be too unnecessarily showy or without practicality. John clung fast to his Staffordshire roots but in property at least adopted the garb of the satisfied and complacent gentleman. And Elizabeth had in the end not been forced to choose between love and a splendid mansion.

In a neat parable, the house had once belonged to John Henry Sparrow, to whom John had been apprenticed when he first left home for the world of work. Master was displaced by servant.

If the outer shell of Oxley House is impressive then John's will gave some sense of the goods it contained and of the lives it supported and comforted. Before exploring this will in detail it is very important to stress that prior to its completion John had already entirely disposed of all of his business interests and assets, for the will notes that:

> whereas several years since I gave to my said sons Thomas Wilkinson Shaw and Edward Dethick Shaw absolutely, and inequal shares all the capital and stock which I had embarked in my trade as Merchant and Factor whether in the United Kingdom or abroad and also the good will of such trade and have from time to time subsequently given to them absolutely additional sums of money to augment their capital in the said trade.

This statement reveals insights into an issue critical for family firms, namely succession. Owens presents strong evidence that many nineteenth-century entrepreneurs viewed the family firm as a means to an end, namely the supply of an income to surviving family members, and thus rather than seeing the firm as an entity that should persist after them took death as opportunity for winding up an enterprise in order to realize the capital invested in it.[19] This was clearly not the approach taken by John who made sure succession was handled well in advance of the crisis of death, enhancing the possibility of the persistence of the firm he had founded. However, these issues will be explored in greater depth in our epilogue. For now, we are more concerned with how, despite this complete ante-mortem gifting of his businesses, John was still able to make extremely generous provision for his family.

John turned first to his bequest to 'my dear wife Elizabeth', who was to receive 'absolutely all the Household furniture and Household goods, plate, linen, china, glass, pictures, prints, printed, books, trinkets, fuel, wines, liquors, housekeeping provisions, horses, carriages and other chattels and effects'. These are truly the accoutrements of a bourgeois life. Moreover, he also gave to Elizabeth 'absolutely all my Tenant right and interest in the Dwellinghouses, Lands and premises which I now hold under Alexander Hordern Esquire'. A propertied man then, who had channelled some of his commercial wealth into real estate holdings. Moreover, after further complex bequests to his five surviving children, all of the remainder of his personal estate, in whatever form, was to be sold and realized as cash, which after meeting all expenses connected to his funeral and the execution of the will, was to be invested so as to generate for Elizabeth an annual income of one thousand two hundred pounds to be paid in equal quarterly payments. Furthermore, this annuity was to be secured before any of the further bequests made in the will were to be put into effect. Elizabeth would not be in material want in her widowhood, of that he was determined.

A further ten thousand pounds was made available to John's trustees to invest 'in or upon the public stocks or funds or other Government securities of the United Kingdom or on Mortgage of freehold hereditaments and premises in England or Wales and to pay the annual income arising therefrom unto my Daughter Elizabeth Shaw'. Critically, this Elizabeth was to be empowered 'to receive the same during her natural life for her separate use free from the control and debts of any husband whom she may marry and so that she shall have no power to alien or anticipate the said annual income'. Despite his own happy experience of marriage, one marked by a pronounced note of equality, John went to lengths to protect his eldest daughter from the depredations of any ill-chosen spouse. This careful protection was extended in turn to any child or children his daughter might in the future have. Identical provision was made for John and Elizabeth's second daughter, Mary Wilkinson Shaw. John and Elizabeth's remaining son, Richard Edward Shaw, 'the state of whose health does not admit of his embarking in an extensive and arduous business', was also left the sum of ten thousand pounds 'for his own absolute use together with interest thereon after the rate of five pounds per centum per annum from the first day of January 1854. Richard's legacy was hedged about with none of the caveats and qualifications with regards to potential future husbands and children attached to the sums left to the daughters. Perhaps there was no expectation that poor Richard would ever marry.

Thus, having previously entirely divested himself of all his business interests, John was able at his death to bequeath a total of £30,000 in cash, sufficient additional property and securities to raise an annuity of £1,200 per annum, and a rich haul of domestic goods. And still he was not done. Thomas was to receive the house on George Street, Wolverhampton 'wherein I lately resided and which is now in the occupation of the said Thomas'. Thomas was also to receive 'all those Warehouses and other buildings yards and premises ... situated in and near Church Lane in Wolverhampton' from which the business was conducted and further properties in Bilston and on Bilston Street, Wolverhampton. Yet more property was assigned to the four executors appointed by John. The will ran on to a total of fourteen complicated pages that deal at length with how its wishes were to be realized, particularly in the light of certain eventualities that might occur. In detail, it is an almost infinitely canny and hedged about instrument for assuring the transfer of wealth. In the round it is a remarkable testament to John and Elizabeth's success in generating that wealth.[20]

Making a Home

John and Elizabeth's start in conjoined domestic life was far more modest than Oxley House. Domesticity was central to John and Elizabeth's lives together. Unlike Yorkshire woollen manufacturer Isaac Holden, who seemed entirely at ease away from home, John valued domestic pleasures and securities fully as much as his wife, perhaps even more.[21] The home offered a place of refuge from both the trials and the threats of world outside; from the anxieties of trade, the perilous temptations of public life, the disorder ushered in by civil unrest, social change, natural peril – storm, fire and disease – and even high politics. It offered a space in which virtue could be nurtured in both themselves and their children and it provided a vital venue for sociability:

> So you cannot be content to live alone in your own house and have every comfort. I should wonder if you could, or any body else of a sociable disposition. Of all things I should dislike to live alone – I used to think I should like [it] – but no hermitage for me. I relish a little company but like to find it at home – don't like to roam for it.[22]

Home, what it meant, what it symbolized, what it contained, was the ultimate creation of their entrepreneurial endeavour. This is then another sense in which the public (masculine) and private (feminine) sphere were anything but separate – or so starkly gendered. As scholarship has increasingly demonstrated in recent years, men had a far more complex relationship with home and domesticity than had been thought at one time. Indeed, it is now clear that all kinds of 'rather unremarkable ... men had somewhat ordinary and everyday engagements with home'.[23]

But home was also a physical space, one whose decoration and furnishing reflected and inculcated the virtues and values important to the family. Never was this more evident than when preparing the first marital home.

As Amanda Vickery notes of the about-to-be-established marital home, 'Discussion of the improvements, wherein the couple projected their future life *en famille*, was part of the regular business of advanced courtship, integral to the consolidation of the match'. It was a discussion carried out via a 'conversation of ... practical intimacy'.[24] At the same time, as Vivian Bruce Conger and others have argued, the home and its different facets, were distinctly gendered spaces. However, it was also the case that 'in reality, many households did not adhere to the ideal structure; wives were not completely powerless, and the seemingly normative male authority appears too rigid and too simplistic'.[25] As a result women 'could advise their husbands, they could even assume male roles when status allowed it and times demanded it; men were expected to be neither tyrannical nor abusive in wielding their power, and they willing ceded masculine responsibilities and authority to their wives as necessary'. As already suggested, one of the principal areas in which these negotiations and compromises might be realized was the home. And just as Elizabeth and John blurred their life roles so their home showed no strict demarcation line between an exterior, and male, public space and an interior, female, domestic one.

These were certainly conversations and negotiations that John and Elizabeth experienced – and recorded. Even if, unlike the heroes of the Austen novels analyzed by Vickery, John was unable to use an existing and genteel property to woo his desired bride then establishing a suitable new home still mattered. Living as he was in unsuitable bachelor lodgings, a new house that would make a proper home had to be found.[26] The search was left to John, for entirely practical reasons – she was absent. In some respects Elizabeth appears somewhat careless and one of the few stipulations she made about the fabric, size, or situation of the home was that it should have chimneys that did not smoke, for such were liable to make her scold.[27] To this extent, she ceded ground over the external, public face the family home would present to the world. Indeed, she did not see the home she was to move into, or even Wolverhampton or any other member of the family she was marrying into, until she was wed and whisked south to the grimy Black Country. She might well have missed the clean cool airs of the Northern moors, where she liked to walk and ride and as marriage approached she showed a natural apprehension about her imminent remove. She was strongly attached to her family and she enjoyed her then current home, with her brother Thomas, in Rochdale: 'There are few places in town where there is prettier living than the top of Yorkshire Street, Rochdale and if your house stands as well I shall not be disposed to think ill of it. The greatest pleasure is having fine walks near ones place of abode'.[28] Of Wolverhampton itself she seems to have decided not to set her expectations too high: 'I have not form'd so bad an opinion of W'h'pton as a town as you imagine – to be sure I don't suppose it is anything very great'.[29]

Perhaps this accepting, realistic attitude helped to soften any disappointment she might otherwise have felt.

However, if she seemed not too concerned about the building itself then Elizabeth took a much more active interest in how and with what it might be furnished and fitted out. The watchwords are modesty, simplicity and economy. These were not mere aesthetic preference; instead we should consider seriously Bonnie Smith's contention that 'fashion and housekeeping habits have an expressive content [that] demands that we consider ... the home as an internally coherent, symbolic form'.[30]

If, as we shall see, she desired economy in her own household then Elizabeth was also not above passing comment on how others, friends and neighbours, managed theirs. When Henry Greenleaves – whom she liked – died of consumption aged twenty-four in the winter of 1812 she could not help but note that 'I should think it will be very distressing to his wife to be left ... She will no doubt have to return to her Mother's along with her little one. Henry told us some time ago that they liv'd after the rate of 600 pr yr therefore they can't have saved much'.[31] Charming and playful, Henry had failed in the proper manly duties of provision and prudence. Still, admitted Elizabeth, softening her tone, 'independent of worldly circumstances – how distressing to lose a partner & particularly where there is a strong affection for each other'.[32] Gossip though this might be we should not dismiss it as entirely idle, gossip can provide a vital societal glue in reinforcing bonds, norms and moralities.[33]

Elizabeth was far more openly judgemental about the habits of another young couple she observed in her local community during the same period, as her own marriage approached and her thoughts no doubt turned to the preparations she had to make herself. Having attended a sale (where she and her brother made some good bargains carefully itemized for John's approval)[34] at a nearby house, Elizabeth found opportunity for reflections on thrift and furnishing:

> The persons who belong'd to it have only been married about 2 yrs they have one child. He (Mr Chadwick) instead of attending to his business (in the woollen line) has rioted in intemperance to that excess that he has worn out his constitution and is on the borders of the grave – His wife, I understand comes of a pretty good family and he had (I am told) 5, or, £700 with her in fortune which seem to have been wasted one way or another. Her disposition is able but from what is reported she knew little of housekeeping so that they have been burning the candle at both ends. They had laid out quite too much money in furnishing their house – not, that they had more things than the fashionable world calls necessary but a great many more than I think requisite, or necessary, for young beginners in the world, who have to live by industry and carefulness.[35]

Here, in Elizabeth's final pronouncement, fashion, taste and indulgence collide with the virtues of industriousness, prudence, necessity and a certain modest seemliness. Elizabeth tests her husband-to-be; it is important to her that they are in accord on this issue. Restraint was linked for her to contentment and domesticity, profligacy with misery, a wandering, restlessness amidst the temptations of the wider world:

> I hope your thoughts are in unison with my own upon this subject. I certainly think families are render'd comfortable by having things convenient and useful – but more than this is only outward show and is not absolutely necessary to happiness, especially to those whose greatest pleasure is to live at home, for they, feel not those wants that rovers abroad, in quest of pleasure, feel – besides, the human mind is ever active to find out wants to and if we have no real ones we shall certainly find out Imaginary ones.[36]

She ends this passage with a simple, but heartfelt, homily, 'I assure you, my ambition (If I have any) lays more in having a good husband than a well-furnish'd house'; and a vision of 'the time when we can sit under our own vine and fig tree none daring to make us afraid'.[37] Even as she assured John that he might defer their wedding if poor business prospects demanded it, so she held firm to an ideal of the life they were working towards together, an ideal that included a vision of the physical space they would occupy together.

By the summer of 1812 Elizabeth was at last in position to set about the task of readying her own home. Her letters on the subject are full of intensely practical detail, almost an instruction manual for John to follow as he equips the marital home. She begins with a request that almost encapsulates her ethos: 'will you oblige me so far as to purchase nothing but what will be useful in one way or another – I mean nothing that is merely to look at – no pictures – They are expensive things and what may very well be done without'.[38] This point established she proceeds with care, displaying a deft awareness of sources of supply, varying qualities of goods, likely prices, the impact of prevailing conditions, and sound principles of domestic economy, qualities to be expected in the dutiful daughter, sister and housekeeper of a family of shopkeepers:

> you nam'd having given some orders for glass – did you remember salts – salt spoons will also be wanted when you order the other spoons – and sugar tongs – Glass and china are getting higher in consequence of the new duty laid upon them – perhaps if you mind may get them at the low prices. Glass will be ½ as much again as it is – Have you seen any bedsteads and hangings which you like – The upholsterers generally in large towns keep patterns by them – I think good handsome prints stand and wear the best of anything – In chusing anything I frequently consider the length of time it will look handsome – therefore my things are often grave to begin with but answer my purpose. My Aunt bought a very handsome carpet little more than a yr since – It was compos'd chiefly of yellow and green – It is now faded with the sun and looks like an old one – If it had been dark and the colours bright it would have look'd well many years.[39]

It is notable that Elizabeth both trusts John to make some purchases whilst feeling the need to impart the simplest intelligence – that larger retailers keep pattern books, for example; and this to a man who spent almost all of his working life working with manufacturers and retailers of a wide range of goods. Her voice has a quiet confidence in what might easily be cast as a distinctly feminine area of interest – yet she herself introduces gender to this discussion only once: 'your Mother and Sister would buy anything in the cloth line better than you because they would know both the quality and quantity wanted for each thing – I hope you are not too reserved to ask them, are you'. Evidently John could not be trusted with *every* purchase, even if suggesting this to him needed some delicacy. Separation undoubtedly played a role here and as Bruce Conger notes of the Franklin household; 'An absent male would radically alter those relationships even further, and the Franklin household was hardly "normal". Deborah spoke the common language of goods as skilfully as he'.[40] Undoubtedly this was true of Elizabeth, and as she exerted her command of that language she too 'constructed a new identity for herself', that of an equal partner in this endeavour.[41]

Elizabeth returned to the same subject, yet more exhaustively, in a letter written just a few days later in the same month. Clearly, it was very important that this task, probably not to be repeated for several years, was done right. A lack of opportunity for direct oversight was not going to make Elizabeth cede control of the process. Indeed the issue was one of some urgency, leading the epistolary pact to be broken: 'A few things which you nam'd respecting furniture have caused me to write a little earlier than I otherwise should have done – I will therefore begin with these first'. What follows seems to treat of almost every possible concern in furnishing a house: carpets for the bedroom, and how they were to be arranged; chests of drawers and dressing tables (be they 'not ... too expensive'); chests ('one tolerable siz'd'); a prolonged discussion of mattresses, truly an issue of 'practical intimacy' ('Hair ones are to [sic] to buy, except in a sales when sometimes they go cheap – straw ones you do not like'); beds ('These things are as you observe heavy articles and also they are things in which, I had like to have said, a judge may be deceived. New ones generally, in the end prove cheapest'), including a detailed discussion of the prices for different qualities of feather and the different parts of the country from which they might come. Still, Elizabeth concludes this section with a surprisingly diffident 'After all please yourself about it and I shall not be displeased'.

Next come blankets ('Is yours a good country for them?') and hangings for beds ('better not to be put up until the last thing when everything is compleated – that they may not get soiled') and curtains ('have the goodness to see that the draperies are hung upon the small tinn'd tacks then they are easily taken down'). At this point Elizabeth was forced to ask 'what kind of window has it – double, single, large, or small?' Really she knew very little of where she was soon to live. Similarly she asked 'Are glasses in parlours very common with you – they are not with us except amongst the highest class. They are expensive and also useless as they are now used', suggesting a regional fragmentation of furnishing styles, or at least a lack of awareness of any commonalities from place to place. John was busy helping to forge ever more integrated markets through his work as a factor, yet, for Elizabeth, Staffordshire remained, to some extent, a domestic *terra incognita*. And amidst all the prosaic details Elizabeth remembers exactly what it is that they are building: 'I hope you will not feel the loss of fine paintings nor want company while I am with you – perhaps I may feel a want of company when your talking your journeys'. A home was for a family.

Now her thoughts turned to china ('as they are ... such brittle ware and liable to so many accidents – I vote to have them as cheap as they can be got – no matter for shape or colour if they be decent') which, in turn, 'brings me to Urns – I have no choice whatever in these only let them be plain'. On she runs through cruets, mustard pots, silver plate and reminders about salt spoons and sugar tongs. Eventually she concludes 'I dare say you have your hands quite full with it'.[42] No doubt John would have agreed.

The overall tone is one that aims at a comfortable but modest sufficiency. Elizabeth adopted a similar attitude with regard to her own apparel. Her most direct reflections on dress were prompted by John's loan of a book; *The Triumph of Fashion*, a moralistic and judgemental tome from which he thought she might learn. If she felt any annoyance at the obvious implication then she managed to keep it in check, for the most part. Instead, she had the self-confidence to largely dismiss his intervention:

> I should think it very severe if <u>I felt</u> the attack, but my foibles are of a different nature to any that are named in it (except the one you know of) – <u>Dress</u> never was my hobby horse in any great degree. I recollect the time when I was fonder of it than I am now – I should not like to be particular one way or the other – I think I may venture to say I never dress'd (or, as it is call'd, undress'd) indelicately – I have frequently been call'd old womanish for wrapping up so much – If you are not yet satisfied in this subject tell me. <u>Your see me in a fault now</u> and, I have not the <u>happy knack</u> of finding <u>myself in one</u>.[43]

John had decidedly not won this point. Her dismissal has a distinct finality: 'I confess I was disappointed in the little Pamphlet ... I expected a particular instead of a general survey of things – I don't think it is calculated to do much good'.[44] Still the suggestion that she is not particular in any direction as to dress is interesting. It suggests an awareness that there could be vanity in an overweening piety just as there was in ostentation. Certainly, she was not above wearing ribbons, buckles and jewellery, telling John for example how 'that pretty bauble you noticed upon my neck one day' had been smashed in returning home from a visit to family.[45]

John was inculcated with a similar sense of restraint in personal appearance. In his youth as an apprentice traveller his mother exhorted him to look to his

cousin Evan as a 'pattern of economy'. In comparison, John seemed to her somewhat profligate, too concerned with the face he presented to the world (perhaps
a legitimate concern for a commercial traveller constantly having to present himself to customers as a confident, prosperous, and thus creditable man):[46]

> Have sent your Brother for your Wastcoat [sic] and likewise for your shirts if you cannot
> were [sic] them dirty first – your hat may be clean'd and moderniz'd before you have a
> new one. If you can do with your old one, that you sent home lately I mean ... It appears
> to me you wish to have a change of apparel equal to Evan, which is wrong, he has done
> growing, which you have not, look back to what his wardrobe was when at your age ...
> Don't think my dear child I wish to cramp your spirits, far from it, I well know in the
> eye of the world that appearances are not to be disregarded and after the next winter is
> past, you shall have an entire new supply. Your cousin Evan wore but one waistcoat of a
> Sabbath day for the whole year, now he has more and as you grow up so shall you. Do
> you know your last waistcoat every way was upwards of seventeen shillings.[47]

The perennial watchword of make-do and mend rings down through the ages.

A public showiness was perhaps most frowned upon in religious circles. The
outward face needed to be sober and restrained, not likely to elicit sinful pride
in the wearer or envy in the observer. But even amongst modest and devout
middling sorts such as the Wilkinsons occasion could be found when these precepts might be honoured only in the breach. The wedding of Elizabeth's brother
Thomas to Miss Chafer in the summer of 1812 was one such opportunity. Elizabeth tells John how:

> We proceeded to church in two handsome carriages, drawn by four greys, as follows
> – first Mr S[ergeant, preacher], Miss C[hafer] and myself – we two had white dresses,
> Gray sursuits Spencers and white satin bonnets – Mr S in black – second chaise Thos
> and J^{no} in blue coats, white waistcoats, light gray pantaloons and silk stockings – My
> Aunt had on a French gray luster, tippet of the same trimm'd with swansdown and
> straw colour muslin bonnet (she look'd the best of all of us). Marg^t all white except
> gloves which you know were buff – The horses had white reins and post boys white
> gloves – you see we cut quite a dash.[48]

As striking as the very public 'dash' this little party undoubtedly cut is Elizabeth's
interest in and ability to observe and relay to John all the particular details of
materials and fabrics – and her belief that John would be interested in hearing
them.[49] Perhaps, though, Miss Chafer was a flightier, more flamboyant figure
than Elizabeth for on the morning after the wedding Elizabeth, who had been
keeping house for Thomas until that point, 'took Mrs TW [née Chafer] ...
through the house and would have delivered up the keys but Mrs W say she
will not have them'. As Amanda Vickery has demonstrated, taking possession
of the keys to a house was a moment of great symbolic and practical importance.[50] Thomas' new bride seemed but ill-prepared for the duties of mistress of
the house and home.

Life's Pleasures

Establishing the marital home was perhaps the most critical point in the material life of any couple. It was – as it still is today – the point at which the literal foundations were laid for a life together. However, John and Elizabeth carried on consuming together and the brief allusions to this in their letters over the following decades give a fleeting glimpse of what it was that gave them pleasure. Here we can find a concentration on what we might think of as possessions that are nurturing of life. The principal material goods referenced in their courtship letters were books – about which they wrote frequently, avidly exchanging both volumes and opinions on them. As physical objects, books are clearly primarily merely vessels for the ideas that they contain and disseminate. After marriage, the discussion of books declines, no doubt because these conversations could now be had easily at those times when they were at home together. The central issue they faced now was not coming to know one another – a process in which books and reading can help guide to us to a clearer sense of the other, their thoughts, opinions and dreams – but instead calling up and remembering each other across distance and absence. Gifts began to bespeak a thoughtfulness of home and those who occupy it.

Sometimes this gifting could take the form of a permission to enjoy a degree of 'liberality', as when John, at home in Wolverhampton, wrote to Elizabeth 'I think you had better try your luck as to both those said clocks – its a thing I have long wanted but the high price demanded for them has delayed be from having one – who knows how fortunate you may be – the two together will only cost 12/- and this will not make any difference an hundred years to come'.[51] John, despite his growing wealth, remained a canny consumer. At other times it took the form of a fond indulgence. November 1819 saw John particularly 'flat in spirits, things are so dreadfully flat and bad that is almost impossible to keep in good spirits'. It is not surprising that in this frame of mind his thoughts should turn to home ('I would give a trifle to have a peep at you all just now'), and how he might make it yet dearer:

> Have the workmen been again to the job ... the passage, the sooner it is done the more clean and comfortable you will find yourself. I quite forgot 'ere I left home to take the dimensions of our Parlour can you give it me in one of your letters and also what is the projection of the fire place and width. I have a great notion of sporting a new carpet at Kiddermin^r – if you have no objection – for our present one appears to grow shabby and tell me also what ground you think will do best – of course you will say not too light that our little folks may not make it darker.[52]

Still, despite his sudden desire to 'sport' a new carpet John must have felt Elizabeth might be ambivalent about such 'frivolous' spending, and also shows deference to her sense of the practical over the ornamental; perhaps these are reasons why he resorts to seeking her opinion, as a strategy to mollify or placate her.

At the same time, as in probably all families, gifting also functioned as a system of reward, especially with children.[53] Again, though, the emphasis falls on what we might construe as creative, joyful and, perhaps, sometimes improving. Thus, in the spring of 1822 Elizabeth asks John to 'Please tell John I am glad to hear he is so good a boy. I shall not forget his fiddle'.[54] Similarly, at a later date, it is John's turn to instruct Elizabeth that she might tell 'Betsey if she has so set her affections upon an accordion I will get her one but can't afford to give Buxton prices which are at least from one to two pounds more than the value. I well know what they are and have played upon one and the best I have just seen and a beautiful thing it is – did not exceed three guineas. They are a German manufactured article'. His appreciation for quality and price is obvious.[55]

Alongside these common tokens of spousal and parental love and remembrance the most common gifts of all were of food and drink. Again, this branch of giving clearly focused on nurture, sustenance and sociability. Cider, wine, fruit, oysters, fish and cake all circulated on a regular basis within the extended Shaw and Wilkinson families, or were set down in storage for future days.[56] In particular, John seems to have assiduous in sending Elizabeth's family such little treats, both before and after their wedding. Thus on the first of January 1813 ('Two years since today I received your first letter') Elizabeth wrote to John of how 'On Xtmas day my Aunt W^m and Bro^r and Sister Thos desired to spend the evening here (We supp'd off your Oysters which were excellent and toasted the Donor'.[57] Good food, simple, seasonal and very often home grown was an affordable and morally uncomplicated physical pleasure. It also acted to bond; husband to wife, suitor to in-laws, generation to generation.

One charming scene saw John and his eldest son (also John), home together in Wolverhampton, sit 'down to dinner alone to the large table with knives and forks laid as ... [though more were] to have dined with us today. John expressed his surprise saying Papa why does there not be somebody else here to eat this nice dinner – Roast Beef, pudding and cabbage, potatoes and new asparagus'.[58] The maintenance of polite form, the dinner that could not be more English; they all speak of the centrality of the table to family life. Moreover, in closing the same letter he laments that 'I wish I could send you some of our asparagus for suppose you get none at Colne. You will please to remember me to all your friends'.[59] Familiar, home-grown foods acted perhaps, like Proust's Madeleine, to evoke that which was dear; so John feels compelled to tell his wife of a meal of 'our fine lettuce – and a dish of spinage and bacon of which we have had great plenty and all seem very fond of it'.[60] Sometimes he is simply sweetly solicitous of Elizabeth's enjoyment and well-being; 'Are you taking anything that will nourish you and do you good. I hope you don't forget the Madeira wine, it must be good living and strengthening things that will restore your strength'.[61]

Conclusions

It is important to see these habits of gifting, of ensuring a secure, sustaining and comfortable family home, as being situated in an ethic of provision and protection – and one of an essential thankfulness and gratitude too:

> But amidst all these distressing things the thought will frequently strike me – how much better of I am than thousands and thousands and what little cause I have for such complaints, no but little – I have often – very often – come to check myself when I find my mind dissatisfied and doubting the goodness of providence.[62]

Here John admits the temptations and seductions of mere physical sufficiency. Elsewhere, these thoughts are taken much further and, most strikingly, used by Elizabeth to reflect on the relationships between faith, duty, ambition and worldly success:

> If we labour for the true riches the Lord will take care that every other thing shall be add'd – sure – don't mistake it. It is every man's duty to do the best he can for himself and family – to use the abilities Providence has bestow'd upon him to pursue his own and their welfare and after praying for a blessing upon his best endeavours leave the rest.[63]

A man not only *might* but *should* strive as hard as possible towards betterment here on this earth – but not for its own sake but because of what it could do, for the family especially. Money, properly made, and in due proportion, had its virtues. As Joanne Bailey has emphasized recently, home and the physical comforts it housed embodied the emotions dimensions of family life and expressed the success of John's enterprising provision.

At the same time, we must never lose sight of how frequently the letters recurred, and most endearingly, to a noticing of life's simplest, most direct pleasures, especially those that cost little or nothing to enjoy: the weather, the garden, the little things that the children did or said. Such moments as when John remembered how 'It [a thunderstorm] wonderfully cleared the air and today is beautifully fine and a nice cool breeze', or as when Elizabeth recounted how 'I have had a most charming walk all alone. The birds invited me to stay but the air blew cool and I retun'd'.[64]

8 CONCLUSION: THE LIFE THEY MADE

I hope this book has told John and Elizabeth's story in rich and compelling detail. One of my aims has simply been to reclaim their story from the dust and silence of the archives as something vivid, moving, and worth telling for its intrinsic value, for its quiet dramas and joys, for the way in which it may resonate with our own lives. Is it, though, anything more than the story of one couple's marriage and business? John and Elizabeth's lives, individually and together, were prisms through which passed and were refracted some of the most powerful forces coursing through English society of their day – a period as significant as any other in the nation's history.

Across the eight tumultuous decades through which they lived the economy, international ties, politics, social structures and relations, the material world, and more were all fundamentally remade. Perhaps the first amongst those was economic change, whether or not we label it as 'revolutionary'. Certainly, in his economic life, John did little that was revolutionary. People had been trading in similar patterns and using similar methods for decades, perhaps centuries. Nor was he one of a small band of brave pioneers. By the later eighteenth-century England's road system teemed with hundreds, perhaps thousands, of similar travellers and factors, many of them pushing the very same sorts of goods.[1] But he saw and seized the openings that were being created to take and make new opportunities. A confluence of forces – urbanization, technological change, institutional evolution and advance, more extensive and efficient means of interconnection – increasingly privileged not only the manufacturers on whom history has tended to concentrate but also the market-makers like John who could bring together ever more dispersed buyers and sellers via specialized and risky processes of intermediation.[2] New products, new ways of making them, and new ways of buying them, for example in a blossoming number of fixed retail units in rapidly growing urban centres, which were in turn busy being transformed by industrialization,[3] new and increasingly sophisticated, widespread, and trusted financial instruments and institutions, new and changing patterns of taste and consumption, population growth, and many other factors were both releasing and creating demand, ferment and activity. These were not, at root, disembodied, impersonal forces. They depended on individuals making decisions and taking action, bearing risks both physical and financial (perhaps moral even), organizing, and often (though not always) creating enterprises with a degree of formal and enduring existence.

Family was the cradle of much of this effort towards enterprise: *to* the firm flowed family resources and labour, family money, the family home in some instances – but also, and above all else, provision, dignity, respectability, and independence were generated *for* the family. Family ordered the priorities of the firm and ensured endeavour was not a lonely struggle; as well as literal labour family could provide moral and psychological succour. For John it seemed very often that family was the only thing that made enterprise both meaningful and endurable, for though enterprise was embraced that embrace was often uncomfortable, constraining and even painful. It assailed his body with its trials, strained his nerves, and separated him from the family for whom it was all done. Never was this a case of heroic individualism, instead it was hard won and came at a certain price – separation and grief for example. Above all, these demands were shared, not faced alone. Thus, perhaps in response to the price that could be paid, enterprise was only going to work if the firm in some sense mimicked the family. John came from a small, tight-knit, and insular family and these properties he seems to have tried to echo in the firm he created. Even as a partnership it remained rooted in personal knowledge and affection, close and frequent contact, an ambition tempered by modest aspirations. It maintained a proper caution about risk and was never sanguine or complacent about success. In this way business was woven into the warp and weft of family life, another thread amongst the others, a part of the bigger pattern. Here was the first way in which we can think of the Shaw family enterprise as an unlimited partnership; the existence of an inseparability between two institutions – firm and family – too often thought of as distinct, even dichotomous, systems.

So enterprise was one of these greater forces threading its way through John and Elizabeth's lives. Attention to these aspects of their lives, and to those many more like them, returns us to a vision of economic change in this period as a bottom-up process. They took and refashioned opportunity in the image of their own desires, aspirations, aptitudes, energies, and resources. And as they did so, they themselves were changed. Elizabeth and John might stand as personification of the great social transformation that took the humble, virtuous, middling-sorts of the eighteenth-century and wrought from them a new class, the high Victorian bourgeoisie.[4] The arc seems clear for both of them, from humble Lancastrian shop counter and Staffordshire farm to an elegant Palladian villa sequestered at a discrete distance from the industrial town from whence their wealth was drawn. The house was only one outward sign of this transformation. Enterprise had made the Shaws rich, and not simply in possessions or in leisure and luxury. Now they also commanded capital; capital to invest, to grow, to bequeath. There might have been no greater reward for enterprise than this at the dawn of what Hobsbawm called the 'age of capital'.[5] The hard work of enterprise also ultimately bought them ease, retreat, and security. In particular, it allowed Elizabeth to withdraw from close contact with the world of work and the firm and back into the realm of home and motherhood. Her involvement with the business on a direct and day-to-day basis undoubtedly declined significantly once she and John had started their own family – and the first fruits of success had been harvested. For Smith, writing on northern France in nineteenth-century, such a retreat was both entirely typical and symptomatic of a decay of an earlier female vigour and autonomy.[6] Moreover, as well as allowing Elizabeth's at least partial retreat wealth, capital especially, created the possibility of dynasticism. John's mother had been able to pass on to him little more than a fierce drive but to his own sons he was able to bequeath both the firm and capital but the sense of a certain position and standing in the world. A status not to be built but rather to be maintained.

Of course, it is the case that these personal transformations took place in context of much wider and more powerful societal transformations. As Kay says of the nineteenth-century female entrepreneurs she studied it 'is important to recognize that they were still largely working *within* Victorian values'.[7] As with their small contribution to economic change, so John and Elizabeth put their own weight behind the impetus for social change. Certainly John and Elizabeth were acutely aware of their position *within* the social structures they inhabited; at one time Elizabeth consciously identified with both the 'poorer' sort and at another with the owners of capital, such as they were becoming, whilst at yet another date John urged a liberality of living befitting to the new condition in which they found themselves – a series of observations that apparently neatly tracked their progress from a pious restraint and complaisance to the hint of a smug complacency.

We can trace a similar faint vein of complacency in their attitudes to the world beyond their own lives, preoccupied as they were not with getting on but with saving their souls. There is a remarkable silence in their letters, and thus in this book too, around politics, which really only appear when the mob appears frighteningly close to touching their own lives. Both John and Elizabeth were both relatively well travelled, traversing many times and across many years the route between the Midlands and the North and yet they comment very little on vast changes they must have seen all around them. Of the world beyond the shores of Britain there is even less, little more than Elizabeth's alarm at the news of Bonaparte's escape from exile. Yet that wider world, and its politics, touched their lives profoundly. In particular, their Indian 'adventure' was both only possible because of Britain's much greater Imperial adventure and, in its own small way, a contribution to it. If industrial revolution is increasingly seen as a bottom-up process made through a multiplicity of small actions then Finn has recently argued that we might begin to see empire in the same way, as the outcome of individual imperatives and initiatives as much as strategy and policy.[8]

But class was much more than the sum of their possessions, the capital at their disposal, their relative social status or power, or their ability to contribute to Britain's imperial project. It was something to which they gave life via the virtues and values they brought to it – and as McCloskey has taught us, the virtues of the bourgeoisie deserve to be taken very seriously.[9] Following in depth the lives of two member of this emerging bourgeoisie as they made their lives only reinforces this point. These were lived tenets and credos, not abstract theories. As their material and social position changed, John and Elizabeth did not simply abandon the virtues and values to which they had been raised; both of them in deeply religious and observant homes. Those virtues and values – thrift, modesty, industriousness, thankfulness, acceptance of providence, openness to familial affect, McCloskey's vital Prudence – were not in fact easily cast-off like some now outmoded apparel.[10] They were deeply engrained through example and experience. Certainly the genesis of these values can also be traced, in part, to external forces: from religious and parental teaching, from the influence of trading and social milieu, from the lessons of improving literature, but in practicing them throughout their lives John and Elizabeth made them their own.

Virtues and values existed then, above all else, in the attempt to live them out. That attempt was always couched in the context of real relationships. So if John and Elizabeth were entrepreneurs, capitalists, and middling sort made bourgeois then they were also daughter and son, sister and brother, mother and father, wife and husband – and woman and man. As such, in each case, they performed roles that were unavoidably gendered and gendered in ways that changed over times, as we saw in Elizabeth's retreat from the real and symbolic space of the warehouse.[11] These ideas immediately bring into play notions of separate spheres and the physical and metaphorical spaces with which those spheres are commonly associated, the public and the private, the worldly and the domestic. As the new century progressed John and Elizabeth's progress on these various fronts seems to map onto our expectations; enterprise led to the status of capitalists (and consumers), precipitating a shift from recognizably eighteenth-century middling origins to an archetypal bourgeoisie destination, a transition matched by one from active, autonomous man and woman engaged on a companionate marriage of equals to the masculine figure about in the world, the feminine figure increasingly confined to the home.

However, these dichotomies, though there may seem to be evidence for them even in John and Elizabeth's lives, belie the subtle inflections and dynamics of their relationship. They were always more than the sum of their historical correlates; entrepreneur, capitalists, *paterfamilias* and *mater*, man and woman. They each had a strong individuality that was never more alive than in their relationship with one another. Absolutely central was a marriage to which the term 'companionate', denoting a stage in the historical evolution of the institution of family in Western Europe, cannot begin to do justice. Marriage gave them the space to create themselves, their family, their enterprise, and their world. It gave them the foundation to shape their roles as they wanted. Here is the second sense in which they lived out an unlimited partnership. As we examine those roles the easy assumptions about gendering, domesticity, and bourgeoisification rapidly fall away. Just as virtues and values were lived – rather than prescribed – then so was gender. Elizabeth may have nominally retreated away from work and into the home over the course of their lives together but she retained the spirit, independence, and a clear sense of her own selfhood and self-worth that had so strongly characterized the way in which she approached courtship and her choice of marriage partner. In this way she remained absolutely central to all that they achieved together. But if her adoption of the cloak of femininity hides a more complex reality then John never fully complied with our image of the Victorian patriarch. He fashioned a version of masculinity every bit as complex – and surprising – as her approach to the feminine. He was at his greatest ease, at his happiest, at home, with Elizabeth, with the children, enjoying such simple pleasures as a plate of asparagus or a spell of fine weather. Despite all the striving of his entrepreneurship he showed little evidence of a genuine need to assert himself against others or against the world. He wanted to craft a quiet world of affection and fellow feeling, business was its support. In examining John and Elizabeth's lives the notion of gendered separate spheres very largely falls away, a straightjacket that simply does not fit them. And no more appropriate are the images we typically associate with the figure of the entrepreneur.

We began this study by asking a deceptively simple question: how is a life made? For John and Elizabeth the answer lay in the living of it. Guided by clear-sighted priorities, principles, and values, encountering the world with its richness, possibilities, and constraints they made their choices and coped as best they could in pursuit of what mattered to them. They give flesh and blood to our historical categories, and those forces and shifts we have briefly explored here. Telling their story in this way adds complexity our understanding of those wider patterns whilst reinvesting Elizabeth and John with a degree of agency and vitality that came not from the roles they filled, the categories they represented, or any conventional source of power, but from their desire for self-determination as both individuals and a couple.

We are privileged to have their letters. It is the testimony contained in the letters that makes the micro-historical approach I have adopted here possible. That is only appropriate. For many years writing was central to their lives. It made each real to the other across long weeks or months of separation. Much more than just a tool for communication, correspondence became of way of thinking, of connecting and of loving. Letters became part of the tissue of their lives, something we can sense as we read and handle their letters today. The letters also place business and enterprise into their proper context and perspective; that is as something foregrounded by the much more fundamental need to make a life as a family that could be satisfying and lived in good conscience. Being in business as a family emerges as a fine and worthwhile art.

EPILOGUE: 'ONE HUNDRED AND FIFTY YEARS OF ACHIEVEMENT'

'One Hundred and Fifty Years of Achievement'[1]

After John Shaw died in 1858 the firm he had founded went on to record a very long and successful history. This epilogue very briefly tells some of that story, concentrating in particular on the second and third generations, critical in the evolution of many family firms. In tracing these later developments we will rely quite heavily on two celebratory anniversary documents produced either by or for the firm. Though far from neutral, these sources have value in that they reveal the firm's perception of itself, how it understood its history, and how it ordered its priorities at two key dates, in 1895 and 1945.

In 1946 John Shaw and Sons Ltd. published a slim pamphlet celebrating its 150th anniversary.[2] The little booklet opens with a sweeping vision of just how dramatically Britain had been changed over that span of years, charting across 'the period of the firm's life' the wars that had been fought (significant in that another great world war had only very recently been concluded), the heroes, Kings, and Queens who had come and gone, the revolutions defeated, the technologies accomplished. Against this backdrop of transformation the firm was made to standout as a still point of continuity, for 'Yet to-day, the House of John Shaw and Sons, Wolverhampton, Limited, still carries on business with customers commercially descended from customers of the first John Shaw'.[3] This is the great legacy to which probably all family businesses aspire; a sense of continuity couched in terms of genealogical descent and inheritance, of Houses rather than warehouses.

The bedrock of this of this continuity and legacy is of course, in classic style, the gritty integrity and labours of the founder who, as *paterfamilias*, provides the foundation to the house. Work is the key motif in a sketch of an age in which 'attention to one's business was almost an article of religion' (the only mention of religion in the booklet and a curious subversion of how John would probably have ordered business and religion as priorities): 'Shaw, it is recorded, regularly put in a couple of hours work in his office and warehouse before breakfast every day. In winter he would go round the warehouse in the early hours by the light of a lantern'. The hagiography continued: 'He was, at first, his own book-keeper, and his own traveller – in days when there no railroads and all country calls had to be made by horse and gig!' In the end, it was only success that demanded change, for 'Shaw carried on single-handed, managing his business as well as doing the travelling, for twenty years, by the end of which time the affairs of the House had so grown that a partner became necessary'.[4]

Fifty years earlier very similar themes of persistence through tumultuous times were to the fore in a centenary celebration published by the *Hardwareman*. In one subtle difference though the emphasis fell not only on continuity but on longevity specifically:

> To have survived a century is an achievement. Our age is not favourable to longevity ... the sands of time are strewn thick with stranded enterprises which go ashore either from lack of ballast to make their helms responsive, or from lack of a good pilot to study the ever-shifting shoals of the way. Still fewer are the businesses which finish their century in the same family to which they owe their origin, but that of John Shaw and Sons, of Wolverhampton, is one of the few. The present owners look back but two generations to the founder and during the whole of this time the founder and his descendents have been the sole proprietors.[5]

At the same time the *Hardwareman* also did more to emphasize family than the *Sesquicentum*, which had portrayed John as the entrepreneur as heroic lone individual and had given little space, if any, to subsequent generations – and certainly none at all to Elizabeth, or any other woman.[6] Indeed, the *Hardwareman* claimed that it 'may be said without exaggeration, that the period of their [that is John's sons, Thomas Wilkinson Shaw and Edward Dethick Shaw] management constituted the Augustan era of the firm'.[7] In their 'abundantly able ... hands ... by their skill, energy and devotion, the advance went on steadily without flagging' after John's death in 1858, with both the home and overseas trade being so 'greatly extended' that the firm's premises had to be expanded three times under their direction.[8] In fact, the journal offered a veritable paean to the brothers' qualities; they were, it claimed, 'men of strong religious principle ... of abundant but unostentatious charity ... liberal supporters of the movement for the spread of Science and Art education ... and all well-directed efforts to improve the well-being and happiness of the people'.[9] Finally, the journal painted a touching portrait of the brothers' deaths, which took place within twelve months of each other in 1886 and 1887: 'there seems to be no doubt but [Thomas'] death was hastened by the loss of his brother, so faithful as comrades and partners had they been, and so deeply did the survivor feel the bereavement'.[10] We are reminded of the emotional charge that accompanied their brother's death in India nearly fifty years earlier. So another chapter came to pass.

The same issue of the *Hardwareman* that celebrated the past of the firm also carried an extensive interview with Charles E. Shaw MP, Managing Director with responsibility for the Foreign Department and son of Edward Shaw and thus grandson of John and Elizabeth. At that time, the firm was 'Needless to say ... strictly private, all shares being taken by the two families of the late partners and brothers'. John P. Shaw, son of Thomas Wilkinson Shaw (and thus a second grandson) was Charles' co-Managing Director. The only other members of the Board of Directors were William E. Shaw and Ernest E. Shaw, relationships not given: the firm was then a classic example of British personal capitalism of that period.[11]

The interview gives a revealing insight into the culture prevailing at the firm at the close of the nineteenth-century and of how this culture was transmitted across generations, how younger members of the family were inculcated into the firm's practices, and thus how, almost by sleight, succession was prepared for, all of which are important issues for family firms. For the journal that culture, internally, was one of 'remarkable fidelity and earnestness of purpose and conscientious endeavour'. In all staff, the article reported 'as a dominant motive a genuine pride in their House'. The wellspring of this familial *esprit de corps* seemed to flow directly from the active family managers, for the 'reciprocal spirit of absolute trust in all who hold positions of responsibility is equally manifest on the part of the managing directors'.[12] It is perhaps too easy to be cynical about such values but it is possible we should take them seriously and ask as to their genesis. In part the answer may lie with how the firm understood itself as an entity. At the centenary banquet Charles E. Shaw reflected very explicitly on the nature of the firm post-incorporation:

> Gentlemen, we are now a limited company. Limited companies have been described as neither having souls to save nor bodies to be kicked ... but I am thankful to say there are companies and there are companies, and I venture to divide them roughly into three classes, first, the doubtful trading concern, which is foisted upon a too credulous public and which more than generally has a meteoric career. Secondly, the honest trading concern who owners are desirous of sharing their responsibilities with the general public or of retiring from business altogether. Thirdly, the old family business which, consequent upon the death of the partners, avails itself of the Limited Liability Acts. Now, gentlemen, the last named was exactly our case, and I venture to say no employee of the firm has ever felt that any wall of separation has been raised thereby, as between the firm and its employees.[13]

Another part of the answer may lie in the way members were inducted. The picture that emerges is a more complex one that it at first seems. Mr Shaw was first asked about his beginnings as a 'hardwareman':

> It was when I was 17, and I am now 36, therefore 19 years ago ... that was while my father was still alive. I commenced in just the same way any other apprentice did – started at the counter, received goods, saw that they were correct, learned the wrapping up, copied invoices, entered orders on to sheets and then copied the same out again for the manufacturer. My first salary was 5s per week, and I rose 1s per week per

annum until I was 21 – that was all the money I ever had. I then kept the stock for over 12 months, and after learning how to put Travellers' sheets in hand, and doing anything and everything that could be done in the Home Department passed thence to the Foreign Department, which had always been under the control of my father; I then ceased my active connection with Home Department ... my department is the Foreign, to which I devote myself exclusively, except when my co-Managing Director [cousin John P. Shaw] is away.[14]

So, as so many sons of business proprietors did, he started at the bottom and learnt the business thoroughly and was shown few if any favours. It would also appear that he was always destined to follow his father into management of the Foreign Department and that a logical division of labour between he and his cousin, who oversaw the Home Department, had long been planned. In fact, the governance and management of the firm at the dawn of the twentieth-century reflected the workings of crisis and reaction intimately tied to family dynamics. Indeed, Charles had never intended to follow a commercial career:

No. My desire then was to read for the Bar, and I accordingly entered at Balliol; but at my father's request, on account of his failing health, I gave that up, and endeavoured to fit myself to take up a portion of his work. His death, in 1886, seemed to reopen the opportunity for following my original inclinations, and I took up my residence at Balliol.

Here a number of classic tropes from the conventional wisdom about family firms appear: the third generation heir attracted to the professions and elite educational establishments rather than grubby Wolverhampton, the impact of illness and death, the clear sense of duty that returns him to the fold. But there are unsettling elements too, particularly the way in which Charles clearly felt his obligation or duty to the firm and family was broken, rather than deepened, by his father's death, which instead seems to come as a moment of liberation. That liberation was short-lived:

When, however, Thomas W. Shaw died very suddenly, within a year of my father's death, and the business was left without a head, the question of its future disposition became urgent. My cousin, Mr John P. Shaw, refused to take it up unless I joined him; and seeing that the affair might go into litigation, and that there were more than forty clerks to be considered, I decided to leave Balliol, and throw myself into the business. For family reasons, a private limited liability company was registered, and one of the Articles of Association of the company is that, if any member of the of the company wishes to sell his shares, he must first offer them to the remaining shareholders. Our next point was to divide the management ... [15]

Succession between second and third generations was clearly a highly traumatic event, beyond the obvious shock of two deaths following on so quickly from one another and notwithstanding both the obvious desire to retain tight family ownership and the years that had been devoted to training the cousins. Dissolution was probably a very real possibility for a time.[16] It was a perhaps stronger commitment on the half of John P. Shaw that saw the firm through. In his speech on the occasion of the firm's centenary banquet in January 1896 he spoke very warmly of the preceding generations: 'I believe my grandfather, and father and uncle were men of sterling principles – carrying those principles in their business. They knew nothing of the tricks of the trade, but were straight as an arrow, and did not deal in any unfair way ... Their hands were clean, their aims high, and their motives pure, and because of this we are permitted to enter on our second century as a firm'.[17] The implication was that this was a legacy that demanded not simply respect but also preservation and continuation. It was a duty. But he also touched, however lightly, on the toll being in business as a family could take: 'They [the preceding generations] worked hard and long, some think too hard and too long, and they might have been with us tonight if they had taken things a little easier'. Here is the voice of the son who has lost his father. Still, he concluded: 'we believe their principles were right'.[18]

Even so, crisis averted though John P. Shaw's force of will and familial commitment, a practical *modus operandi* had to be found, a considerable challenge, especially after Charles entered Parliament, representing Stafford as a Liberal, in 1892. Charles was candid enough to admit that 'the last three years have been a very trying period. It was here that the value of our secretary, Mr Arlett, came in'. Still, he concluded, 'From the time that the Company has been incorporated, until now, we have more than held our own'.[19] However rudimentary, Mr Arlett perhaps represented the first step on the road to a more professionalized management.[20]

The interview went on to cover many other aspects of the business, as well as a world tour undertaken by Charles Shaw in 1889–1890 that combined both business and pleasure. Several points of interest emerge that give an indication of the culture of the firm. First was the way in which the overseas branches were managed from home and in particular how 'We make a rule with our Calcutta House, whether there is anything to communicate or not, that a letter shall be written from each end once every week, and I do not think this rule has been broken during the last 19 years'.[21] Remarkably, though, the interview also reveals that Charles's visit to Calcutta during his world tour of 1890 was the first made by any member of the firm for more than forty years.[22]

Perhaps more revealing of the culture of the firm though was a discussion of attitude to cash and cash reserves:

> In those days we had no Cashier other than a member of the family for we never allowed the Cash Department to go out of the hands of the firm, on account of the large amount of cash and the extensive and valuable securities requiring to be dealt with ... If my father or cousin were away, then I took charge of the cash ... it may interest your readers to know, it was a rule of the firm never to keep less than £12,000 lying at the bank. This rule grew out of the anxiety and suspense generally prevailing in the

> commercial world during the period following the Overend and Gurney suspension; and since that Black Thursday the firm has made it a rule never to accept a Bill.

These are remarkably prudent, if not cautious, policies, especially as they were still being followed in the mid-1880s and later. The Overend and Gurney banking failure that had precipitated them had, of course, taken place in 1866. The *Hardwareman* was surely right to conclude its review of the firm's history to that point with the observation that:

> here is a house which excels in those qualities that are the distinguishing marks of British commercial enterprise, energy guarded by prudence, a business foresight that rarely if ever errs, sound commercial principle, and that caution that leaves no loophole for grave disaster, an instinctive courtesy to all without, and an unvarying thoughtfulness to all within.[23]

And just as the *Sesquicentum* had, the *Hardwareman* made very great play of the astounding length of the relationships between the firm and some of its customers, including small retail customers in provincial Shropshire, who must have been increasingly marginal to the firm's overall trade.[24] These relationships were easily matched for durability and warm feeling by those with the manufacturers who supplied the firm with goods.[25] Equally much weight was given to the long service (and gratitude) of many employees and of the personal touch given to management by family members. Sometimes it seems as though *not* changing is regarded as a positive virtue.

Still, even if this picture of conservatism, caution, loyalty, and politeness is accurate it is also the case that the firm continued to prosper and expand and in some respects was more forward looking and aggressive than the general tenor of the article would suggest. For example, Mr Burgess of the Calcutta house analysed the threat of American competition in the following terms:

> Then, they [Americans] are adaptable people. They will make what is wanted, whereas the Englishman too often prefers to make what he wants, not what his customer abroad wants. The Americans, again, are always bringing out something new, while the Englishman is more prone to go on the old lines. If the English maker will set himself to study the tastes of markets abroad, and get up new patterns and work out novel lines, he will have a much easier time of it.[26]

This sounds like the judgements advanced by later generations of business and economic historians. Both Burgess and Charles Shaw also expressed trenchant and probably advanced views on a range of issues, including bimetallism, The Merchandise Marks Act (which had 'done more harm than good. It has injured Great Britain's trans-shipment trade, and in many lines injured the direct export trade'),[27] a sharp awareness of the coming competitive threat of such nations as Germany, America, and Japan (visited on the 1890 world tour),[28] general commercial practice and common follies, the potential of South Africa and its gold reserves in particular (visited by Charles in 1894, when he met both Cecil Rhodes and Paul Kruger), and British policy in India, which was roundly condemned: "A financial equilibrium must be established in India, and you cannot lay any more burdens on the shoulders of the native – he is one of the most heavily taxed creatures on the face of the earth: you even tax his salt."[29]

How did this curious admixture of longevity, continuity, old-fashioned courtesy and rather more bull-headed competitiveness manifest itself in action? We can detect essentially two phases of development led by the second and third generations. First, Thomas Wilkinson Shaw and Edward Dethick Shaw never really changed what the firm did – it remained a factor and wholesaler (and in India a retailer too) of a huge range of British made hardware and other goods for both business and domestic use – but they did begin an expansion of the scale and reach of its operations, particularly the addition of further overseas agencies (though not directly owned subsidiaries as in Calcutta) in Canada (1857), Australia (1868), building on prior extensions to the East and West Indies (Jamaica), and Ireland (Cork), both in 1845. These endeavours, the journal averred, brought 'the house to the very front rank of hardware factors and merchants in the Midlands'.[30] The significance of the foreign operations to the development and future of the firm at that time was reflected in the very considerable space given to tracing the history of the Calcutta operation.

After a period of consolidation following the traumatic events of 1886 and 1887 the cousins of the third generation began to significantly re-orientate the firm away from a dependence on factoring and intermediation, which had always formed the backbone of the enterprise. As the *Sesquicentum* observed, the firm now began to 'more and more associated with Hand Tools, in addition to general Hardware'. The undeniably celebratory little pamphlet claims that as 'mechanical processes advanced, the Company kept pace, in design, in resources, and in organization ... and ultimately achieved an outstanding reputation in the Hand Tool industry'.[31] Shaw and Sons, which had, after all, always been purely a selling operation, achieved this new position through a rapid campaign of acquisitions, integrating backwards through the purchase of firms in its home region. Thus in 1896, the company acquired J and W Hawkes of Birmingham, in 1899 both William and Henry Bate and Owen and Fendelow (Owen and Fendelow having themselves over the years acquired a number of other firms, including Windle and Blyth of Walsall, Henry Stuart and Company, and Plimley and Company). The campaign resumed in 1906, with purchase of Onions and Company of Birmingham.[32] Another pause ensued, followed by conversion to public limited liability status in 1919, which event ushered in a second wave of take-overs that saw the absorption of Jenks Brothers Ltd., The British Tool and Engineering Company, and eventually Moore and Wright (Sheffield) Ltd., which firm brought with it Avia Steel and Tool Company Ltd. These last two marked the expansion of the firm outside its home in the Midlands and established the structure, scale, and scope of operations on the eve of World War Two. Now heavily committed to the production of hand and machine tools and other aspects of metal-wares and engineering the war necessarily made very heavy demands on the firm's organizational and productive capacities.

This extensive programme of expansion and re-orientation must have represented a very considerable challenge but the firm was positive that it handled them effectively. Indeed, the *Sesquicentum* claimed that:

> It is not in the the multiplicity of Departments that the House prides itself, or on which it relies for progress. These are the results, not the causes of the firms present strong position. It is the organization inside those Departments which is, we hope pardonably, the pride of the Directors of John Shaw and Sons.[33]

However, by the close of the war other much more far-reaching changes had been wrought in the DNA of the firm. Charles E. Shaw, grandson of John and Elizabeth, having been made a Baronet in 1908, had died in 1942. The firm exited the war with G. Clement Jenks as both Chairman and Managing Director. Jenks' death in 1946 saw him replaced by Reginald P. Jenks. This was still in some sense a family firm then, but no longer could it really be said to be John Shaw and Sons.

NOTES

Introduction: An Unlimited Partnership

1. Wilkinson Ms No. 23, Elizabeth Wilkinson to John Shaw, 14 August 1812. Elizabeth quoted these words to her betrothed in a letter, describing them as a 'never failing source of delight & happiness – I sincerely hope we shall ever enjoy it in the married state'. Ibid.

2. Shaw Ms No. 35, John Shaw to Elizabeth Shaw, 22 April 1832. The Shaws in fact had another twenty-six years of marriage ahead of them.

3. See K. Thomas, *The Ends of Life: Roads to Fulfilment in Early Modern England* (Oxford: Oxford University Press, 2010).

4. This is too rarely even attempted. See, for one example of the study of the entanglement of life, family, and business, K. M. Guy, 'Drowning Her Sorrows: Widowhood and Entrepreneurship in the Champagne Industry', *Business and Economic History*, Vol. 26 No. 2 (1997): pp. 505–14

5. See, M. R. Hunt, *The Middling Sort: Commerce, Gender, and the Family in England, 1680–1780* (Berkeley, CA: University of California Press, 1996).

6. C. Spinosa, F. Flores and H. L. Dreyfus, *Disclosing New Worlds: Entrepreneurship, Democratic Action, and the Cultivation of Solidarity* (Cambridge, MA: MIT Press: 1997).

7. Ibid., p. 1.

8. For contemporary perspectives on this interweaving see, E. Hamilton, 'Whose Story is it Anyway? Narrative Accounts of the Role of Women in Founding and Establishing Family Businesses', *International Small Business Journal*, 24:3 (2006), pp. 253–71; E. Hamilton, 'Narratives of Enterprise as Epic Tragedy', *Management Decision*, 44:4 (2006), pp. 536–50.

9. In fact, the firm founded by John Shaw, probably in 1805, went through a number of changes in ownership and legal status during his lifetime, but all of them were characterized by personal ownership and management and unlimited liability. Chapter 2 will give more detail on the development of the firm. In Chapter 4 we will follow John and the firm to India and in the Epilogue we will sketch the later history of the firm across the rest of the nineteenth-century and on into the twentieth.

10. E. Berenson, *The Trial of Madame Caillaux* (Berkeley, CA: The University of California Press: 1992); p. 8.

11. See though A. Popp, 'Building the Market: John Shaw of Wolverhampton and Commercial Travel in the Early Nineteenth-Century', *Business History*, 49:3 (2007), pp 321–47; A. Popp, 'From Town to Town: How Commercial Travel Connected Manufacturers and Markets in the Industrial Revolution', *Journal of Historical Geography*, 35:4 (2009), pp. 642–67.

12. M R. Trouillot, *Silencing the Past: Power and the Production of History* (Boston, MA: Beacon Press, 1995).

13. For a recent example of this line of argument and approach see: L. Colley, *The Ordeal of Elizabeth Marsh: How a Remarkable Woman Crossed Seas and Empires to Become Part of World History* (London: Harper Perennial, 2007).

14. See also J. Tosh, 'From Keighley to St-Denis: Separation and Intimacy in Victorian Bourgeois Marriage', *History Workshop Journal*, 40:1 (1995), pp. 193–206.

15. Sadly it seems no letters survive for the last nineteen years of their marriage. It seems likely that as they aged both John and Elizabeth would have travelled less, thus spending less time apart and writing fewer letters. It is possible, however, that others have been lost.

16. For other historical studies of epistolary courtship see M. Hanna, *Your Death Would be Mine: Paul and Marie Pireaud in the Great War* (Cambridge, MA: Harvard University Press, 2006); O. Figes, *Just Send Me Word: A True Story of Love and Survival in the Gulag* (London: Allen Lane, 2012).

17. See A. Popp and R. Holt, 'Emotion, Succession, and the Family Firm: Josiah Wedgwood and Sons', *Business History* (forthcoming) for an extended discussion of emotion and the family firm.

1 'Did You Really Think Your Letter Would Prove Too Long?'

1. Shaw Ms No. 6, John Shaw to Elizabeth Wilkinson, 21 November 1811.

2. Shaw Ms No. 10. John Shaw to Elizabeth Wilkinson, 25 December 1812.

3. John Keats to J.H. Reynolds, 3 February 1818. Robert Gittings (ed.), *John Keats Selected Letters* (Oxford: Oxford University Press, 2002), p. 59.

4. Shaw Ms No. 8, John Shaw to Elizabeth Wilkinson, Sunday evening, 5 August 1812.

5. 'You must excuse me [not] giving you a long letter. I have not time just now as it is twelve o'clock ... and if I do not finish tonight you will not get it on Thursday.' Shaw Ms No. 13, John Shaw to Elizabeth Shaw, Liverpool, 4 December 1816.

6. 'My hands are so full all day long out of doors and till late at night and early in the morning. I have so much entering up to do that I really cannot write so much as I would wish and feel inclined to ... if I do not give so long letters it is not for want of inclination but of ability and time so to do.' Shaw Ms No. 14, John Shaw to Elizabeth Shaw, Manchester, 3 July 1817.

7. In one letter, Elizabeth, newlywed, tells John how she spends her days whilst he is away, including the charming detail that 'I sometimes read in the arbour.' Shaw Ms No. 40a, Elizabeth Wilkinson to John Shaw, 1813.

8. Ibid. The privacy of correspondence engendered a belief in the possibility of complete honesty. John echoes the words of Geneviève de Malboissière, a young woman in Paris in the later eighteenth-century, who in a letter to her closest female friend insisted: 'Be very sure, my friend, that we are much happier than they are ... Between ourselves, we know no dissimulation.' D. Goodman, 'Letter Writing and the Emergence of Gendered Subjectivity in Eighteenth-Century France', *Journal of Women's History*, 17 (Summer 2005), p. 16.

9. Shaw Ms No. 12, John Shaw to Elizabeth Shaw, 9 April 1816.

10. Isaac and Sarah Holden, North country Methodists married in 1850, suffered similar agonies, Sarah being '"kept on the rack" by his silences'; J. Tosh, 'From Keighley to St-Denis', p. 196.

11. Ibid.

12. Elizabeth, a little later, describes John's letter 'as a cordial to my drooping soul.' Wilkinson Ms No. 28, Elizabeth Wilkinson to John Shaw, 25 November 1812.

13. Shaw Ms No. 103, Mary Shaw to John Shaw, 20 November 1805.

14. Shaw Ms No. 40a, Elizabeth Shaw to John Shaw, 1813.

15. Hanna, *Your Death Would be Mine*, p. 23.

16. Wilkinson Ms No. 28, Elizabeth Wilkinson to John Shaw, 25 November 1812. She continued: 'You may smile at the last sentence but I assure you I have in imagination held many a long conversation with you.

17. Wilkinson Ms. No. 23, Elizabeth Wilkinson to John Shaw, 14 August 1812. Emphasis added.

18. See for example S. E. Rowe, 'Writing Modern Selves: Literacy and the French Working Class in the Early Nineteenth Century', *Journal of Social History* (Autumn 2006), pp. 55–83.

19. D. A. Gerber, 'Acts of Deceiving and Withholding in Immigrant Letters: Personal Identity and Self-Presentation in Personal Correspondence', *Journal of Social History*, 39:2 (2005), pp. 315–30; G. Stott, 'The Persistence of Family: A Study of a Nineteenth-Century Canadian Family and their Correspondence', *Journal of Family History*, 31:2 (2006), pp. 190–207.

20. Wilkinson Ms No. 18, Elizabeth Wilkinson to John Shaw, nd. In fact, Elizabeth seems to have suffered numerous interruptions, on which she provided a running commentary, during the writing of this particular letter, complaining that 'I have been writing all the afternoon save when company came, or [I] had to go in the shop.' In transcript the letter is more than five closely typed A4 pages long. In the end she was forced to lock the door whereupon: 'While I was writing another rap came to the door – & Mr Midgley surprised me with a lock'd door – upon my opening it he laugh'd and hop'd I was writing to a gentleman he thought I could [not] be able to say so much to a lady.' Ibid. While one can understand Elizabeth's desire not to be interrupted one can also sense that to lock a door in the house during the day was probably looked on slightly askance. Though undated this letter recounts as very recent events the Luddite assaults on Burton's Mill, Middleton, which took place on 20 and 21 of April 1812.

21. Shaw Ms No.47, Elizabeth Shaw to John Shaw, 11 March 1816; Shaw Ms No. 42, Elizabeth Shaw to John Shaw, 21 March 1815. On the latter occasion Elizabeth was pregnant with their first child, news that had not yet been shared with his family. Disclosing the letter would have revealed this news.

22. Shaw Ms No. 94, Elizabeth Wilkinson to Elizabeth Shaw, 24 March 1828.

23. In another incident Miss Lomax, a friend, relates to Elizabeth how 'My Brother ... showed me a letter he had received from Mrs Parker and showed me a copy one he had written in answer to hers – you were mentioned in it in very high terms I can tell you.' This predates Elizabeth's correspondence with John. Shaw Ms No. 97, M. Lomax to Elizabeth Wilkinson, 1 December 1810.

24. Wilkinson Ms No. 13, Elizabeth Wilkinson to John Shaw, n.d. Similarly, in November 1811, Elizabeth had begun a letter by noting that 'I should not address you so soon but for the fear of either directing wrong or my falling into the hands of some person who may know you and thereby publish what may as well be kept secret. Wilkinson Ms No. 11, Elizabeth Wilkinson to John Shaw, November 1811. This anxiety was not restricted to Elizabeth; in March 1812 she reassured John that 'You may rest satisfied that your letters will not be seen.' Wilkinson Ms No. 15, Elizabeth Wilkinson to John Shaw, 6 March 1812.

25. Wilkinson Ms No. 13, Elizabeth Wilkinson to John Shaw, 1 January 1812. There is an echo of Mrs Larpent's reflections, quoted by Amanda Vickery: 'These letters brought back many events, but above all marked the progress of time & how it sweeps into its course over friends over feelings', A. Vickery, *The Gentleman's Daughter: Women's Lives in Georgian England* (New Haven, CT: Yale University Press, 1999), p. 1.

26. See, for example, the contrivances adopted by the subjects of Mark Seymour's 'Epistolary Emotions: Exploring Amorous Hinterlands in 1870s Southern Italy', *Social History*, 35:2 (2010), pp. 148–64.

27. Shaw Ms No. 49, Elizabeth Shaw to John Shaw

28. Ibid. Emphasis in the original. In her next letter she describes one from him as a 'kind and affectionate token of remembrance.' Shaw Ms No. 50, Elizabeth Shaw to John Shaw

29. M. Lyons, 'Love Letters and Writing Practices: On *Écritures Intimes* in the Nineteenth Century', *Journal of Family History*, 24:2 (1999), pp. 232–9, p. 236.

30. The exceptions are a reference to the letters of Lord Lyttelton (perhaps *Observations on the Conversion and Apostleship of St. Paul. in a Letter to Gilbert West, Esq.* by George Lyttelton, first Baron Lyttelton) and to Hester Chapone's famed letters to her niece, published as *Letters on the Improvement of the Mind* in 1773.

31. Wilkinson and Shaw Letters No. 2, Richard Wilkinson to Elizabeth Wilkinson, 27 August 1802. In March of the following year Richard still wondered 'much at my Brother's Silence, as he never writes me ... I should write to him at present , only I think he is indebted to me a letter first.' Wilkinson and Shaw Letters No. 3, Richard Wilkinson to Elizabeth Wilkinson, 11 March 1803.

32. Wilkinson and Shaw Letters No. 28, Elizabeth Shaw to John Shaw, n.d.

33. Shaw Ms No. 43a, Elizabeth Shaw to John Shaw, 31 March 1815.

34. Shaw Ms No. 82, Elizabeth Shaw to Elizabeth Wilkinson, 14 June 1828. The omissions could be reciprocal; a letter from Elizabeth's mother from 1822 begins 'No doubt you have tho't me very long in writing but the obstructions which have accrued are to [*sic*] tedious to mention.' The letter was signed 'your affect Mo'r in haste.' Shaw Ms No. 96, Elizabeth Wilkinson to Elizabeth Shaw, 19 November 1822.

35. Shaw Ms No. 97, M. Lomax to Elizabeth Wilkinson, 1 December 1810.

36. Shaw Ms No. 98, M. Lomax to Elizabeth Wilkinson, 13 May 1811.

37. Shaw Ms No. 99, M. Lomax to Elizabeth Wilkinson, 'The last day of the last year' – without doubt 1811.

38. Shaw Ms No. 101, M. Lomax to Elizabeth Wilkinson, 29 May 1812.

39. Wilkinson Ms No. 16, Elizabeth Wilkinson to John Shaw, 25 March 1812.

40. M. Smith (ed.), *Charlotte Brontë: Selected Letters* (Oxford: Oxford University Press, 2010), p. 238.

41. Ibid., p. 239.

42. A. Vickery, *Behind Closed Doors: At Home in Georgian England* (New Haven, CT: Yale University Press, 2009), pp. 110–11.

43. Goodman, 'Letter Writing and the Emergence of Gendered Subjectivity'.

44. Vickery, *Behind Closed Doors*, p. 238.

45. Tosh, 'From Keighley to St-Denis', p. 199.

46. John and Elizabeth were hardly alone in presenting this more complex form of gendering and other historians have found a range of varieties of masculinity. See for example the middling life-writings examined in H. Barker, 'Soul, Purse and Family: Middling and Lower-class Masculinity in Eighteenth-Century Manchester', *Social History*, 33:1 (2008), pp. 12–35.

47. D. Goodman, *Becoming a Woman in the Age of Letters* (London: Cornell University Press, 2009). Goodman, 'Letter Writing and the Emergence of Gendered Subjectivity'.
48. Gerber, 'Acts of Deceiving and Withholding in Immigrant Letters'; Stott, 'The Persistence of Family'.
49. Hanna, *Your Death Would be Mine*; Seymour, 'Epistolary Emotions'; N. Eustace, '"The Cornerstone of a Copious Work:" Love and Power in Eighteenth-Century Courtship', *Journal of Social History* (Spring 2001), pp. 517–46; R. K. Nelson, '"The Forgetfulness of Sex:" Devotion and Desire in the Courtship Letters of Angelina Grimke and Theodore Dwight Weld', *Journal of Social History* (Spring 2004), pp. 663–79; E. K. Rothman, 'Sex and Self-Control: Middle-Class Courtship in America, 1770–1870', *Journal of Social History* (2001), pp. 409–25. But see, especially, all of the letters in R. Earle (ed.), Epistolary Selves: Letters and Letter-Writers. 1600-1945 (Franham: Ashgate, 1999)
50. M. Hanna, 'A Republic of Letters: The Epistolary Tradition in France during World War I', *American Historical Review* (December 2003), pp. 1338–61; Rowe, 'Writing Modern Selves'.
51. C. Acton, 'Writing and Waiting: The First World War Correspondence between Vera Brittain and Roland Leighton', *Gender & History*, 11:1 (1999), pp. 54–83; V. B. Conger, '"There is Graite Odd between A Mans being At Home and A Broad": Deborah Read Franklin and the Eighteenth-Century Home', *Gender & History*, 21:3 (2009), pp. 592–607; M. Roper, 'Splitting in Unsent Letters: Writing as a Social Practice and a Psychological Activity', *Social History*, 26:3 (2001), pp. 318–39.
52. Though see, for example: J. Smail, 'Coming of Age in Trade: Masculinity and Commerce in Eighteenth-Century England', in M. C. Jacob and C. Secretan (eds), *The Self-Perception of Early Modern Capitalists* (Basingstoke: Palgrave Macmillan, 2008), pp. 229–52.
53. G. Boyce, 'Language and Culture in a Liverpool Merchant Family Firm, 1870–1950', *Business History Review*, 84:1 (2010), pp. 1–26.
54. Müller, Leos. '"Merchants" and "Gentlemen" in Eighteenth-Century Sweden: Worlds of Jean Abraham Grill.' In, Jacob, Margaret C. And Catherine Secretan (eds.), *The Self-Perception of Early Modern Capitalists* (Basingstoke: Palgrave Macmillan, 2008), pp. 125–147.
55. Lyons, 'Love Letters and Writing Practices', p. 236.
56. Ibid., p. 233.
57. Ibid., p. 232.
58. Ibid., p. 237. An important element of the specific pact studied by Lyons was that letters be answered in full. John and Elizabeth held to this too, Elizabeth tasking John to not 'be long before you answer this letter – & please answer it all – not part as you did last time.' Wilkinson Ms No. 26, Elizabeth Wilkinson to John Shaw, 19 October 1812.
59. Seymour, 'Epistolary Emotions', p. 149.
60. Roper, 'Slipping Out of View'. Elsewhere, Roper identifies letters as a 'good means of showing the work of negotiation which authors perform between experience, internal states and the cultural forms through those states are rendered'. Roper, 'Splitting in Unsent Letters', p. 319.
61. Goodman, 'Letter Writing and the Emergence of Gendered Subjectivity', p. 26.
62. Ibid., p. 11. Emphases added. Goodman notes that this chance to see the construction of intersubjectivity through writing is in addition to letters as 'a window into [subjects'] selves'. Ibid., p. 12.
63. Seymour, 'Epistolary Emotions', p. 149.
64. Tosh, 'From Keighley to St-Denis', p. 204.

65. Ibid., p. 205 and p. 193.
66. Goodman, 'Writing and the Emergence of Gendered Subjectivity', p. 9.

2 John Shaw in Business

1. W. Cobbett, *Rural Rides*, ed. G. Woodcock (1830; London, 1967), pp. 479–80.
2. J. F. Wilson and A. Popp, *Industrial Clusters and Regional Business Networks in England, 1750–1970* (Aldershot: Ashgate, 2003). P. Hudson, *Regions and Industries: Perspectives on the Industrial Revolution* (Cambridge: Cambridge University Press, 1989).
3. J. Stobart, *The First Industrial Region: North-west England c. 1700–60* (Manchester: Manchester University Press, 2004), p. 1.
4. Shaw and Wilkinson Ms. 35, Elizabeth Shaw (mother) to John Shaw, 9 September 1802. That William, though based in Liverpool, has no direct experience of Manchester is a reminder of how the reality of distance changes with changes in transportation.
5. Shaw and Wilkinson Ms. 38. William Shaw (brother) to John Shaw, 10 June 1801. These contrasts were not all pleasing and in the same letter William also expressed his wish to 'see my Papa and mama for though I am in such a place as L'pool my heart is still at Penn. But however if it is to be my Lot to be Placed here I must do as well as I can. I have no very great Bad Objections to the place except of being cut of so from you all which is a very heavy misfortune but I hope it is all for the best.' If it was not home then William found that Liverpool also had another disadvantage: 'it has a great misfortune. I mean its inhabitants of being a wicked and Loose people and [I] believe there are but few truly virtuous women in the town.' Ibid.
6. Wilkinson and Shaw Ms 3, Richard Wilkinson (brother) to Elizabeth Wilkinson, 11 March 1803. Richard was with Messrs Jones, Lloyd, Hume and Co. Six years later younger brother John was attempting to derive the same advantage from location: 'I have not been spending my time idly since I came up [to London], I have been improving myself in accounts and other branches of learning, besides getting a knowledge of the town, which is requisite for everyone who goes into a retail house'. Shaw and Wilkinson Ms. 15, John Wilkinson (brother) to Elizabeth Wilkinson, 20 July 1809.
7. Parson and Bradshaw, *Staffordshire General and Commercial Directory for 1818* (Manchester: J. Leigh, 1818).
8. DB–24/A/29 Indenture of Apprenticeship between W.E. Shaw and Messrs Henry Pooley and Thomas Walker, 1801
9. Wilkinson and Shaw Ms 29, Elizabeth Shaw (mother) to John Shaw, 15 June 1801.
10. For a detailed exploration of the transition to adulthood amongst the commercial middling classes, and of the parental role in that transition, see: Smail, 'Coming of Age in Trade'.
11. Wilkinson and Shaw Ms 28, Elizabethe Shaw (mother) to John Shaw, n.d.
12. Ibid.
13. Wilkinson and Shaw Ms 34, Elizabethe Shaw (mother) to John Shaw, 27 February 1802.
14. Wilkinson and Shaw Ms 31, Elizabethe Shaw (mother) to John Shaw, 10 September 1801.
15. Wilkinson and Shaw Ms 29, Elizabethe Shaw (mother) to John Shaw, 15 June 1801.
16. Wilkinson and Shaw Ms 32, Elizabethe Shaw (mother) to John Shaw, 10 June 180?.
17. Wilkinson and Shaw Ms 30, Elizabeth Shaw (mother) to John Shaw, 30 August 180?. Shame at worldly loss and failure was another motivating force. When, in the same years, brother William suffered some unspecified financial losses their mother wrote to John

to 'scritly [strictly?] charge ... should you be ask'd questions by anny one not to acknowledge his lose. You may say it is redus'd wich is but to true, Ward was very pressing with
him to acknowledge it to know one but his parents; what he has encounter'd and the
thoughts what his future health may be hangs a heavy weight upon my spirits'. Wilkinson
and Shaw Ms 32, Elizabeth Shaw (mother) to John Shaw, 10 June 180?. Reputation and
its maintenance were of vital importance.

18. Wilkinson and Shaw Ms 34, Elizabeth Shaw (mother) to John Shaw, 27 February 1802.
19. Shaw Ms 10, John Shaw to Elizabeth Shaw, 25 December 1812.
20. Shaw Ms 9, John Shaw to Elizabeth Shaw, 12 November 1812. This observation on
    forms of business organization was prompted by the news that the partnership of one
    Elizabeth's brothers was to be 'so soon dissolved ... Your brother will no doubt do much
    better alone.' Ibid.
21. See, J. Smail, 'Credit, Risk, and Honor in Eighteenth-Century Commerce', *Journal of
    British Studies*, 44:3 (July 2005), pp. 439–56.
22. Wilkinson and Shaw Ms 3a, Richard Wilkinson (brother) to Elizabeth Wilkinson, 11
    March 1803.
23. Wilkinson Ms 27, Elizabeth Wilkinson to John Shaw, 3 November 1812. This letter
    gives a vivid picture of the hustle and bustle attending the launch of a new venture: 'I
    came last and am my Bror Thos until we can get some bedsteads set up. We have got
    a servant girl and a shop man who board here also at present. The workmen are in the
    shop – hope they will get out on Wednesday night. If possible we must be open next
    Saturday as it is the fair – I sadly fear we shall not. The house is in a sad condition – full
    of workmen – everything to get in and little time for it. Ibid. In her next letter Elizabeth
    was able to paint a more optimistic picture: 'My Bror open'd his shop at the time props'd
    (with very great difficulty for the workmen were in it to the last day) and am happy to
    say he meets with very good encouragement considering the badness of times. I have not
    the smallest doubt but it will answer.' Shaw Ms 28, Elizabeth Wilkinson to John Shaw,
    25 November 1812
24. Shaw Ms 26, Elizabeth Wilkinson to John Shaw, 19 October 1812. Despite these hopes
    Elizabeth wrote in her very next letter to John of the failure of the putative partnership:
    'I have before told you that JS was going into partnership with my Bror Jno – a circum-
    stance which I cannot now inform you of ... happn'd that entirely frustrated their design.
    The partnership was dissolved and my Bro^r carries on the business alone.' Shaw Ms 27,
    Elizabeth Wilkinson to John Shaw, 3 November 1812.
25. Wilkinson and Shaw Ms 14, John Wilkinson (brother) to Elizabeth Wilkinson, 8
    December 1808.
26. Wilkinson and Shaw Ms 16, John Wilkinson (brother) to Elizabeth Wilkinson, 20
    August 1809. It seems unlikely that a travelling salesman would have been viewed much
    more favourably. As Elizabeth herself reflected in a letter from the period of courtship
    'Who would have thought two years ago that any thing like it would have taken place ...
    I would have as soon have thought of anything as a traveller falling to my lot. How things are
    brought about.' Shaw Ms 20, Elizabether Wilkinson to John Shaw, 5 June 1812.
27. During their courtship, Elizabeth had characterized John and herself as of those who
    should be restrained in expenditure as they 'have to live by industry and carefulness'.
    Shaw Ms 16, Elizabeth Wilkinson to John Shaw, 25 March 1812.
28. Ibid. In the same letter she recounted the salutary tale of a neighbour, a Mr Chadwick,
    who 'instead of attending to his business (in the woolen line) has rioted in intemperance

to that excess that he has worn out his constitution and is on the borders to the grave.' Ibid. Good business required diligence and sobriety of behaviour, in every sense.

29. N. McKendrick, 'The Consumer Revolution of Eighteenth-Century England', N. McKendrick, J. Brewer and J. Plumb (eds), *The Birth of the Consumer Society: the Commercialization of Eighteenth-century England* (London, 1982), p. 21.

30. Stobart, *The First Industrial Region*.

31. Ibid., p. 37.

32. For more information on the account data contained by the Journey Books, and how it has been utilized, please see Popp, 'From Town to Town', *Journal of Historical Geography*, pp. 642–67.

33. Again, for further detail on how customers have been identified please see Popp, 'From Town to Town'.

34. The one exception to the rule of little variation in customers by geography was Sheffield, another metal making and using district of course, where John Shaw did an often very large trade with other merchants, one of whom was later to provide a very valuable route into overseas business.

35. In the summer of 1817 John wrote explaining that Elizabeth must accept a short letter from him as 'my hands are so full all day long out of doors and till late at night and early in the morning. I have so much entering to do that I really cannot write so much as I would wish and feel inclined to do ... I am most sadly behind hand in copying my orders'. Shaw Ms No. 14, John Shaw to Elizabeth Shaw, 3 July 1817.

36. 'Your parcel from Manchester and the two sheets of orders are just to hand and shall have immediate attention'. Shaw Ms No. 41, Jos Latham to John Shaw, 13 March 1815.

37. 'The spike nails I am doubtful I shall not be able to get so low as 18/- from Carters knowing the makers price to be 5/6 ... beside the waste of iron in the making but I intend walking over to Dudley myself and will endeavour to get them from the cheapest person. Shaw Ms. No. 40b, unknown to John Shaw, 8 June of unknown year. Similarly, 'Edward went up this morning to before breakfast to the ironworks for the prices', Shaw Ms No. 41, Elizabeth Shaw to John Shaw, 13/4 March 1815.

38. One letter from the warehouse to John on the road captures these pressures nicely, reporting how 'Jones of Oswestry wrote ... to request his order may be cancelled owing to him not having a copy of it according to promise, I shall not order them until I hear from you or him again' and that 'I took a pretty good order from [Mr Threlfall] which must be at Blackburn very shortly.' Ibid.

39. 'You say they are busy at the Warehouse – do they seem attentive also?' Shaw Ms No. 21, John Shaw to Elizabeth Shaw, 25 December 1823. In March 1815 Elizabeth reported that 'I think it was well that Crane came into the Warehouse when he did because Latham was so strange to workmen – did not know where they lived – consequently mishaps occurred. They seem to go on very well now.' Shaw Ms No. 42, Elizabeth Shaw to John Shaw, 21 March 1815. See also, 'I think they are very attentive at the W'house and got off the orders as fast as they can get them in – but the workmen have been very lazy lately – however they are making up for it against quarter day'. Shaw Ms 43, Elizabeth Shaw to John Shaw, 31 March 1815. The business naturally also experienced fallow periods, thus: 'I should think William could have little or nothing to do at the W'house so that you have him to put the garden quite in order'. Shaw Ms No. 13, John Shaw to Elizabeth Shaw, 4 December 1816.

40. DB/24/A/183.

41. To a very large degree every aspect of John's experience of factoring and commercial travelling is corroborated, to a greater or lesser extent, by that of Worcester based pin factor John English. The close parallels between the two cases (both Midlands based hardware factors operating in overlapping time periods) give confidence as to the representativeness of the Shaw case. See, S. R. H. Jones, 'The Country Trade and the Marketing and Distribution of Birmingham Hardware, 1750–1810', *Business History*, 26:1 (1984), pp. 24–42.

42. DB–24/A/1. Articles of Partnership between John Shaw and Henry Crane, 1815. The partnership seems to have emerged from an unsettled period in the relationship between Shaw and his young employee; a letter from Elizabeth written in March 1815 reports that 'Mr Crane ... called upon me in the morning ... and sat talking until nearly one and again in the evening he came a little after as we were first sitting down to supper he took some with us ... I think he seems quite tired of playing and wants to be at work again – I told him pretty nearly what you said – but he seems to have made up his mind to come to you.' Shaw Ms. No. 41. Elizabeth plays a very subtle, almost un-noticeable but nonetheless important role here, brokering the relationship between John and Henry through an easy sociability.

43. In addition they each promised to be 'just, true and faithful to each other in all their transactions, accounts and dealings concerning or relating to the said Copartnership and shall severally endeavour by their utmost Skill, Care and Diligence to advance and promote the same and employ or their time and attention solely to the said Trade or Business and to the utmost of their ability and in as extensive a manner as may be.' Ibid.

44. In April 1819, explaining to Elizabeth an overlong silence, John noted how 'not well knowing the fresh ground I was going on I had given you too much time to answer my letter.' The new route evidently took in Carlisle and Richmond, North Yorkshire. Shaw Ms. No. 12, John Shaw to Elizabeth Shaw, 9 April 1816.

45. DB–24/A/51. Morton continued 'Of course, it is impossible for me to say to what extent [Mr Shaw is disadvantaged], but from the view which I am enabled to take of it I cannot think it would extend to £200 and I think it may be best arranged by a settlement between them.' Ibid.

46. http://eh.net/hmit/

47. M. Finn, *The Character of Credit: Personal Debt in English Culture, 1740–1914* (Cambridge: Cambridge University Press, 2003). D. A. Kent, 'Small Businessmen and their Credit Transactions in Early Nineteenth-Century Britain', *Business History*, 36:2 (1994), pp. 47–64.

48. Shaw Ms No. 16, John Shaw to Elizabeth Shaw, 28 November 1819; Shaw Ms No. 13, John Shaw to Elizabeth Shaw, 4 December 1816; Shaw Ms. No. 15, John Shaw to Elizabeth Shaw, 3 July 1817. The case of John English again supports these insights into Shaw's business; see, Jones, 'The Country Trade'.

49. Shaw Ms No. 9, John Shaw to Elizabeth Shaw, 12 November 1812.

50. Shaw Ms No. 49a, Elizabeth Shaw to John Shaw, 1 April 1816.

51. Smail, 'Credit, Risk, and Honor'.

52. See, for example, Smail, 'The Culture of Credit in Eighteenth Century Commerce.

53. Shaw Ms No. 29, John Shaw to Elizabeth Shaw, 18 January 1828.

54. Goodall and Alston collection. In private hands. I am deeply indebted to Mrs Enid Shanahan for access to these letters.

55. John Alston Snr to Thomas Alston, 11 January 1830. Alston continued, 'when I consented to give him the £100 it was that he was to give you it all and when he refused that

he should have been made to feel the effects of it for as he was behind, he would have eather [*sic*] to have paid up what he was behind and brought in more, or made him bankrupt.' Goodall's disloyalty seems to have been motivated by financial troubles. Alston correspondence, in private hands.

56. John Alston to Thomas Alston, 29 June 1830. John Alston to Thomas Alston, 1 July 1830. Alston even contemplated 'changing the route a little and by that means, will probably get before Goodall in these places.' John Alston to Thomas Alston, 22 September 1830. It is clear though that sociability and cooperation between travellers was a common experience on the road. In the same letter John also noted that 'Brown's traveller is here just now and I understand from him that Corny is worse and not able to take his journey.'

57. John Alston to Thomas Alston, 26 June 1830.

58. See for example Shaw Ms No. 42, Elizabeth Shaw to John Shaw, 21 March 1815, in which Elizabeth reports an approach from a Sheffield-based traveller seeking work having six years experience on the road, a good reference and married (and thus perhaps respectable) but without children and needing employment as his previous house had become insolvent. Similarly see, Shaw Ms No. 41, Elizabeth Shaw to John Shaw, n.d., for reports of the difficulties other local factors were having in securing the service of reliable travellers.

59. See, R. Pearson and D. Richardson, 'Business Networking in the Industrial Revolution', *Economic History Review*, Vol. 54, No. (2001), pp. 657–79, and the ensuing debate, J. F. Wilson and A. Popp, 'Business Networking in the Industrial Revolution: Some Comments', *Economic History Review*, 56:2 (2003), pp. 355–61; R. Pearson and D. Richardson, 'Business Networking in the Industrial Revolution: Riposte to Some Comments', *Economic History Review*, 56:2 (2003), pp. 362–8.

60. Wilson and Popp, 'Business Networking', p. 358

61. Ibid., p. 359.

62. Sometimes such opportunities seem to have been seized through much less formal means. In (probably) 1815 Elizabeth reported to John that 'Crane tells me also that Boscoe and Wheeldon are about to dissolve their partnership and the latter leaves the town – C[rane] thinks it would be a good opportunity to take his journey – if you think proper.' Shaw Ms. No. 41, Elizabeth Shaw to John Shaw, nd.,,

63. Shaw Ms. No. 41, Jos Latham to John Shaw, 13 March 1815.

3 John and Elizabeth in Love

1. Wilkinson M Nos 28; Elizabeth Wilkinson to John Shaw, 25 November 1812.

2. Ibid.

3. Though his findings are now very widely disputed it is nonetheless worth noting Stone's observation that the companionate model perhaps 'first developed as a norm among the more pious, often non-conformist, middle-class families'; a description that fits perfectly Elizabeth and John's backgrounds. L. Stone, *The Family, Sex and Marriage in England, 1500–1800* (London: Weidefeld and Nicholson, 1977), p. 361. Stone describes this new family type as emerging during the eighteenth-century amongst the urban bourgeoisie and the squirachy and 'playing a new role and experiencing new internal and external relationships: a family serving rather fewer practical functions, but carrying a much greater load of emotional and sexual commitment. It was a family type which was more conjugal and less kin and community oriented; more bound by ties of affection or habit

...; more internally liberal, and less patriarchal and authoritarian ...; more sexually liberated ...; more concerned with children and their needs and less adult-oriented; more private and less public', p. 657.Whatever the value of Stone's wider thesis, this provides a good description of John and Elizabeth's marriage and family.

4. For example, early in their correspondence, Elizabeth tells John that she has been reading '"Friendly Hints to the Youth of Both Sexes" ... by J Doncaster – in treating upon Marriage he says it is highly imprudent for two persons whose sentiments differ or who frequent different places of worship to marry.' This issue was central to early development of Elizabeth and John's relationship. Wilkinson Ms No. 4, Elizabeth Wilkinson to John Shaw, July 1811.

5. As Stone notes, strongly affective relationships, whether with parents, siblings, spouses or children, are deeply hazardous in times of very high mortality. Stone, *The Family*, pp. 651–2. When they first met, John's father was relatively recently dead and both of Elizabeth's parents were still alive and would remain so for many years. They were, of course, far from cushioned from the effects of death however; in his second extant letter to her John told Elizabeth that he has lost eleven relatives in the prior seven years. Shaw Ms No. 2, 16 April 1811.

6. Shaw and Wilkinson Ms No. 36. Elizabeth Shaw (née Edwards, mother) to John Shaw, nd.

7. Shaw and Wilkinson Ms No. 35. Elizabeth Shaw (née Edwards) to John Shaw, 9 September 1802. At another time John's sister, also Elizabeth, reminds John how 'you know my Papa is not blest with too great a [store] of patience.' Shaw and Wilkinson Ms No. 41. Elizabeth Shaw (sister) to John Shaw, n.d. One senses an irascible, difficult presence in the Shaw household.

8. Shaw and Wilkinson Ms No. 29. Elizabeth Shaw (née Edwards, mother) to John Shaw, 15 June 1801; Shaw and Wilkinson Ms No. 36. Elizabeth Shaw (née Edwards, mother) to John Shaw, 15 June 1801.

9. Shaw and Wilkinson Ms No. 30. Elizabeth Shaw (née Edwards, mother) to John Shaw, 15 June 1801

10. John's sister seemingly never married. Elizabeth noted in 1828 that 'She has been so long in this blessed state of singleness that she will have something to do to persuade herself to marry.' Shaw Ms No. 82. Elizabeth Shaw to Elizabeth Wilkinson, 14 June 1828.

11. Shaw and Wilkinson Ms No. 39. William Shaw (brother) to John Shaw, 20 June 1801

12. Shaw and Wilkinson Ms No. 33. Elizabeth Shaw (née Edwards, mother) to John Shaw, 18 August

13. In a letter to her mother written in June 1828, Elizabeth asks 'do you think [father] gets any more like himself – he will always be nervous.' Shaw Ms No. 82. Elizabeth Shaw to Elizabeth Wilkinson, 14 June 1828. In a letter to her daughter dated 24 January 1822 Elizabeth's mother relates how her husband is 'certainly much better though upon speaking to him of his mental complaint he now uses the same expression he did at first – the other day I said Mr W is it not time for you to return home and make yourself useful in your shop with a shake of the head he answered – no I shall never go home ... I shall never be fit to go home ... [but] there is a considerable abatement of his ravings – he is seldom heard only in a morning – a short time when he first gets up'. Shaw Ms No. 85. Elizabeth Wilkinson to Elizabeth Shaw, 24 January 1822.

14. Shaw and Wilkinson Ms No. 26. Thomas Wilkinson (father) to Eliza Wilkinson, 18 February 1810.

15. Shaw Ms No. 79, Elizabeth Shaw to Thomas Shaw (father), 23 February 1832.

16. Shaw and Wilkinson Ms No. 23, Thomas Wilkinson (brother) to Elizabeth Wilkinson, 4 November 1808.

17. Shaw and Wilkinson Ms No. 4, Richard Wilkinson (brother) to Elizabeth Wilkinson, 14 November 1803.

18. Shaw and Wilkinson Ms No. 5, Richard Wilkinson (brother) to Elizabeth Wilkinson, 24 March 1806. The paragraph continues in a gossipy vein; 'Is there any truth that Miss Wilkinson and W Hargreaves are mutually engaged en amour, I think it must all be nonsense, as I have a higher Idea of her than to think would countenance any person in his situation'. He further notes that he will be 'obliged by a call' if a Miss W. visits town for 'Had I continued in the Country, I fear I might have fallen a victim to her fascinating charms.'

19. Shaw and Wilkinson Ms No. 6, Richard Wilkinson (brother) to Elizabeth Wilkinson, 4 June 1806.

20. Shaw and Wilkinson Ms No. 7, Richard Wilkinson (brother) to Elizabeth Wilkinson, 22 December 1806.

21. Shaw and Wilkinson Ms No. 8, Richard Wilkinson (brother) to Elizabeth Wilkinson, 11 March 1807.

22. Shaw and Wilkinson Ms No. 9. Richard Wilkinson (brother) to Elizabeth Wilkinson, 7 June 1807. The suitor is unknown but was not John Shaw. The archive also contains an anonymous Valentine to Elizabeth, from 'WG A Travler,' dated 19 February 1805, prompted by a visit to Colne where he had 'the pleasure to behould the most Divine Female figure I ever gazed upon before'. Shaw and Wilkinson Ms No. 25, WG (anon) to Elizabeth Wilkinson, 19 February 1805.

23. In a letter to John written on 15 August 1811, early in their courtship, Elizabeth includes the following passage: 'There is one thing in your letter I particularly noticed – you say "It appears from your last letter but one that you have before been engaged"' – as much as if you had said, 'I did not know it before.' I believe I told you that the first time we conversed alone and also the reason why that engagement was broken off – as the best argument why you should not address me, for, if I had voluntarily given up an attachment (which was certainly dear to me) for the sake of difference in religious sentiment Why commence another with the same prospect. – I fear'd to answer your last letter lest through correspondence you might be led to hope what you could not realize – I can truly say I do not wish to give pain on my account tho' I have unfortunately done it.' Shaw Ms 13, Elizabeth Wilkinson to John Shaw, 15 August 1811.

24. Shaw Ms No. 80 Thomas Wilkinson (father) to Elizabeth Shaw, 15 December 1815. Similarly, in the same year Elizabeth warned her mother not let her brother William and his wife to move back into the parental home for 'If he fancies his wife is not noticed by you as much as Sarah [brother Thomas's wife?] it will be a cause of constant jealousy.' Shaw Ms No. 84, Elizabeth Shaw to Elizabeth Wilkinson (mother), 1 July 1815. None did like William's wife and by the mid-1820s she and William were deeply at odds with the rest of the Wilkinson family.

25. Shaw and Wilkinson Ms No. 81, Thomas Wilkinson (father) to Elizabeth Shaw, 23 January 1816.

26. Shaw Ms No. 22, Elizabeth Wilkinson to John Shaw, 25 July 1812. In the same letter though she goes on to reveal that she had 'never been a brides maid – but once at a Wedding – You don't need any lesson before the ceremony takes place – a novice acts as well as any one.' Ibid.

27. For example, in a letter of June 1807 Richard Wilkinson asked Elizabeth 'Does no person solicit the Hand of either of the Miss Sagars of Southfield. I suppose Mr Sagar would be very particular as to any person bold enough to make an offer of the kind.' Clearly, parental approval was still required in some families. Shaw and Wilkinson Ms No. 9, Richard Wilkinson (brother) to Elizabeth Wilkinson, 7 June 1807.
28. Wilkinson Ms No. 2, Elizabeth Wilkinson to John Shaw, 6 May 1811.
29. Ibid.
30. Wilkinson Ms No. 4, Elizabeth Wilkinson to John Shaw, July 1811.
31. In a later letter Elizabeth recalled that 'you gave me your affections the second time you saw me ... I hope you will never have to repent it (altho' it was rather injudicious of you).' Wilkinson Ms No. 19 Elizabeth Wilkinson to John Shaw, 14 May 1812.
32. Wilkinson Ms No. 6, Elizabeth Wilkinson to John Shaw, 15 August 1811.
33. Wilkinson Ms No. 9, Elizabeth Wilkinson to John Shaw, 21 October 1811. In an echo of Elizabeth, Manon Phlipon, one of the eighteenth-century French women letter-writers studied by Dena Goodman, insisted that 'Well-founded esteem, delicacy, and feeling will conduct me to the altar, or I won't go there at all.' Goodman, *Becoming a Woman in the Age of Letters*, p. 299.
34. Wilkinson Ms 12, Elizabeth Wilkinson to John Shaw, 24 December 1811.
35. Goodman, *Becoming a Woman in the Age of Letters*, p. 276.
36. Ibid.
37. At one point Elizabeth confessed to John that 'receiving letters from and writing to you I reckon amongst my greatest pleasures,' Wilkinson Ms No. 23, Elizabeth Wilkinson to John Shaw, 14 August 1812. Nervous at the prospect of frequent separation once married, Elizabeth consoled herself that 'Perhaps I shall enjoy your company the more if I am to have so little of it and we shall enjoy the pleasure or writing often one to the other', Wilkinson Ms No. 28, Elizabeth Wilkinson to John Shaw, 25 November 1812.
38. Shaw Ms No. 98, Miss M. Lomax to Elizabeth Wilkinson, 13 May 1811.
39. Ibid.
40. Shaw Ms No. 97, Miss M. Lomax to Elizabeth Wilkinson, 1 December 1810. As well as letters, the women exchanged small gifts, for example Miss Lomax could tell Elizabeth 'your cotton is ready both the white and buff and will send it ... tomorrow and hope you will like it'. Shaw Ms 98, Miss M. Lomax to Elizabeth Wilkinson, 13 May 1811. They wrote too about books they had read ('You speak of self-examination – there is a book with that title that I heard very highly spoken of', Shaw Ms No. 100, Miss M. Lomax to Elizabeth Wilkinson, 20 February 1812), and were quite as gossipy about marriage amongst their circle as ever the Wilkinson siblings were. However, some misunderstanding led the women to fall out, Miss Lomax 'There was a time when I could have thought you would have done anything sooner than have written me such a letter ... I thought it a very sharp one.' Shaw Ms No. 101, Miss M. Lomax to Elizabeth Wilkinson, 29 May 1812.
41. Goodman refers to this as 'epistolary reasoning', arguing that 'the private space of letter writing became the major site in which women enjoyed the freedom to exercise the power of the pen.' Letters reveal women as 'reasoning beings for whom epistolarity facilitated reflection, especially about men and marriage'. Goodman, *Becoming a Woman in the Age of Letters*, pp. 277–8.
42. Ibid., p. 276.
43. Elizabeth did not like to be 'continually caviling at Doctrine', but 'still it appears to me to be my duty to maintain my own principles, it is not from pride but for conscience sake

and I should wish the man that marries me to hold the same principles with myself for the sake of his offspring as well as me.' Wilkinson Ms No. 5, Elizabeth Wilkinson to John Shaw, 24 July 1811.

44. Elizabeth at least was fully alive to the dangers inherent to corresponding; 'We must settle this immediately one way or another – for continuing to write backward and forward only increases the agitation of our mind. Wilkinson Ms No. 13, Elizabeth Wilkinson to John Shaw, 1 January 1812.

45. The first extant letter from John begins thus; 'Although I could not obtain your consent to a correspondence, I cannot longer refrain addressing [you] upon a subject on which I find my happiness so very materially depends and when I assure you of this must throw myself upon your goodness and for the first offence I trust I shall find forgiveness'. Shaw Ms No. 1, 31 December 1810.

46. Wilkinson Ms No. 1, Elizabeth Wilkinson to John Shaw, 21 March 1811. In her third extant letter to John, Elizabeth suggests that 'As neither of us see our path so clear as could wish would it not be best to drop the subject of our correspondence, at least for the present, and consider ourselves as friends'. Wilkinson Ms No. 3, Elizabeth Wilkinson to John Shaw, 28 May 1811.

47. Wilkinson Ms No. 4, Elizabeth Wilkinson to John Shaw, 11 July 1811.

48. Shaw Ms No. 5, 16 July 1811. John goes on to lay out his understanding of her father's sentiments; namely that, 'please God, please yourself and you would please him'. Ibid.

49. Wilkinson Ms No. 4, Elizabeth Wilkinson to John Shaw, July 1811.

50. Wilkinson Ms No. 22, Elizabeth Wilkinson to John Shaw, 25 July 1812. The amount of money Elizabeth's father is to settle on the young couple becomes a subject of discussion in John and Elizabeth's correspondence in late 1812, only a few months before they were married. John shows a sense of grievance that he is not being treated fairly in comparison to Elizabeth's brothers. Elizabeth defends her father's actions robustly. However, though the subject clearly pains Elizabeth there is never a sense that the marriage was either initially predicated on the couple receiving a particular sum or that the dispute might lead to the connection being broken. This issue will be discussed in greater detail in Chapter 6, which will deal with the importance of networks and sociability.

51. Tosh, 'From Keighley to St-Denis'.

52. Wilkinson Ms No. 1, Elizabeth Wilkinson to John Shaw, 21 March 1811.

53. Elizabeth does not seem to have been alone in her circle in marrying a man from outside the locality however. Elizabeth's friend Miss Lomax wrote to her thus in February 1812, 'What do you mean pray about Miss Sagers and you going to make some one happy there too. Don't forget to tell me when you write. I am sure there is nothing like Staffordshire Beaux for Lancashire girls – how many do I know that are gone, Miss A Sager, Miss Wilcock and Miss C Peel the handsomest girl in our county is to be married in May to a Staffordshire gentleman'. Shaw Ms No. 100, Miss Lomax to Elizabeth Wilkinson, 20 February 1812.

54. The fifth and sixth extant letters from Elizabeth both discuss enquiries she and her father have made in Wolverhampton. The second of these is the most interesting: 'My father has not, nor does he, intend to write to the persons, whose names you gave him, for the respectability of your character. – he, and I am sufficiently satisfied with a letter he received, in answer to his enquiries, from Mr Holmes (the Methodist preacher) who, altho' he did know either you or my father – took the pains to enquire after you, and his letter, which my father copied and sent me … pleased me so much that I could not

help loving the man who could write in so liberal, unprejudiced and pleasing a manner.' Wilkinson Ms No. 6, Elizabeth Wilkinson to John Shaw, 15 August 1811.

55. Wilkinson M Nos. 1, Elizabeth Wilkinson to John Shaw, 21 March 1811; Wilkinson Ms 26, Elizabeth Wilkinson to John Shaw, 19 October 1812. Stone quotes Thomas Gisborne (1797) to the effect that "'the stiffness and, the proud and artificial reserve which in former ages infected even the intercourse of private life are happily discarded.'" Stone, *The Family, Sex and Marriage*, p. 330

56. In the same letter Elizabeth observes, 'I have heard it asserted that the days of a courtship are the most pleasant ones but they have ever been to me the most miserable ones – I have had more anxiety of mind in them than in all the other days of my life put together.' Wilkinson Ms No. 12, Elizabeth Wilkinson to John Shaw, 24 December 1811.

57. Wilkinson Ms No. 14, Elizabeth Wilkinson to John Shaw, 27 January 1812.

58. Wilkinson Ms No . 3, Elizabeth Wilkinson to John Shaw, 28 May 1811.

59. Wilkinson Ms 13a, Elizabeth Wilkinson to John Shaw, n.d.

60. Wilkinson Ms 10, Elizabeth Wilkinson to John Shaw, 7 November 1811.

61. Wilkinson Ms 12, Elizabeth Wilkinson to John Shaw, 24 December 1811.

62. When he learnt that she had previously been engaged, Elizabeth had to reassure John: 'Perhaps you may ask, are you not yet attach'd to the person you speak of. I answer that my sentiments are the same now that they were when I broke the connection and I am happy to say that through the influence of religion ... I have been enabled to withdraw my affections, Yea, in a great measure, before I became acquainted with you and as it is merit alone that will win then you have at present a greater chance than any other.' Wilkinson Ms No. 6, Elizabeth Wilkinson to John Shaw, 15 August 1811. As late as summer 1812 Elizabeth was being provoked to write 'I beseech you not to be jealous after we are united – or we must bid adieu to happiness.' Wilkinson Ms No. 21, Elizabeth Wilkinson to John Shaw, 18 July 1812.

63. Wilkinson Ms No. 17, Elizabeth Wilkinson to John Shaw, 10 April 1812.

64. Wilkinson Ms No. 26, Elizabeth Wilkinson to John Shaw, 19 October 1812.

65. Shaw Ms No. 1, John Shaw to Elizabeth Wilkinson, 31 December 1810.

66. Shaw Ms No. 2, John Shaw to Elizabeth Wilkinson, 16 April 1811.

67. Shaw Ms No. 4, John Shaw to Elizabeth Wilkinson, 5 July 1811.

68. Shaw Ms No. 7, John Shaw to Elizabeth Wilkinson, 21 November 1811.

69. Wilkinson Ms No. 6, Elizabeth Wilkinson to John Shaw, 11 August 1811.

70. Shaw Ms No. 9, John Shaw to Elizabeth Wilkinson, 12 November 1812.

71. Shaw Ms No. 11, John Shaw to Elizabeth Wilkinson, 3 April 1813.

72. Stone, *The Family, Sex and Marriage*, p. 325. Here Stone draws on de Tocqueville's observation that 'Freedom is then infused into the domestic circle'. Stone, *The Family, Sex and Marriage*, p. 666.

73. Goodman, *Becoming a Woman in the Age of Letters*, p. 301. Most clearly Goodman states that 'For women, marriage meant loss of freedom, equality and human dignity. How then were they to choose the path to happiness through marriage?', p. 275.

74. Ibid., p. 306

75. Vickery, *The Gentleman's Daughter*.

76. Wilkinson Ms No. 17, Elizabeth Wilkinson to John Shaw, 10 April 1812.

77. Wilkinson Ms No. 28, Elizabeth Wilkinson to John Shaw, 25 November 1812. In her final extant letter before marriage she again avers 'My mind would shrink from the very idea of being join'd to a man who did not love me – his love must be the basis of mine.' Wilkinson Ms No. 30, Elizabeth Wilkinson to John Shaw, 12 January 1813.

78. Stone, *Family, Sex and Marriage*, p. 326.
79. The books she discusses in her letters are overwhelming religious tracts and guides and manuals, such as those discussed here or, for example, Zimmerman on solitude. Another book she profits from greatly is a 'Guide to Domestic Happiness.' She is more active than John in recommending specific works.
80. Wilkinson Ms No. 19, Elizabeth Wilkinson to John Shaw, 14 May 1812.
81. Stone, *Family, Sex and Marriage*.
82. Ibid., p. 327.
83. Amidst all her discussions of books and reading Elizabeth mentions only one novel, entitled 'Self-Control,' author not given. It has not as yet proved possible to trace this book.
84. Though it is worth noting that conservative male writers of the time, such as Richard Polwhele in *The Unsex'd Females* (1798) bluntly categorized contemporary female authors as either 'good' or 'bad' girls, with Chapone, along with other such as Elizabeth Montagu and Fanny Burney, in the good camp and Wollstonecraft very firmly in the bad. H. K. Linkin, 'Skirting Around the Sex in Mary Tighe's *Psyche*', *Studies in English Literature 1500–1900*, 42:4 (2002), pp. 731–52.
85. Wilkinson Ms No. 19, Elizabeth Wilkinson to John Shaw, 14 May 1812.
86. Ibid.
87. Shaw Ms No. 5, John Shaw to Elizabeth Wilkinson, 16 July 1811.
88. Wilkinson Ms No. 24, Elizabeth Wilkinson to John Shaw, 31 August 1812.
89. Wilkinson Ms No. 28, Elizabeth Wilkinson to John Shaw, 25 November 1812.
90. Shaw Ms No. 3, John Shaw to Elizabeth Wilkinson 15 May 1811; Wilkinson Ms No. 3, Elizabeth Wilkinson to John Shaw, 28 May 1811.
91. John seemed very comfortable with these decisions: 'this I leave entirely to yourself, please yourself and you will please me.' Shaw Ms No. 11, John Shaw to Elizabeth Wilkinson, 3 April 1813.
92. Wilkinson Ms No. 23, Elizabeth Wilkinson to John Shaw, 14 August 1812. In this letter Elizabeth gives a rich and vivid sketch of the wedding of her brother Thomas and the rebellious Miss Chafer; its timings, the company's dress and food eaten. Thomas and his bride, though Methodist, were married in Church, as they had to be by law at that time; the service itself though lasted a full five minutes. The material aspects of this wedding, particularly what was worn and what was eaten, will be discussed further in Chapter 6.
93. Ibid.
94. Wilkinson Ms No. 16, Elizabeth Wilkinson to John Shaw, 25 March 1812.
95. Wilkinson Ms No. 20, Elizabeth Wilkinson to John Shaw, 5 June 1812.
96. Stone, *The Family, Sex and Marriage*, p. 325.
97. Vickery, *The Gentleman's Daughter*, p. 285.
98. Wilkinson Ms No. 23, Elizabeth Wilkinson to John Shaw, 14 August 1812. On 25 December 1812 John, who was clearly being quizzed by all who knew about the engagement, wrote, 'Methinks our union ought to be attended with every possible happiness to compensate for the length of time we have been waiting for it.' Shaw Ms No. 10, John Shaw to Elizabeth Wilkinson, 25 December 1812.
99. Shaw Ms No. 40a, John Shaw to Elizabeth Shaw, 6 June 1813.
100. Shaw Ms No. 12, John Shaw to Elizabeth Shaw, 9 April 1816. Elizabeth replied: 'Accept of a thousand thanks for the kind and affectionate token of remembrance which I rec'd last night. I do not know whether pain or pleasure preponderated whilst I perused it; pain for having inadvertently caused you so much sorrow and pleasure to find you still the same fond and affectionate husband. I do most sincerely and freely forgive you my

love and if you were here I would seal it with a strong embrace.' Shaw Ms No.50, Elizabeth Shaw to John Shaw, 1816,

101. Shaw Ms No. 35, John Shaw to Elizabeth Shaw, 22 April 1832.
102. Wilkinson Ms No. 8, Elizabeth Wilkinson to John Shaw, 15 October 1811.
103. Wilkinson Ms No. 19, Elizabeth Wilkinson to John Shaw, 14 May 1812.
104. Tosh, 'From Keighley to St-Denis'; Rothman, 'Sex and Self Control'.
105. A. Finer, and G. Savage (eds), *The Selected Letters of Josiah Wedgwood* (London: Cory, Adams and Mackay, 1965), p. 26.
106. For example in only John's third extant letter he asks Elizabeth 'Will you ... take another ride with me to Colne.' Shaw Ms No. 3, John Shaw to Elizabeth Wilkinson, 15 May 1811.
107. Wilkinson Ms No. 28, Elizabeth Wilkinson to John Shaw, 25 November 1812.
108. Nelson, '"The Forgetfulness of Sex"'.
109. Shaw Ms No. 40a, Elizabeth Shaw to John Shaw, 6 June 1813
110. Shaw Ms No. 48b. Elizabeth Shaw to John Shaw, 16 April 1816. Flirtatiously, in one letter, John looked forward to coming home and 'the hearty welcome I know I shall receive – and so you will give me an extra kiss will you – what then am I to conclude – that you have made up your mind to give me only a limited number – I really cannot think so its quite a new plan if you do so. I dare lay a wager you don't tell to Dozens how many I shall have.' Shaw Ms No. 39, John Shaw to Elizabeth Shaw, nd. It seems quite possible that this undated letter was written in response to Elizabeth's quoted in the main text, suggesting a playful mutual enjoyment of each other.
111. Shaw Ms No. 47, Elizabeth Shaw to John Shaw, 11 March 1816.
112. Shaw Ms No. 25, John Shaw to Elizabeth Shaw, 4 August 1825.
113. It is perhaps dangerous to speculate too widely on a few scattered references, but Elizabeth and John do not appear to support either Stone's claims that many who were 'dissenting or Methodist in religion ... were very prudish in their sexual behaviour,' or that whilst the professional and bourgeoisie were 'probably the first to adopt the ideal of married love, [they were] the last to build frank sexual passion into the marital relationship.' Stone, *The Family, Sex and Marriage*, pp. 393 and 658.
114. Shaw Ms No. 10, John Shaw to Elizabeth Wilkinson, 25 December 1812.
115. Shaw Ms No. 4, John Shaw to Elizabeth Wilkinson, 5 July 1811. It has not proved possible to trace the source of the verse.
116. For a strongly functionalist interpretation of the links between family, social capital and business see D. Sunderland, Social Capital, Trust and the Industrial Revolution, 1780-1880 (London: Routledge, 2007).
117. Wilkinson Ms No. 28, Elizabeth Wilkinson to John Shaw, 25 November 1812.
118. Shaw Ms No. 7, John Shaw to Elizabeth Wilkinson, 20 December 1811.

4 'Our Present Adventure' India and Beyond

1. Shaw Ms. No. 27, John Shaw to Elizabeth Shaw, 10 July 1826.
2. Shaw Ms. No. 72, Elizabeth Shaw to John Shaw, 8 July 1829.
3. J. Hoppit, *Risk and Failure in English Business, 1700–1800* (Cambridge: Cambridge University Press, 1987).
4. And given average life expectancy at that time John and Elizabeth were by no means 'young' any more.

5. The new Calcutta business was so named after its first manager, T. E. Thomson, who had worked for Shaw and Crane as a commercial traveller for a number of years, DB–24/A/34, Agreement for 5 Years Service between Mr T. E. Thomson and Messrs Shaw and Crane. This agreement stipulated that Thompson 'conduct himself as a faithful and honest servant,' a stipulation he obviously fulfilled. The new business was undoubtedly owned by Shaw and Crane however. It seems likely Thomson may have had some share in the new business but no evidence confirming this has as yet been found.

6. See, Popp and Holt, 'The Presence of Opportunity'.

7. WALS, DB/24/A/52. Joseph Rogers and Sons to Shaw and Crane, 23 August 1827.

8. Ibid.

9. Ibid.

10. WALS, DB/24/A/53.

11. Ibid.

12. Ibid.

13. Ibid.

14. S. Haggerty, *The British-Atlantic Trading Community, 1760–1810: Men, Women, and the Distribution of Goods* (Leiden: Brill, 2006), p. 109.

15. WALS, DB/24/A/54.

16. WALS, DB/24/A/56. It was not only Rawson and Holdsworth on whom Shaw and Crane were dependent; a whole host of other service providers were necessary to make this trade a reality, such as the Liverpool shipping agents Leech and Harrison.

17. See for example, DB–24/A/82: Letter from Anderson, Wise and Co. to Shaw and Crane, August 1832, which lays out sales made so far on Shaw and Crane's account and is solicitous of further trade.

18. See, for example, DB–24/A/83, Letter from Robert Wise and Company, Batavia to Shaw and Crane, July 1833, complaining of and perhaps excusing the flatness of trade (and thus of sales of Shaw and Crane's goods) 'owing to the detention of the Netherlands vessels'. The vagaries to which such long distance trade was subject is most apparent.

19. WALS, DB/24/A/98.

20. WALS, DB/24/A/97. The letter goes on to warn however that 'the sailings of the vessels for India are ... so uncertain'.

21. See DB–24/A/35, Memorandum of Agreement between Shaw and Crane and Joseph Anderson for five years service as an assistant at Calcutta, 1834.

22. WALS, DB/24/A/35.

23. WALS, DB/24/A/103. This letter from Thomson to Shaw and Crane is full of details: of goods, such as weighing machines and glass, though for the latter 'the excise at Birmingham have not forwarded the certificate so cannot ship it'; insurance, the shipment was to have a total coverage of £3,000; the ship, its captain; other passengers for the voyage; and other final arrangements. A series of letters and documents – including certificates of shipping and insurance and bills of lading – from or forwarded by Rawson and Co. in Liverpool, WALS, DB/24/A/105 and DB/24/A/108, provide further interesting details. Two shipments were made on behalf of Shaw and Crane in late November 1834, eleven casks and three cases on the Gunga (?), Joseph Mackinney master, and one hundred and five casks of nails, thirty cases, thirteen casks and one hogshead of hardware, eleven casks and five crates of earthenware, and one weighing machines on the Anne Baldwin, master Henry Crawford. Rawson and Co. also enclosed their account, comprised of expenses for arranging freight, carting and porterage, passage, excise, and insurance premiums, amounting to a total of £324, 5s., 3d., less £67, 1s., 6. for insurance

at six months credit, leaving £256, 7s., 9d. to be remitted 'at any time at your convenience'. Shaw and Crane were clearly still heavily depended on the services of a series of specialist located in Liverpool.

24. S. Chapman, *Merchant Enterprise: From the Industrial Revolution to World War I* (Cambridge: Cambridge University Press, 2004); G. Jones, *Merchants to Multinationals: British Trading Companies in the Nineteenth and Twentieth Centuries* (Oxford: Oxford University Press, 2000); C. M. Connell, 'Entrepreneurial Enterprise and "Image" in the Nineteenth Century Trading Firm: Shaping the Legal Environment for Business', *Business History*, 48:2 (2006); pp. 193–219.

25. Chapman, *Merchant Enterprise*, p. 108.

26. Jones, *Merchants to Multinationals*, p.21.

27. Ibid., p.29.

28. T. Webster, 'An Early Global Business in a Colonial Context: The Strategies, Management, and Failure of John Palmer and Company of Calcutta, 1780–1830', *Enterprise & Society: The International Journal of Business History*, 6:1 (2005), p. 102 and 109.

29. Connell, 'Entrepreneurial Enterprise and "Image"', p. 204.

30. Chapman, *Merchant Enterprise*, p. 112.

31. WALS, DB/24/B/450. For students of the industrial district concept, there is interest in the way this business decision came about through a face-to-face meeting in the heart of manufacturing centre, illustrating the importance of proximity to relationships.

32. Ibid. The letter noted that Crane had advised that Chubb correspond directly with Thomson and that very shortly £200–300 of locks would be sent out. Chubb also made considerable play of their existing connections with the Governor General and the government in Calcutta.

33. WALS DB–24/B/531: List of Goods for Sale, 1841.

34. DB–24/B/.

35. Vickery, *Behind Closed Doors*.

36. WALS, DB/24/B/450.

37. Ibid. The complaints about slow payment continued; 'no profit can cover three years credit and when the bill of Shaw and Crane falls dues which you last remitted three years will have transpired. You are supplied with goods upon the same terms as the respectable furnishing Ironmongers are who [pay] first journey, we only allow 10% if second journey is taken ... I shall be happy to do all in my power to serve you [circumstances] impel me to say I cannot afford to give you the credit you have taken'.

38. Ibid. A similar promise to reserve particular goods for exclusive supply to Thomson and Co. was made in a letter dated April 1841 despite an offer from a 'London merchant which he wanted for Calcutta [which] I could have had for cash subject to the same discount'.

39. Ibid.

40. Shaw Ms No. 26, John Shaw to Elizabeth Shaw, 20 September 1835.

41. In a letter dated 1831 held at Rochdale Library John tells Elizabeth that the previous night be had (unsuccessfully) bid £1,450 for a house at auction. He concluded 'so it is not likely we shall have a place in the Country soon'. The aspirations are clear.

42. M. Finn, 'Anglo-Indian Lives in the Later Eighteenth and Early Nineteenth-Centuries', *Journal of Eighteenth Century Studies*, 33:1 (2010), p. 49.

43. Ibid. She continues: 'the family was at once both a place of political power, a prime site of capital accumulation, a focal point of identity formation and a key locus of emotional development and expansion'. Ibid., p. 49–50.

44. Ibid., p. 55.
45. Ibid.
46. Moreover, the archives contain no definite evidence of pregnancies lost through either miscarriage or stillbirth. This is all the more remarkable given that all of Elizabeth's pregnancies seem to have been attended by considerable difficulties. Indeed, in April 1816 Elizabeth wrote to John to tell him of a violent illness she had endured but that happily 'I have once more a chance of bringing you a son – but Mr F[ouke, the Shaw's doctor] seems to think it a very small one'. Shaw Ms 48b, Elizabeth Shaw to John Shaw, 15 April 1816. It is not clear whether or not this mysterious illness related to a pregnancy not successfully brought to term.
47. 'Mrs Crane is not yet confined'. Shaw Ms No. 51, Elizabeth Shaw to John Shaw, 1822?
48. Shaw Ms No. 75, Elizabeth Shaw to John Shaw, 12 August 1834.
49. Scattered references suggest John was working in the office/warehouse by 1829, at which date he would have been fourteen. See for example, 'John has written all your order heads and we have got some more that he does like so well from Mr C[rane]'. Shaw Ms No. 72, Elizabeth Shaw to John Shaw, 8 July 1829.
50. It is evident at several points that Shaw had not shared with Crane the contents of his own letter to Thomson.
51. Neither of which, we may infer, contained any hint as to the impending disaster. These various letters place John's illness and death as occurring very suddenly in the first ten days of November 1839.
52. WALS DB/24/B/450; Assorted Correspondence, 1839–46.
53. Ibid.
54. Ibid. These final words are the clearest indication we have that Thomson had some form of ownership stake in the Calcutta business.
55. Ibid. Thomson was destined also to die on service in India.
56. WALS DB/24/A/.
57. The belief that English parents had not long and bitterly grieved the loss of children has been most effectively debunked by Keith Thomas. See *The Ends of Life*. John and Elizabeth's experience of and attitude towards parenting will be explored further in Chapter 5 of this book.
58. WALS DB/24/A/.
59. See A. Popp, 'From Wolverhampton to Calcutta: The Low Origins of Merchant Capital', in R. Lee (ed.), *Commerce and Culture: Nineteenth-Century Business Elites* (Aldershot: Ashgate, 2011), pp. 37–61.

5 'To Work Hard for a Larger Family': Managing Work and Family.

1. Shaw Ms No. 40a, Elizabeth Shaw to John Shaw, 6 June 1813.
2. Shaw Ms No. 17, John Shaw to Elizabeth Shaw, 10 May 1821.
3. Wilkinson Ms No. 21, Elizabeth Wilkinson to John Shaw, 18 July 1812. Michael French presents substantial corroborating evidence of the burden of separation endured by women married to travellers. Michael French, 'On the Road: Travelling Salesmen and Experiences of Mobility in Britain before 1939', *Journal of Transport History*, 31:2 (2010), pp. 133–50.
4. Wilkinson Ms No. 8, Elizabeth Wilkinson to John Shaw, 15 October 1811. Nor was this match what she had necessarily looked for: 'Who would have thought two years ago that any thing like it would have taken place – you never thought of coming to Rochdale for

a wide – and I should as soon have thought of any thing as a traveller falling to my lot'. Wilkinson Ms No. 20, Elizabeth Wilkinson to John Shaw, 5 June 1812.

5. A. Vickery, '"Golden Age or Separate Spheres?" A Review of the Categories and Chronology of English Women's History', *Historical Journal*, 36:2 (1993), pp. 38–414.

6. Ibid., p. 384.

7. Ibid., p. 405.

8. Ibid. As Vickery notes, many of these complaints were age-old, pushing the supposed 'Golden Age' of female liberation every further back in time. Defoe, for example, had complained that the women of his age 'act as if they were ashamed of being tradesmen's wives, and never intended to be tradesmen's widows'. Quoted in Vickery, '"Golden Age or Separate Spheres,"' p. 407.

9. J. Tosh, *A Man's Place: Masculinity and the Middle-Class Home in Victorian England* (New Haven, CT: Yale University Press, 1999).

10. E. Gordon and G. Nair, 'Domestic Fathers and the Victorian Parental Role', *Women's History Review* Vol. 15 No. 4 (2006), p. 544.

11. Ibid., p. 554.

12. Ibid., p. 557.

13. E. Gordon and G. Nair, 'The Myth of the Victorian Patriarchal Family', *History of the Family* Vol. 7 (2002), p. 125.

14. Vickery, '"Golden Age or Separate Spheres,"' p. 385. As Vickery goes on to note 'The endless permutations in matrimonial power relations that can result from accidents of circumstance and character have led some scholars to argue for the unpredictable variety of private experience, in any age, whatever the dominant ideology'. Ibid., p. 390.

15. Ibid., p. 412. Emphasis added.

16. E. Gordon and G. Nair, 'Domestic Fathers', p. 552.

17. As Gordon and Nair note 'Until relatively recently fatherhood has not been seen as central to the Victorian middle-class male identity. Its importance was either overlooked or conceptions of fatherhood equated simply with the role of breadwinner', 'Domestic Fathers', p. 554. As we shall see John held to and acted out a conception of fatherhood that was both far wider and deeper than that of the disciplinarian provider.

18. Shaw Ms No. 21, John Shaw to Elizabeth Shaw, 25 December 1823.

19. Wilkinson Ms No. 16, Elizabeth Wilkinson to John Shaw, 25 March 1812.

20. Ibid.

21. Later in the letter just quoted Elizabeth again plays to these stereotypes, suggesting that being forbidden to discuss gossip would be 'as great a task as can be imposed upon a woman'. Ibid.

22. Wilkinson Ms No. 21, Elizabeth Wilkinson to John Shaw, 18 July 1812.

23. Wilkinson Ms No. 19, Elizabeth Wilkinson to John Shaw, 14 May 1812.

24. Shaw Ms No. 13, John Shaw to Elizabeth Shaw, 4 December 1816. Towards the close of the letter he add, 'Please tell Mr Crane I hope to write him tomorrow and send him all the money I possibly can wh^{ch} goodness know will not be much'. Ibid.

25. The stresses of life as a commercial traveller are brought home most vividly in a letter John wrote in 1829, which is very probably alluding to cases of suicide amongst the ranks of the occupation: 'What a shocking thing for poor Firth. I am afraid his circumstances are getting bad [that] was the cause. A traveller from London did the same thing at Manchester the other day. He also was travelling in the tea trade'. If suicide this truly shocking at a time of very strong legal, religious, and societal sanctions against suicide. Shaw Ms No. 31, John Shaw to Elizabeth Shaw, 30 January 1829.

26. 'I do feel so anxious and wishful to see you. I cannot describe and much inclined to think I shall decline the next journey. I shall propose to Mr C[rane] his keeping that journey and I will keep his'. Ibid.
27. Ibid.
28. Shaw Ms No. 14, John Shaw to Elizabeth Shaw, 3 July 1817.
29. Ibid.
30. It was not only money that had to be kept working but employees too, to whom John felt a responsibility. Still underemployed workers might be put to good use around the home, further blurring the line between public and private spheres: 'I should think William could have little or nothing to do at the W'house so that you may have him put the garden quite in'. Shaw Ms No.13, John Shaw to Elizabeth Shaw, 4 December 1816.
31. And in addition he found himself 'so underhanded at the warehouse ... and these meetings of one kind or another and this banking concern together with diverse customers – I am almost run off my feet'. Shaw Ms No. 34, John Shaw to Elizabeth Shaw, 19 October 1831.
32. Shaw Ms No. 16, John Shaw to Elizabeth Shaw, 28 November 1817.
33. Shaw Ms No. 28, John Shaw to Elizabeth Shaw, 6 January 1828. The woes continued, in July of the same year trade was still 'exceeding flat and bad which makes folks twice as tedious to do with ... I am well in health but sadly out of sorts and spirits as to business which I find getting good for nothing and wonderfully different to what it should and what it used to be'. Shaw Ms No. 30, John Shaw to Elizabeth Shaw, 20 July 1828.
34. Shaw Ms No. 16, John Shaw to Elizabeth Shaw, 28 November 1817.
35. This sentence began thus: 'It makes me heave some long and heavy sighs when I think of the length of time that must elapse ere I shall see you'. Shaw Ms No. 18, John Shaw to Elizabeth Shaw, 17 December 1821.
36. Ibid.
37. Shaw Ms No. 14, John Shaw to Elizabeth Shaw, 3 July 1817. This letter concludes with the simple but heartfelt 'Adieu my dear love and in hopes of soon having the pleasure of holding you in my arms'.
38. Shaw Ms No. 12, John Shaw to Elizabeth Shaw, 9 April 1816.
39. In a letter home written in 1821 John records that their eldest son John had 'told me he would write me a letter and would say in it please papa to come home again'. Shaw Ms No. 18, John Shaw to Elizabeth Shaw, 17 December 1821.
40. Shaw Ms No. 33, John Shaw to Elizabeth Shaw, 14 March 1831. John's last few extant letters show no diminution of his sentiments towards or attachment to Elizabeth: 'You can't conceive how much you have been upon my thoughts since I left home ... I got here [Cheadle, Staffs] last night all alone and thought myself very low spirited'. In concluding he looked forward to the 'unspeakable joy and satisfaction of again clasping you to my fond and anxious bosom'. Shaw Ms No. 38, John Shaw to Elizabeth Shaw, nd. but almost certainly 1838 or 1839.
41. Shaw Ms No. 79, Elizabeth Shaw to Thomas Wilkinson, 23 July 1832.
42. Shaw Ms No. 15, John Shaw to Elizabeth Shaw, 13 August 1818. A little further down the page he bursts out again with 'I don't know how we shall manage without you'.
43. Shaw and Wilkinson Ms No. 17, John Shaw to Elizabeth Shaw, 10 May 1821.
44. John was frequently critical of Elizabeth's brother Thomas in this period, particularly over his approach to marriage, which he felt to be both too fickle and too much motivated by money rather than love.
45. Shaw and Wilkinson Ms No. 17, John Shaw to Elizabeth Shaw, 10 May 1821.

46. John and Elizabeth were evidently successful in their attempts to persuade her mother to leave business for on Christmas day 1823 John wrote that 'I would advise you recommending your Mother not to go into business again at Colne … I think your Mother much to blame even again to attempt it for so soon as she again enters into it so much will she repent it – she even knows what she has coming and she also must know what she expends – but on the other hand she will never know it besides being plagued'. Mrs Wilkinson was clearly a driven and somewhat restless woman. Shaw Ms No. 21, John Shaw to Elizabeth Shaw, 25 December 1823.

47. Wilkinson Ms No. 19, Elizabeth Wilkinson to John Shaw, 14 May 1812.

48. John and Elizabeth's attempts to persuade her parents out of business evidently fell on deaf ears. In 1832 Elizabeth noted to her father, who by then had been widowed a year, 'I am aware your time is much occupied in the shop but you should allow yourself some leisure'. Shaw Ms No. 79, Elizabeth Shaw to Thomas Wilkinson, 23 July 1832.

49. For example, in early 1822, John expressed the following concerns: 'what do you think of your Mother's plan … I hardly think she will be able to manage with your father at home and do think you had better endeavour to persuade her from it – my idea is that he will not get any better at home but most likely worse'. Shaw and Wilkinson Ms No. 19, John Shaw to Elizabeth Shaw, 8 February 1822.

50. Prior to their marriage John's sister seems to have shown some jealousy of Elizabeth, whom she had not yet met, and this was naturally a source of some tension. Happily it was a tension that did not persist. See Wilkinson Ms No. 18, Elizabeth Wilkinson to John Shaw, n.d. but undoubtedly spring 1812.

51. Ms No. 18, Elizabeth Wilkinson to John Shaw, n.d.

52. Ms No. 17, Elizabeth Wilkinson to John Shaw, 10 April 1812.

53. See for example, Ms No. 16, Elizabeth Wilkinson to John Shaw, 25 March 1812.

54. Wilkinson Ms No. 22, Elizabeth Wilkinson to John Shaw, 25 July 1812.

55. For female enterprise in the nineteenth century see H. Barker, *The Business of Women: Female Entreprise and Urban Development in Northern England, 1760–1830* (Oxford: Oxford University Press, 2006) and A. C. Kay, *The Foundations of Female Entrepreneurship: Enterprise, Home and Household in London, c. 1800–1870* (Abingdon: Routledge, 2009).

56. See for example one parcel that 'went to the W'house and they opened it but finding what the contents were thought it likelier for the house'. Shaw Ms No. 43a, Elizabeth Shaw to John Shaw, 31 March 1815.

57. 'There have been no letters of consequence since I last wrote – nothing but invoices and a few small orders – Tomlinson sent a scolding letter about his goods and said he had in mistake paid you 1£ too much'. Shaw Ms No. 44a, Elizabeth Shaw to John Shaw, Wednesday Morn, n.d. but certainly 1815.

58. Shaw Ms No. 44a, Elizabeth Shaw to John Shaw, Wednesday Morn, n.d. but certainly 1815.

59. See for example, Shaw Ms No. 40a, Elizabeth Shaw to John Shaw, 6 June 1813: 'the 4th June has brought no rich intelligence to make up for flatness of trade. We had an account of two banks the last we know nothing of'.

60. 'He [Crane will] tell you what confusion the shutting up of Gibbons bank occasion'd. Nobody seems to have suspected it but it appears to have been quite a premeditated thing … It has occasion'd a terrible run upon Horderns and Co. … I hope that confidence will be restor'd by tomorrow'. Shaw Ms No. 47, Elizabeth Shaw to John Shaw, 11 March 1816. By April 1 Elizabeth was relaying advice from the warehouse to 'take but

few orders – for it was out of Horderns hands to assist any of his friends ... things are so precarious that the less business that is done ... the safer'. Shaw Ms No. 49, Elizabeth Shaw to John Shaw, 1 April 1816.

61. Shaw Ms No. 43a, Elizabeth Shaw to John Shaw, 31 March 1815.
62. Shaw Ms No. 43a, Elizabeth Shaw to John Shaw, 31 March 1815.
63. Shaw Ms No. 43a, Elizabeth Shaw to John Shaw, 31 March 1815. She does, however, continue that 'of course [he] takes them back with him – therefore I am unable to give you any just account of them'.
64. Shaw Ms No. 43a, Elizabeth Shaw to John Shaw, 31 March 1815.
65. Shaw Ms No. 44a, Elizabeth Shaw to John Shaw, n.d. Again in the next letter she relays that 'I think they are going on well at [the] Warehouse – they keep Mr Latham constantly employ'd at the desk – Mr Crane is here, there and everywhere'. Shaw Ms No. 45a, Elizabeth Shaw to John Shaw, Tuesday night, 15 April [815].
66. Shaw Ms No. 42, Elizabeth Shaw to John Shaw, 21 March 1815.
67. Shaw Ms No. 21, John Shaw to Elizabeth Shaw, 25 December 1823.
68. Shaw Ms No. 25, John Shaw to Elizabeth Shaw, 4 August 1825.
69. Over time Elizabeth seems to have become for the most part a conduit between John and his partner when and as circumstances demanded: 'I sent to ask if C[rane] had anything to ask – he says he is writing [to you at] Bury – I must direct there too I suppose'. Shaw Ms No. 69, Elizabeth Shaw to John Shaw, 9 January 1828.
70. Thus, in one letter she told John that 'I have called upon your customers here [Colne]'. Shaw Ms No. 54, Elizabeth Shaw to John Shaw, 25 May 1822.
71. 'Crane comes up almost every day about one thing or another, he seems of a very cheerful disposition'. Shaw Ms No. 44a, Elizabeth Shaw to John Wilkinson, Wednesday Morn, n.d but certainly 1815. 'I think he [Crane] seems quite tired of playing and wants to be at work again – I told him pretty nearly what you said – but he seems to have made up his mind to come to you'. Shaw Ms No. 41, Elizabeth Shaw to John Shaw, n.d.
72. Hamilton, '"Whose Story is it Anyway?"', p. 254.
73. Ibid., p. 255.
74. Ibid., p. 263.
75. In these attitudes to parenthood John exemplified many of the characteristics of the 'good father' then current in society, as explored by Joanne Bailey, '"A Very Sensible Man": Imagining Fatherhood in England c. 1750-1830', *History*, 95:3 (2010), pp. 267-92.
76. Shaw Ms No. 6, John Shaw to Elizabeth Wilkinson, 21 November 1811.
77. Shaw Ms No. 11, John Shaw to Elizabeth Wilkinson, 3 April 1813.
78. Shaw Ms No. 10, John Shaw to Elizabeth Wilkinson, 25 December 1812.
79. Ibid.
80. Shaw Ms No. 17, John Shaw to Elizabeth Shaw, 10 May 1821. In another letter from Wolverhampton written almost exactly one year later John looks forward to Elizabeth's return from Lancashire but quickly goes on to add 'but not that I wish you to hurry for two or three days as I find we can get on very well without you – otherwise should we wish to see you'. Again, as so often, he concluded with a message from the children: 'This morning John has given me about Thirty Kisses in lieu to send you'. Shaw Ms No. 20, John Shaw to Elizabeth Shaw, 12 May 1822.
81. Shaw Ms No. 17, John Shaw to Elizabeth Shaw, 10 May 1821
82. See for example, Shaw Ms No. 20, John Shaw to Elizabeth Shaw, 12 May 1822.
83. Shaw Ms No. 26, John Shaw to Elizabeth Shaw, 20 September 1835.

84. Shaw Ms No. 33, John Shaw to Elizabeth Shaw, 14 March 1831. He continued to relate how Mary, their youngest, was 'quite well and looks well – she is quite alive and laughing and taking notice of everything. She is doing very well in her short clothes and very desirous of finding her feet'.

85. Shaw Ms No. 34, John Shaw and Elizabeth Shaw, 19 October 1831.

86. Shaw Ms No. 35, John Shaw to Elizabeth Shaw, 22 April 1832. He continued with another very sweet and fetching description of how 'She can now prattle away when she in the harness and walks very steadily after you all round the room. She has now left off her cap and she such a little white flaxen head of hair – it's as soft as silk'.

87. A modernity we see reflected not only in their attitudes towards one another, or to the supposed public-private separation, or to marriage or parenthood, but also time and again in the little details, such as in their advanced attitudes towards both breastfeeding and childhood vaccination.

6 'The Whole Circle of Our Acquaintance': Networks and Sociability

1. Wilkinson Ms No. 16, Elizabeth Wilkinson to John Shaw, 25 March 1812.

2. 'I did not tell you in my letter that Mr Shaw was gone to Holland and as he had not been accustomed to go over the sea and I knew it was extremely tempestuous during his voyage out I was a good deal concern'd and agitated which brought on, as I suppos'd symptoms of a miscarriage'. Shaw Ms No. 83, Elizabeth Shaw to Elizabeth Wilkinson (mother), 19 September 1828. It is not clear that this was a miscarriage; Elizabeth concluded that it might have been 'the turn of years', e.g. the menopause.

3. Certainly Elizabeth's parents shared this habit; in August 1812 her mother was 'at Blackpool on account of her health'. Regretfully though 'she was but ill accommodated with lodgings. B. is uncommonly full'. Displaying her slightly parsimonious side, Elizabeth found herself wondering 'how people find the money to go'. Wilkinson Ms No. 24, Elizabeth Wilkinson to John Shaw, 31 August 1812.

4. S. Caunce, 'Banks, Communities and Manufacturing in West Yorkshire Textiles, c. 1800-1830', in Wilson and Popp (eds), *Industrial Clusters and Regional Business Networks*, pp. 112-29; G. Cookson, 'Quaker Networks and the Industrial Development of Darlington, 1780-1870', in *Industrial Clusters and Regional Business Networks*, pp. 155-73; R. Coopey, 'The British Glove Industry, 1750-1970: The Advantages and Vulnerability of a Regional Industry', in *Industrial Clusters and Regional Business Networks*, pp. 174-91.

5. Shaw Ms No. 40a, Elizabeth Shaw to John Shaw, 6 June 1813.

6. Wilkinson Ms No. 26, Elizabeth Wilkinson to John Shaw, 19 October 1812.

7. Ibid.

8. Ibid.

9. Ibid.

10. Wilkinson Ms No. 27, Elizabeth Wilkinson to John Shaw, 3 November 1812.

11. For his part John greeted this news with sanguinity; 'I am glad to hear the partnership of your Brother and Spencer is so soon disolved [*sic*] ... of this [advantage] I could see none here'. Shaw Ms No. 9, John Shaw to Elizabeth Wilkinson, 12 November 1812. In the same letter he nonetheless conceded that 'It gives me pleasure to hear you Brother Thos' business is going on so well'.

12. Ibid. The Wilkinson family had little luck with partnerships in this period. In May 1812 Elizabeth related how her brother Richard had not taken a partner in London 'with an intention of staying himself [there] – He intended coming to Colne and leaving his partner in L. so that they wish'd to make sure of business [the nature of which is not made clear] by having 2 strings to their bow – However, their designs at present are frustrated Mr Greenwood (the partner) was seiz'd with a fever and all hope of his life despair'd of – but, his constitution got the better of the disorder and he is again recovering slowly – his native air is recommended when he is able to travel – so my bro'will be obliged to stay some time longer'. Wilkinson Ms No. 19, Elizabeth Wilkinson to John Shaw, 14 May 1812.

13. Wilkinson Ms No. 27, Elizabeth Wilkinson to John Shaw, 3 November 1812.

14. Ibid.

15. 'I told you my father had got together the money he had promis'd ready whenever it should be call'd for – that as it was not wanted immediately. It came in to be very useful and saved my father a great deal of anxiety of mind. It seem'd prepared for the purpose. My father has a Bro'a bachelor who came to live in Colne about that time and he wish'd to put out £200, he was glad to lend it to my father , which made 500. John was to have four and the other in goods. The other two Third is to come (if it is not come already) from some of Mrs W's friends at least my father expects it soon which will enable him to be according to his word. My Uncle John will let his money rest in Bro' John's hands'. Ibid. Elizabeth, though a relatively young unmarried daughter is clearly privy to a great deal of potentially very personal information about family finances.

16. Ibid. In the middle of this passage, where we have placed the ellipse, she adds, 'If my eldest Bro'had behaved as he ought to have done, you would have had no cause for complaint, but there is no mending a thing that is over and past'. Clearly her brother Richard had caused the family some financial loss, the nature of which is now obscure, though he was at this time relatively recently returned to Lancashire from London, where he had been trying to establish a career in banking. John too knew the effect of financial embarrassment on a family. Not long after he had first left home his mother had written to 'therefore [strictly] charge you should you be ask'd questions by anny one not acknowledge his [brother William's] lose [sic, for loss]'. Wilkinson and Shaw Ms No. 32, Elizabeth Shaw to John Shaw, n.d. but *c*. 1800.

17. Ibid.

18. Shaw Ms No. 9, John Shaw to Elizabeth Wilkinson, 12 November 1812.

19. Ibid.

20. This dispute over Wilkinson money was not confined to John as an outsider. In 1823 Elizabeth's mother was moved to reflect that 'a mercenary mind can never be satisfied and may I be delivered from such a spirit. Sometimes Sarah is very good and at other times very cross – the £400 I let Wm Shaw have I have a joint Bond – W^m and Rich and your uncle John Shaw. I have £415 per cent. I thought it would be safe – in your Father's will he order'd £400 to be plac'd out to interest for John during his natural life and to set the principal among the ch[ildren] at his death – there is £400 more for Rich upon the same principle only with the exception of his chil^n have the principal at his demise'. This last was significant as Richard had just died. Shaw Ms No. 87, Elizabeth Wilkinson (mother) to Elizabeth Shaw, 28 March 1828.

21. Ibid.

22. Wilkinson Ms No. 28, Elizabeth Wilkinson to John, 25 November 1812. Elizabeth does recur to the subject in her next extant letter, dated 1 January 1813, but only to relay her

mother's explanation of the course of events and circumstances, and that in a tone that suggests the dispute, if it can be called that, is now resolved: 'she says "Your father has given no more to John and Tho'than he purpos'd to give to Mr S[haw] with you. Tis' true, they have money upon interest you know. It was not your father's mind that John should have engaged in so large a concern but what could he do when Spencer declin'd partnership? The shop was taken and it must be furnish'd – so it was unavoidable what he did for John (You yourself wish'd him to begin his business). I have not the least doubt but your father will make you equal with other children and do anything he is able for you but you know what an aversion he has to borrow money upon interest – or to be engaged for more than he can pay when demanded." She goes on to say she is sorry your feelings should have been so much hurt and that I may tell you with safety that my father has nothing against doing anything he can to make me comfortable'. Wilkinson Ms No. 29, Elizabeth Wilkinson to John, 1 January 1813.

23. At times Elizabeth directly facilitated this trade. In one letter she reported 'My bro' got your Invoice yesterday – he wishes you to send 1 Gross Brass Per Buttons 2 3/8 In long with Cast Iron 2 ½ Hinges ordered and by land carriage as soon as possible. If I have made a mistake in this attribute it to my ignorance of the trade'. Wilkinson Ms No. 13a, Elizabeth Wilkinson to John Shaw, nd.

24. Popp, 'From Town to Town'.

25. Wilkinson Ms No. 16, Elizabeth Wilkinson to John Shaw, 25 March 2012.

26. WALS, DB/24/A/167, Kendal Journey, August 1814; WALS, DB/24/A/168, Liverpool Journey, November 1814

27. A number of references suggest that Thomas had an amiable but somewhat inconsistent or biddable character. John certainly did not always approve of his behaviour in relation to women and courtship.

28. 'I understand Thomas met with trouble in paying the creditors – I hope he will not mind that the pleasure attendant upon doing what is right will overbalance that upon reflection and that we shall be as losers by it in the end'. Shaw Ms No. 82, Elizabeth Shaw to Elizabeth Wilkinson (mother), 14 June 1828.

29. Shaw Ms No. 80, Thomas Wilkinson (father) to Elizabeth Shaw, 15 December 1815.

30. Shaw Ms No. 9, John Shaw to Elizabeth Wilkinson, 12 November 1812.

31. After her marriage some of the familial roles Elizabeth performed passed to her younger sister Sarah. In December 1815 Elizabeth's father told her how 'Your Mo[ther] and I work as we used to do and more, what shall we do if we loose Sarah [who wished to visit Wolverhampton] except we can get a good Serv' ... your moth' tired of shopkeeping completely'. Shaw Ms No. 80, Thomas Wilkinson (father) to Elizabeth Shaw, 15 December 1815.

32. Shaw Ms No. 40a, Elizabeth Shaw to John Shaw, 6 June 1813.

33. Ibid.

34. This cannot have been easy. John's sister expressed some quite strong jealousy towards Elizabeth before they had even married and John himself admitted very early in their correspondence that he came from a particularly small and tight-knit family: 'Herself [mother], [sister] Mary [and] my Bother and servant compose the whole of the family and they ... feel so happy in the enjoyment of each other's company that when one is absent the others are quite lost'. Shaw Ms No. 6, John Shaw to Elizabeth Wilkinson, 21 November 1811.

35. For example in an undated letter from the winter of 1811–12 Elizabeth reports how 'We have had my bro' Wm here nearly a week ... Also a young lady (Cousin Shaw) from

Burnley has been here better than fortnight at my Aunts and she talks of prolonging her visit at least two weeks longer. She is a very sensible well inform'd woman about thirty ... She often comes here and yesterday my Aunt had two Nephews came who are to spend a week of ten days (I suppose) and my Aunt having but one spare bed I have got my cousin for a bed-fellow'. Wilkinson Ms No. 13a, Elizabeth Wilkinson to John Shaw, nd.

36. Wilkinson Ms No. 15, Elizabeth Wilkinson to John Shaw, 6 March 1812.

37. Ibid.

38. Wilkinson Ms No. 11, Elizabeth Wilkinson to John Shaw, November 1811.

39. The Mander family business, founded in 1773, became one of the county's largest manufacturers of paints, varnishes and other coatings during the course of the nineteenth-century, conducting a truly international trade. By the turn of the twentieth-century all remaining components of Manders PLC had been acquired by other firms and the name effectively disappeared from British business history. The firm remained a family owned and managed concern until well into the twentieth-century and showed an extremely long-lasting commitment to both philanthropy and progressive business practices, for example in the field of labour relations. In many ways the long-run histories of the Shaw and Mander enterprises traced very many significant parallels. C. N. Mander, *Varnished Leaves: a biography of the Mander Family of Wolverhampton, 1750–1950* (Gloucestershire: Owlpen Press, 2004). The Mander family left behind very considerable papers and a fascinating and important business history remains to be written.

40. As Elizabeth once noted 'We have not had much visiting except calls'. Wilkinson Ms No. 24, Elizabeth Wilkinson to John Shaw, 31 August 1812.

41. H. Whitbread (ed.), *I Know My Own Heart: The Diaries of Anne Lister, 1791–1840* (New York: New York University press, 1992).

42. Shaw Ms No. 58, Elizabeth Shaw to John Shaw, 11 January 1823.

43. Wilkinson Ms No. 14, Elizabeth Wilkinson to John Shaw, 27 January 1812. In portraying women as more likely to lose their heads over fashion, status and sociability Elizabeth was following an extremely common and persistent cultural trope.

44. Elizabeth went on to tell John how the lecturer 'also had a microscope of a wonderful magnifying nature and of which he was the inventor – his name is Rogers'. It is notable how Elizabeth continues to socialize in the same circle that John had already established when they first married; his own small family, the Manders, and a few other select friends. Shaw Ms No. 63, Elizabeth Shaw to John Shaw, 3 December 1823.

45. Shaw Ms No. 77, Elizabeth Shaw to John Shaw, 11 July 18??.

46. A conscious rejection of worldly pleasures – and temptations – formed a consistent strain in John's writings. In his second extant letter to Elizabeth he made the following claim: 'Was is not from imperious necessity, little very little should I mingle with the world, for in the words of, I think, that beautiful writer Dr Blair, "Happy should I be to lose the remembrance of its busy song and hear no more of its distant tumults. Vain grandeurs of the earth's perishing riches and fantastic pleasures. Can they yield undecaying delights? Joys becoming the capacities of an immortal mind?" No, impossible, 'ere one great business here should be our future bliss to ensure'. Shaw Ms No. 2, John Shaw to Elizabeth Wilkinson, 16 April 1811.

47. Shaw Ms No. 25, John Shaw to Elizabeth Shaw, 4 August 1825. Likewise, see Shaw Ms No. 27, John Shaw to Elizabeth Shaw, 10 July 1826, in which he hopes 'to hear you have embraced the opportunity [of fine weather] and been out two or three times in chaise. I beg you will think nothing of the expense – maybe a caring physic [doctor] costs more

than a chaise and so let me beg you will do as I request and go as often as you feel able and the weather will permit'.

48. Shaw Ms No. 5, John Shaw to Elizabeth Wilkinson, 16 July 1811. Later letters certainly contain news and gossip about church affairs, but little indication of John's active involvement. See Shaw Ms No. 37, John Shaw to Elizabeth Shaw, 21 June 1839, for example.

49. http://www.localhistory.scit.wlv.ac.uk/Museum/metalware/general/shaw.htm

50. M. French and A. Popp, "'Ambassadors of Commerce:' The Commercial Traveller in British Culture, 1800–1939', *Business History Review*, 82:4 (2008), pp. 789–814

51. Shaw Ms No. 31, John Shaw to Elizabeth Shaw, 30 January 1829: 'I went last evening to take supper with Mr Holgate ... and had quite a treat – with his daughters playing – three of them sat down to the pianoforte and another to the Welsh harp – and most delightfully they performed – he has a fine family of nine children all at home – a governess in the house'. For another example see Shaw Ms No. 23, John Shaw to Elizabeth Shaw, 24 August 1825, in which John tells Elizabeth how he 'dined yesterday with a customer who has perhaps been afflicted with it [an illness] as much as you'.

52. A. Popp, "'This Sad Affair:' Separation, Sentiment and Familism in a Nineteenth-century Family Multinational', in C. Lubinski, P. Fernández Pérez and J. Fear (eds), *Family Multinationals: Entrepreneurship, Governance, and Pathways to Internationalization* (London: Routledge, forthcoming, 2012).

53. J. F. Wilson and A. Popp, 'Business Networks in the Industrial Revolution: Some Comments', *Economic History Review*, 56:2 (2003), pp. 355–61.

54. A. Popp, "'Though it is but a Promise:' Business Probity in Arnold Bennett's *Anna of the Five Towns*', *Business History*, 48:3 (2006), pp. 332–53.

55. WALS DB–24/A/173, Shaw and Crane Bill Book, c.1815–19.

56. J. F. Wilson and A. Popp (eds), *Industrial Clusters and Regional Business Networks in England, 1750–1970* (Aldershot: Ashgate, 2003).

57. Shaw Ms No. 84, Elizabeth Shaw to Elizabeth Wilkinson (mother, July 1815.

58. Shaw Ms No. 85, Elizabeth Wilkinson (mother) to Elizabeth Shaw, 24 January 1822.

59. Ibid. This would be a difficult trap to escape and 'we have not fix^t on any situation for Rich. Something I hope will turn up whereby he may be able to keep his family on'. Enterprise was alighted on as the natural response in this archetypal middling family: 'your uncle John hath taken a house in Colne but his wife says she will not come and if he doth not come Rich may take his place [and] if there shd be business here for your uncle why not for Rich^d'.

60. Ibid. She continued to note that 'Sarah is noth^g better. I am ready to conclude they make bullets and set W^m to shoot them'. Alas, there was no happy ending for brother Richard who died early the next year (1823), a death no doubt attributed in part to shame. Sadly the family remained divided: 'I fear Rich^{ds} death was no more than an arrow that passeth through the air to some of the family who told me it was well he was gone. I was sorry to find so little love to a Bro^r'. Shaw Ms No. 87, Elizabeth Wilkinson (mother) to Elizabeth Shaw, 28 March 1823. Certainly bankruptcy could be taken very hard. In 1822 Elizabeth's mother told her how 'poor Mrs Irvin died of a broken heart immediately after her delivery (Irvin had never made her acquainted with his circumstances when he was insolvent only about three weeks before her confinement)'. Shaw Ms No. 86, Elizabeth Wilkinson (mother) to Elizabeth Shaw, 29 March 1822. The mid-1820s were extremely turbulent times for Elizabeth's Lancashire family, which was rocked by successive traumas and tragedies including death, bastardy, feuds, and further business failings. All in all a series of events too complex to relate here.

61. Finn, *The Character of Credit*.
62. Pearson and Richardson, 'Business Networking in the Industrial Revolution', pp.657–79.
63. Though for a later date see, for example: H. Berghoff, 'Regional Variations in Provincial Business Biography. The case of Birmingham, Bristol, and Manchester, 1870–1914', *Business History*, 37:1 (1995), pp. 64–85. More contemporaneously see A. Wilson, *William Roscoe: Commerce and Culture* (Liverpool: Liverpool University Press, 2008).
64. Shaw Ms No. 23, John Shaw to Elizabeth Shaw, 24 August 1825.
65. Shaw Ms No. 34, John Shaw to Elizabeth Shaw, 19 October 1831.
66. For the spatiality of nineteenth-century investing see Lucy Newton, 'Capital Networks in the Sheffield Region, 1850–1885', in Wilson and Popp, *Industrial Clusters*.
67. Most notably when in 1823 Elizabeth's sister Sarah, who was pregnant, was jilted at the altar by her intended groom. Shaw Ms No. 88, Elizabeth Wilkinson (mother) to Elizabeth Shaw, 23 September 1823.
68. Though there were exceptions, notably that centred on money and inheritance at the time of the death of Elizabeth's eldest brother Richard in Spring 1823 explored briefly in notes above.

7 'Happiness (in Earthly Things)': Getting and Having

1. Wilkinson Ms No. 28, Elizabeth Wilkinson to John Shaw, 25 November 1812. We have deliberately reused this quotation, with which Chapter 2 also begins, to highlight how it is not simply about love but about love in a particular setting: the home.
2. Wilkinson Ms. No. 29, Elizabeth Wilkinson to John Shaw, 1 January 1813.
3. Wilkinson Ms. No. 28, Elizabeth Wilkinson to John Shaw, 25 November 1812.
4. W. R. Ward, 'Methodism and Wealth, 1740–1860', in D. J. Jeremy (ed.), *Religion, Business and Wealth in Modern Britain* (London: Routledge, 1998), p. 66.
5. Ibid.
6. Ibid. Moreover he acknowledges that 'Whether Wesley's followers agonized over the issue of wealth as much as he did is unlikely'; instead Methodist businessman faced a daily challenge of reconciling 'their evangelical personal ethic of love with the impersonal market economics of their weekday commercial orthodoxy'. Ibid., p. 68 and p. 69.
7. Wilkinson Ms No. 3, Elizabeth Wilkinson to John Shaw, 28 May 1811.
8. Wilkinson Ms No. 18, Elizabeth Wilkinson to John Shaw, n.d.
9. D. Cohen, *Household Gods: The British and their Possessions* (New Haven, CT: Yale University Press, 2006), p. 2.
10. Ibid., p. 6.
11. Ibid., p. 6.
12. Ibid., p. 3.
13. Shaw Ms No. 34, John Shaw to Elizabeth Shaw, 19 October 1831.
14. Shaw Ms No. 35, John Shaw to Elizabeth Shaw, 22 April 1832.
15. For the tensions between religion, industriousness, and wealth, albeit at an earlier date, see: M. Kadane, 'Success and Self-Loathing in the Life of an Eighteenth-Century Entrepreneur', in M. C. Jacob and C. Secretan (eds.), *The Self-Perception of Early Modern Capitalists* (Basingstoke: Palgrave Macmillan, 2008), pp. 253–72.
16. In the same letter he goes on to note that he had not been able to write the preceding Sunday, as intended, as he attended chapel a total of three times. Shaw Ms No. 35, John Shaw to Elizabeth Shaw, 22 April 1832.

17. It is not clear when the Shaw's moved to Oxley House, but a letter of March 1831 strongly indicates the growing family was actively looking to move out of George St. John relates how 'I did not purchase the Old Manse at Penn [the village of his birth] – it was quite above my price – indeed there was no sale – that is the highest bidding which was £1800 was not enough – the reserve bidding being £2300 ... [and to do] as I should have done it will cost a deal of money – that is to pull the old house down and erect a good modden one in a quite different style as the old one is good for nothing and quite too near the road'. Shaw Ms No. 33, John Shaw to Elizabeth Shaw, 14 March 1831. These plans show a definite ambition.

18. Shaw Ms No. 58, Elizabeth Shaw to John Shaw, 11 January 1823. Vickery calls the coach 'the most flamboyant masculine accoutrement ... always ultra expensive in itself'. Vickery, 'His and Hers', p. 33.

19. A. Owens, 'Inheritance and the Life-Cycle of Firms in the Early Industrial Revolution', *Business History*, 44:1 (2002), pp. 21–46.

20. Last Will and Testament of John Shaw, Wolverhampton Archives and Local Studies.

21. Tosh, 'From Keighley to St-Denis'.

22. Wilkinson Ms. No. 29, Elizabeth Wilkinson to John Shaw, 1 January 1813.

23. K. Harvey, 'Making Home: Masculinity and Domesticity in Eighteenth-Century Britain', *Gender and History*, 21 (2009), p. 524.

24. Vickery, *Behind Closed Doors*, p. 88 and p. 86

25. Conger, '"There is Graite Odds between A Mans being At Home and A Broad"', p.595.

26. Most of Elizabeth's letters to John prior marriage were directed to him at 'Mrs Green's, Craddocks Walk, Wolverhampton.

27. This should not be mistaken for disinterest, for in one letter she warns that 'I shall ask you twenty questions about this house which you have in view when you come – so I would have you prepare your lungs – that I may not tire you with talking'. Wilkinson Ms No. 20, Elizabeth Wilkinson to John Shaw, 5 June 1812.

28. Wilkinson Ms No. 26, Elizabeth Wilkinson to John Shaw, 19 October 1812. Images from the turn of the early twentieth-century show a bustling shopping street, curving as it gently climbs the slope. Today it remains one of the town's principal shopping streets.

29. Ibid.

30. B. Smith, *Ladies of the Leisure Class: The Bourgeoises of Northern France in the Nineteenth Century* (Princeton, NJ: Princeton University Press, 1981), p. 7.

31. Wilkinson Ms No. 26, Elizabeth Wilkinson to John Shaw, 19 October 1812.

32. Ibid.

33. John may have upbraided her for her words, for in her next letter she admits 'I do not know a single word how G[reenleaves] left his affairs. I merely conjectured that if they liv'd so extravagantly they could not save much. I believe he stood very high in the estimation of his Partners'. Wilkinson Ms No. 27, Elizabeth Wilkinson to John Shaw, 3 November 1812. Even in death a businessman's reputation and character mattered.

34. Elizabeth was evidently very pleased with the purchases she and her brother Thomas had made for his Rochdale home; 'I think I told you in my last that that our sitting room was likely to be metamorphis'd but I did not then know what finery we were about to have, you will scarcely know the room when you come we are so fine, with a sopha – cover'd with scarlet moreen, trimm'd with black velvet, and window hangings to correspond – We bought them at a sale – They are thought to be very cheap – The sopha is well stuff'd with hair and excellent mahogany frame – It cost 7 pounds without cover scarcely two years ago. We gave 5-15-0 for cover and all & 1-19-0 for curtains but they look very

handsome – The cornice is worth 12/-'. Wilkinson Ms. No.16, Elizabeth Wilkinson to John Shaw, 25 March 1812

35. Ibid. If, as Vickery claims 'A standing theme of misogynist humour was the spendthrift wife, who had her husband by the nose and in her excesses made a complete fool of him' then Elizabeth placed at least equal blame on these profligate male wastrels and was herself determined not to spend John's money unnecessarily. Vickery, *Behind Closed Doors*, p. 102.

36. Ibid.

37. Ibid.

38. Wilkinson Ms. No.16, Elizabeth Wilkinson to John Shaw, 25 March 1812.

39. Wilkinson Ms. No.21, Elizabeth Wilkinson to John Shaw, 18 July 1812. Even after signing off with their customary 'Adieu' Elizabeth cannot help returning, almost breathlessly to the same subject: 'Respecting the house – you say it is got painted and white wash'd – will you have the goodness to see that it is kept clean – for paint looks ill when it is dirtied and workman of any kind are far from being careful – Do you send to the persons you nam'd for the furniture and linen – or rather, cotton that which you nam'd to me. I think, must be cheap if the carriage would not be expensive – we could try if both for table, and bed linen, if you please – only, be careful not to buy too much – Linen will be best for towels'. Ibid.

40. Conger, '"There is Graite Odds between A Mans being At Home and A Broad"', p. 598

41. Ibid., p. 600.

42. Wilkinson Ms No. 22, Elizabeth Wilkinson to John Shaw, 25 July 1812.

43. Wilkinson Ms No. 11, Elizabeth Wilkinson to John Shaw, November 1811.

44. Ibid. Moreover, Elizabeth tested the book's precepts against another's opinion, for she had just sat down to read it when a neighbour, Mrs Sergeant, wife to one the preachers and 'a very steady pious woman and one whose advice I was as soon take as any persons ... [and] one of the old school in dress', entered for a visit. She tells John how she had explained to Mrs Sergeant that 'A friend lent it to me that I might discover in it some thing of which I am guilty – Now I beg ... that you will take particular notice of me while I read, for altho' I confess I cannot see it yet you may. I am only a partial judge – She acquiesced – When I had done she made me stand up and turn around – "perhaps you do not wear pockets", said she – I reply'd, generally one. After examining me well all over she said, "I don't see any thing ails you."' Ibid.

45. Wilkinson Ms No. 10, Elizabeth Wilkinson to John Shaw, 7 November 1811.

46. For travellers' dress codes see, A. Popp and M. French, '"Practically the Uniform of the Tribe:" Dress Codes Amongst Commercial Travellers', *Enterprise and Society*, 11:3 (2009), pp. 437–67.

47. Shaw and Wilkinson Ms. No. 28, Elizabeth Shaw (mother) to John Shaw, n.d. One wonders how John felt about cousin Evan, whose 'filling up his time is equally good, he'll make a valuable man, two of his Evenings (after the warehouse is shut up) he devotes to the study of French, two more to reading, two more to learning to play the German flute, the seventh is always spent as you know in the servise [*sic*] of his maker'. Ibid.

48. Wilkinson Ms No. 23, Elizabeth Wilkinson to John Shaw, 14 August 1812. Elizabeth was much less concerned about her own marriage: 'If as you say, I am to please myself about the performing of the ceremony at our marriage I shall neither have carriages nor Gray horses. I shall be more thoughtful about the thing itself than it accompaniments'. Wilkinson Ms No. 24, Elizabeth Wilkinson to John Shaw, 31 August 1812.

49. The élan of the wedding party was matched by sumptuousness of the refreshments. After a moorland walk above the town of Hebden Bridge, dinner was served at 4pm. 'At the top of table was a couple of boil'd fowls cover'd with white sauce, [at the] bottom a good piece of roast beef – in the middle a couple of roasted ducks – a piece of hot ham, veal cutlets – a very nice pudding – pies, puffs, etc, etc. – Gooseberries were all the desert we could procure'. Supper was served at 9pm and consisted of 'veal cutlets – at the bottom a roasted leg of lamb – in the middle stood our fine glass salver 3 heights ornamented with jellies, and preserves with whipt cream on the top – pies, tarts, and puffs stood on each side – besides ham and tongue sliced – (a fine pigeon pie) which was never tasted and a few other little things, everything look'd well and I felt pleased at it. My Aunt had been very kind in assisting ... after supper a large brides Cake came upon the table and everyone drank health and happiness to the bride and groom'. Ibid.
50. Vickery, *Behind Closed Doors*.
51. Shaw Ms No. 34, John Shaw to Elizabeth Shaw, 18.
52. Shaw Ms No. 16, John Shaw to Elizabeth Shaw, 28 November 1819.
53. In one example, John told 'Betty' that 'the quieter the house was kept and the better order and regularity was observed so much the better present would I make her on my return but I fear from what you say she will gone right to forfeit it already'. Shaw Ms No. 27, John Shaw to Elizabeth Shaw, 10 July 1826.
54. Elizabeth was responding to John's letter of 12 May, in which he told her 'John has given me about Thirty Kisses in lieu to send you and hopes I will tell you he is a very good boy that he may have a fiddle and some Ladys Comfits alias Sugar plumbs – of which he is very fond'. Shaw Ms No. 20, John Shaw to Elizabeth Shaw, 12 May 1822.
55. Shaw Ms No. 36.
56. For example, John related in 1822 that 'I have got a few hogshead of Herefordshire cyder assessed and placed securely in the cellars – hope it will turn out good so that it be good in bottles for some years to come – so that we now have in our Cellar Ale, Porter and Cyder'. Shaw Ms No. 20, John Shaw to Elizabeth Shaw, 12 May 1822.
57. Wilkinson Ms. No. 29, Elizabeth Wilkinson to John Shaw, 1 January 1813.
58. Shaw Ms No. 20, John Shaw to Elizabeth Shaw, 12 May 1822.
59. Ibid.
60. Shaw Ms No. 37, John Shaw to Elizabeth Shaw, 21 June 1839.
61. Shaw Ms No. 27, John Shaw to Elizabeth Shaw, 10 July 1826.
62. Shaw Ms No. 9, John Shaw to Elizabeth Wilkinson, 12 November 1812.
63. Shaw Ms No. 49a, Elizabeth Shaw to John Shaw, 1 April 1816.
64. Wilkinson Ms No. 21, Elizabeth Wilkinson to John Shaw, 18 July 1812.

8 Conclusion: The Life They Made

1. See, for example: Jones, 'The Country Trade'; French, Michel. '*Commercials, Careers and Culture: Travelling Salesmen in Britain 1890s–1930s*', *Economic History Review*, 58:2 (2005), pp. 352–77.
2. Popp. 'Building the Market' and 'From Town to Town'.
3. Stobart, *The First Industrial Region*.
4. Hunt, *The Middling Sort*; L. Davidoff and C. Hall, *Family Fortunes: Men and Women of the English Middle Class, 1780–1850* (London: Routledge, 1987).
5. E. Hobsbawm, *The Age of Capital: 1848–1875* (London: Weidenfeld and Nicholson, 1975).

6. Smith, *Ladies of the Leisure Class.*
7. Kay, *The Foundations of Female Entrepreneurship*, p. 134
8. M. Finn, 'Anglo-Indian Lives in the Later Eighteenth and Early Nineteenth-Centuries', *Journal of Eighteenth Century Studies*, 33:1 (2010), pp. 49–65.
9. D. McCloskey, *The Bourgeois Virtues: Ethics for an Age of Commerce* (Chicago, IL: University of Chicago Press, 2007).
10. Ibid.
11. Of course, even with the best intentions, are histories are always gendered too. This study, for example, has discussed child-rearing, a role that John and Elizabeth shared to quite a considerable extent but has given much less experience to Elizabeth's experience of pregnancy, which was very rarely pleasant, often deeply unhappy, and extensively discussed in her letters. I have personal experience of both marriage and parenthood but, as a man, none of pregnancy or childbirth.

Epilogue: 'One Hundred and Fifty Years of Achievement'

1. John Shaw and Sons Ltd, *Sesquicentum.* The pamphlet is not paginated.
2. This celebration may have been premature. The firm dated its founding to 1795, in which year John Shaw would have thirteen. He may have been apprenticed by that age but to have commenced in business on his own account seems particularly precocious.
3. Ibid.
4. Ibid.
5. Johns Shaw and Sons, Wolverhampton, Ltd, *Hardwareman*, 31 August 1895, p. 237. At a later date Charles even took to the road when one of the firm's travellers suffered a prolonged illness. In early 1896 *The Hardwareman* carried a very extensive report on the centenary banquet held by the firm on 3 January 1896 at the Star and Garter Hotel, Wolverhampton. Again the theme of longevity was prominent and Sir Henry Fowler MP, proposing 'The Firm', observed how 'it was a rare thing for a firm to carry on business in one town, with so short a succession from father to son, and from sons to grandsons, for a period already exceeding a century'. *Hardwareman*, 11 January 1896, p. 260. Sir Henry placed considerable stress on the relationship between the firm and the town.
6. However, at the firm's centenary banquet in January 1896, amongst the letters from customers read out, one referred to how '"It is nearly 47 years since I gave you an opening order. John Shaw and his good lady were then to the front, their sons, Thomas and Edward, working like niggers." Clearly, this customer perceived Elizabeth to have played an important role in the firm'. *Hardwareman*, 11 January 1896, p. 261.
7. Ibid., p. 238.
8. Ibid.
9. Ibid. Interestingly, given that his father was a founding shareholder, Thomas Wilkinson Shaw was also praised for 'his splendid services in averting a financial disaster on the occasion of the temporary suspension of the Wolverhampton and Staffordshire Bank in 1857, for it was generally admitted that his exertions enabled the Bank to weather the storm successfully and regain the confidence of the community'. Ibid.
10. Ibid.
11. For a detailed exploration of this concept see, for example: R. Lloyd-Jones and M. J. Lewis, *Raleigh and the British Bicycle Industry: An Economic and Business History, 1870–1960* (Aldershot: Ashgate, 2000). The Chairmanship of the board rotated on an annual

basis between John P. Shaw and Charles E. Shaw. The home business had a capitalization of £120,000 on incorporation in 1887, the foreign business £60,000.

12. Johns Shaw and Sons, Wolverhampton, Ltd, *Hardwareman*, 31 August 1895, p. 243.

13. *Hardwareman*, 11 January 1896, p. 263.

14. Ibid., p. 253.

15. Ibid.

16. Charles seems to have taken his constituency work seriously, moving to Stafford as soon as possible, but took a laxer approach to Parliament itself, admitting that 'I have chiefly interested myself in commercial and industrial questions and the only time I have spoken [in over two years] was on the Employers' Liability Bill. I have served on several Committees – Railway Rates, Manchester Ship Canal, and again on the Marking of Files Bill'. Ibid., p. 254.

17. *Hardwareman*, 11 January 1896, p. 261.

18. Ibid.

19. Johns Shaw and Sons, Wolverhampton, Ltd, *Hardwareman*, 31 August 1895, p. 254.

20. Charles E. Shaw reflected at some length on the firm's dependence on its managers at the centenary banquet.

21. Ibid., p. 253. He continued: 'We of course like to know how things are on that side of the water, the health of staff, state of trade, course of exchange, Bank rate, silver market etc'.

22. Similarly, during the same world tour, Shaw took the opportunity of his visit to Australia to spend a 'few weeks with our friends Messrs W. and A. Bennetts and Son, who are very large merchants in Fitzroy, and I may here mention that, although the two firms had had business connections for over thirty years, this was the first time that any members of the respective firms had met'.

23. Ibid., p. 257. Later, the article quotes from the memories of James R. Wilson, the firm's oldest traveller, to the following effect: 'in 1885, I lost a son, at the age of ten, by spasmodic croup. I shall never forget the kind letter of condolence sent me by the late Mr. T.W. Shaw. In this letter he informed me that he had – several years before – lost a little daughter eight years old by the same dire disease. In 1893 I had the misfortune to lose my wife ... and I have now by me (written by Mr John P. Shaw) one of the most sympathetic and kindly letters I then received", p. 252.

24. 'Mr Matthew Wilson, of Liverpool, recalls the visits to his employer 50 years ago of "either Mr Shaw or Mr Crane," who "was very kind to us lads in the shop, which made us like the business," and he remembers his "old governor paying much attention to the traveller."' Ibid., p. 244. Similarly, Mr Coffin of Ellesmere, Shropshire, described 'the strong impression made upon him, when, in early life, he first visited Wolverhampton, by the cordial reception he had and by his entertainment at the private residence of one of the then partners'. Ibid., p. 252.

25. At the firm's centenary banquet in January 1896, for example, Frank James of Walsall noted that he represented a firm that '"had had the pleasure of transacting business with this firm during the whole term of their existence. For himself he could speak for a period of a half-a-century."' *Hardwareman*, 11 January 1896, p. 262.

26. Ibid., p. 246.

27. Ibid., p. 246.

28. This was clearly much more than a holiday, his observations included as 'some evidence of Japanese enterprise, let me say that I found their cities lighted with electricity at a time when not a single English town had taken it up'. Whilst in America on the same tour, he visited 'several of the large hardware establishments, and when asked what impres-

sion they produced in his mind, answered, that in size, perfection of appointments, and generally up-to-date character, they struck him as being much in advance of similar establishments in this country'. Ibid., p. 253 and 254. Many of the numerous speeches at the centenary banquet in January 1896 concentrated very heavily on the spectre of foreign competition.

29. Ibid., p. 254.
30. Ibid., p. 238.
31. John Shaw and Sons Ltd., *Sesquicentum*.
32. John Shaw and Sons administrative history: http://blackcountryhistory.org/collections/getrecord/GB149_DB-24/
33. John Shaw and Sons Ltd., *Sesquicentum*.

WORKS CITED

Archival Sources

DB/24/A/1–432: Archives of John Shaw and Sons, Wolverhampton Ltd., 1667–1960, Wolverhampton Archives and Local Studies (WALS)

DB/24/B: Archives of T.E. Thomson and Co. Ltd., 1839–1946, WALS

WALS, Wilkinson and Shaw Letters, 1799–1831, WALS

Shaw Letters, Ms No.s 1–119, *c*. 1800–39. University of Birmingham Library.

Wilkinson Letters, Ms No. 1–30, 1811–13. WALS.

Printed Primary Sources

Parson and Bradshaw, *Staffordshire General and Commercial Directory for 1818* (Manchester: J. Leigh, 1818).

'The "Hardwareman's" Monograph on John Shaw and Sons Wolverhampton Ld: A Century of Progress in Hardwareland, 1795–1895,' *The Hardwareman* (1895).

The Hardwareman, 11 January 1896.

Sesquicentum, Being a Century and a Half of Progress, John Shaw and Sons Wolverhampton Limited and their Subsidiary Companies (Wolverhampton, 1945).

Secondary Sources

Books

Barker, H., *The Business of Women: Female Enterprise and Urban Development in Northern England, 1760–1830* (Oxford: Oxford University Press, 2006).

Berenson, E., *The Trial of Madame Caillaux* (Berkeley, CA: The University of California Press: 1992).

Chapman, S., *Merchant Enterprise: From the Industrial Revolution to World War I* (Cambridge: Cambridge University Press, 2004).

Cobbett, W., *Rural Rides*, ed. George Woodcock (London,, 1967; 1ˢᵗ ed. 1830).

Cohen, D., *Household Gods: The British and their Possessions* (New Haven, Conn.: Yale University Press, 2006).

Colley, L., *The Ordeal of Elizabeth Marsh: How a Remarkable Woman Crossed Seas and Empires to Become Part of World History* (London: Harper Perennial, 2007).

Davidoff, Leonore and Catherine Hall. *Family Fortunes: Men and Women of the English Middle Class, 1780–1850* (London: Routledge, 1987).

Earle, R., (ed.), Epistolary Selves: Letters and Letter-Writers, 1600-1945 (Farnham: Ashgate, 1999).

Figes, O., *Just Send Me Word: A True Story of Love and Survival in the Gulag* (London: Allen Lane, 2012).

Finn, M., *The Character of Credit: Personal Debt in English Culture, 1740–1914* (Cambridge: Cambridge University Press, 2003).

Finer, A. and George Savage (eds), *The Selected Letters of Josiah Wedgwood* (London: Cory, Adams and Mackay, 1965).

Gittings, R., (ed.), *John Keats, Selected Letters* (Oxford: Oxford University Press, 2002)

Goodman, D., *Becoming a Woman in the Age of Letters* (London: Cornell University Press, 2009).

Haggerty, S., *The British-Atlantic Trading Community, 1760–1810: Men, Women, and the Distribution of Goods* (Leiden: Brill, 2006)

Hanna, M., *Your Death Would be Mine: Paul and Marie Pireaud in the Great War* (Cambridge, MA: Harvard University Press, 2006).

Hobsbawm, E., *The Age of Capital: 1848–1875* (London: Weidenfeld and Nicholson, 1975).

Hoppit, J., *Risk and Failure in English Business, 1700–1800* (Cambridge: Cambridge University Press, 1987).

Hudson, P., *Regions and Industries: Perspectives on the Industrial Revolution* (Cambridge: Cambridge University Press, 1989).

Hunt, M R., *The Middling Sort: Commerce, Gender, and the Family in England, 1680–1780* (Berkeley, CA: University of California Press, 1996).

Jones, G., *Merchants to Multinationals: British Trading Companies in the Nineteenth and Twentieth Centuries* (Oxford: Oxford University Press, 2000)

Kay, A. C., *The Foundations of Female Entrepreneurship: Enterprise, Home and Household in London, c. 1800–1870* (Abingdon: Routledge, 2009).

Lloyd-Jones, R., and M. J. Lewis, *Raleigh and the British Bicycle Industry: An Economic and Business History, 1870–1960* (Aldershot: Ashgate, 2000).

Mander, C. N., *Varnished Leaves: a biography of the Mander Family of Wolverhampton, 1750–1950* (Gloucestershire: Owlpen Press, 2004).

McCloskey, D., *The Bourgeois Virtues: Ethics for an Age of Commerce* (Chicago, IL: University of Chicago Press, 2007).

Smith, B., *Ladies of the Leisure Class: The Bourgeoises of Northern France in the Nineteenth Century* (Princeton, NJ: Princeton University Press, 1981).

Smith, M., (ed.), *Charlotte Brontë: Selected Letters* (Oxford: Oxford University Press, 2010).

Spinosa, C., F. Flores, and H. L. Dreyfus, *Disclosing New Worlds: Entrepreneurship, Democratic Action, and the Cultivation of Solidarity* (Cambridge, MA: MIT Press: 1997).

Stobart, J., *The First Industrial Region: North-west England c. 1700–60* (Manchester: Manchester University Press, 2004).

Stone, L., *The Family, Sex and Marriage in England, 1500–1800* (London: Weidefeld and Nicholson, 1977).

Sunderland, D., *Social Capital, Trust and the Industrial Revolution, 1780-1880* (London: Routledge, 2007).

Thomas, K., *The Ends of Life: Roads to Fulfilment in Early Modern England* (Oxford: Oxford University Press, 2010).

Tosh, J., *A Man's Place: Masculinity and the Middle-Class Home in Victorian England*, (New Haven, CT: Yale University Press, 1999).

Trouillot, M. R., *Silencing the Past: Power and the Production of History* (Boston, MA: Beacon Press, 1995).

Vickery, A., *The Gentleman's Daughter: Women's Lives in Georgian England* (New Haven, CT: Yale University Press, 1999).

—, *Behind Closed Doors: At Home in Georgian England* (New Haven, Conn.: Yale University Press, 2009).

Whitbread, H. (ed.), *I Know My Own Heart: The Diaries of Anne Lister, 1791–1840* (New York: New York University press, 1992).

Wilson, A., *William Roscoe: Commerce and Culture* (Liverpool: Liverpool University Press, 2008).

Wilson, J. F., and A. Popp (eds), *Industrial Clusters and Regional Business Networks in England, 1750–1970* (Aldershot: Ashgate, 2003).

Journal Articles and Chapters in Books

Acton, C., 'Writing and Waiting: The First World War Correspondence between Vera Brittain and Roland Leighton', *Gender & History*, 11:1 (1999), pp. 54–83.

Bailey, J., '"A Very Sensible Man": Imagining Fatherhood in England c. 1750 - 1830', *History*, 95:3 (2010), pp. 267-92.

Barker, H., 'Soul, Purse and Family: Middling and Lower-Class Masculinity in Eighteenth-Century Manchester', *Social History*, 33:1 (2008): pp. 12-35.

Berghoff, H., 'Regional Variations in Provincial Business Biography. The Case of Birmingham, Bristol, and Manchester, 1870–1914', *Business History*, 37:1 (1995), pp. 64–85.

Boyce, G., 'Language and Culture in a Liverpool Merchant Family Firm, 1870–1950', *Business History Review*, 84:1 (2010), pp. 1–26.

Caunce, S., 'Banks, Communities and Manufacturing in West Yorkshire, c. 1800-1860', in J. F. Wilson and A. Popp (eds), *Industrial Clusters and Regional Business Networks in England, 1750-1970* (Aldershot: Ashgate, 2003), pp. 112-29.

Cookson, G., 'Quaker Networks and the Industrial Development of Darlington, 1780-1870', in J. F. Wilson and A. Popp (eds), *Industrial Clusters and Regional Business Networks in England, 1750-1970* (Aldershot: Ashgate, 2003), pp. 155-73.

Coopey, R., 'The British Glove Industry, 1750-1970: The Advantages and Vulnerability of a Regional Industry', in J. F. Wilson and A. Popp (eds), *Industrial Clusters and Regional Business Networks in England, 1750-1970* (Aldershot: Ashgate, 2003), pp. 174-91.

Conger, V. B., '"There is Graite Odd between A Mans being At Home and A Broad": Deborah Read Franklin and the Eighteenth-Century Home', *Gender & History*, 21:3 (2009), pp. 592–607.

Connell, C. M., 'Entrepreneurial Enterprise and "Image" in the Nineteenth Century Trading Firm: Shaping the Legal Environment for Business', *Business History*, 48:2 (2006), pp. 193–219.

Eustace, N., '"The Cornerstone of a Copious Work:" Love and Power in Eighteenth-Century Courtship', *Journal of Social History* (Spring 2001), pp. 517–46.

Finn, M., 'Anglo-Indian Lives in the Later Eighteenth and Early Nineteenth-Centuries', *Journal of Eighteenth Century Studies*, 33:1 (2010), pp. 49–65.

French, M., '*Commercials, Careers and Culture: Travelling Salesmen in Britain 1890s–1930s*', *Economic History Review*, 58:2 (2005), pp. 352–77.

—, 'On the Road: Travelling Salesmen and Experiences of Mobility in Britain before 1939', *Journal of Transport History*, 31:2 (2010), pp. 133–50.

French, M., and A. Popp, '"Ambassadors of Commerce:" The Commercial Traveller in British Culture, 1800–1939', *Business History Review*, 82:4 (2008), pp 789–814.

Gerber, D. A., 'Acts of Deceiving and Withholding in Immigrant Letters: Personal Identity and Self-Presentation in Personal Correspondence', *Journal of Social History*, 39:2 (2005); pp. 315–30.

Goodman, D., 'Letter Writing and the Emergence of Gendered Subjectivity in Eighteenth-Century France', *Journal of Women's History*, 17 (Summer 2005), pp. 9–37.

Gordon, E., and G. Nair, 'The Myth of the Victorian Patriarchal Family', *History of the Family*, 7 (2002), pp. 125–38.

—, 'Domestic Fathers and the Victorian Parental Role', *Women's History Review*, 15:4 (2006), pp. 551–9.

Guy, K M., 'Drowning Her Sorrows: Widowhood and Entrepreneurship in the Champagne Industry', *Business and Economic History*, 26:2 (1997), pp. 505 – 14.

Hamilton, E., 'Whose Story is it Anyway? Narrative Accounts of the Role of Women in Founding and Establishing Family Businesses', *International Small Business Journal*, 24:3 (2006), pp. 253–71.

—, E., 'Narratives of Enterprise as Epic Tragedy', *Management Decision*, 44:4 (2006), pp. 536–50.

Hanna, M., 'A Republic of Letters: The Epistolary Tradition in France during World War I', *American Historical Review* (December 2003), pp. 1338–61.

Harvey, K., 'Making Home: Masculinity and Domesticity in Eighteenth-Century Britain', *Gender and History*, 21 (2009), pp. 520–40.

Jones, S. R. H., 'The Country Trade and the Marketing and Distribution of Birmingham Hardware, 1750–1810', *Business History*, 26:1 (1984), pp. 24–42.

Kadane, M., 'Success and Self-Loathing in the Life of an Eighteenth-Century Entrepreneur', In, Jacob, Margaret C. And Catherine Secretan (eds.), *The Self-Perception of Early Modern Capitalists* (Basingstoke: Palgrave Macmillan, 2008), pp. 253–72.

Kent, D. A., 'Small Businessmen and their Credit Transactions in Early Nineteenth-Century Britain', *Business History*, 36:2 (1994), pp. 47–64.

Linkin, H. K., 'Skirting Around the Sex in Mary Tighe's *Psyche*', *Studies in English Literature 1500–1900*, 42:4 (2002), pp. 731–52.

Lyons, M., 'Love Letters and Writing Practices: On *Écritures Intimes* in the Nineteenth Century', *Journal of Family History*, 24:2 (1999), pp. 232–9.

McKendrick, N. 'The Consumer Revolution of Eighteenth-century England', in N. J. McKendrick, J. Brewer and J. Plumb (eds), *The Birth of a Consumer Society: the Commercialisation of Eighteenth-century England* (London: Bloomington, 1982).

Müller, Leos. '"Merchants" and "Gentlemen" in Eighteenth-Century Sweden: Worlds of Jean Abraham Grill.' In, Jacob, Margaret C. And Catherine Secretan (eds.), *The Self-Perception of Early Modern Capitalists* (Basingstoke: Palgrave Macmillan, 2008), pp. 125–47.

Nelson, R K., '"The Forgetfulness of Sex:" Devotion and Desire in the Courtship Letters of Angelina Grimke and Theodore Dwight Weld', *Journal of Social History* (Spring 2004), pp. 663–79.

Newton, L., 'Capital Networks in the Sheffield Region, 1850–1885', in J. F. Wilson and A. Popp, *Industrial Clusters and Regional Business Networks in England, 1750–1970* (Aldershot: Ashgate, 2003).

Owens, A., 'Inheritance and the life-cycle of Firms in the Early Industrial Revolution', *Business History* Vol. 44 No. 1 (2002), pp. 21–46.

Pearson, R., and D. Richardson, 'Business Networking in the Industrial Revolution', *Economic History Review*, 54:4 (November 2001), pp. 657–79.

Pearson, R. and D. Richardson, 'Business Networking in the Industrial Revolution: Riposte to Some Comments', *Economic History Review*, 56:2 (2003), pp. 362–68.

Popp, A., '"Though it is but a Promise:" Business Probity in Arnold Bennett's *Anna of the Five Towns*.' *Business History*, 48:3 (2006), pp. 332–53.

—, 'Building the Market: John Shaw of Wolverhampton and Commercial Travel in the Early Nineteenth-century', *Business History*, 49:3 (2007), pp. 321–47

—, 'From Town to Town: How Commercial Travel Connected Manufacturers and Markets in the Industrial Revolution.' *Journal of Historical Geography*, 35:4 (2009), pp. 642–67.

—, 'From Wolverhampton to Calcutta: The Low Origins of Merchant Capital' in R. Lee (ed.), *Commerce and Culture: Nineteenth-Century Business Elites* (Aldershot: Ashgate, 2011), pp. 37–61.

—, "'This Sad Affair:" Separation, Sentiment and Familism in a Nineteenth-century Family Multinational.' In Lubinski, Christina, Paloma Fernández Pérez, and Jeff Fear (eds.) *Family Multinationals: Entrepreneurship, Governance, and Pathways to Internationalization* (London: Routledge, forthcoming, 2012).

Popp A., and M. French, "'Practically the Uniform of the Tribe:" Dress Codes Amongst Commercial Travellers', *Enterprise and Society*, 11:3 (2009), pp. 437–67.

Popp, A., and Holt, R., 'The Presence of Opportunity', *Business History* (forthcoming).

Roper, M., 'Splitting in Unsent Letters: Writing as a Social Practice and a Psychological Activity', *Social History*, 26:3 (2001), pp. 318–39.

—, 'Slipping Out of View: Subjectivity and Emotion in Gender History', *History Workshop Journal*, 59 (2005), pp. 57–72.

Rothman, E K., 'Sex and Self-Control: Middle-Class Courtship in America, 1770–1870', *Journal of Social History*, 15:3 (1982), pp. 409–25.

Rowe, S E., 'Writing Modern Selves: Literacy and the French Working Class in the Early Nineteenth Century', *Journal of Social History*, 40:1 (2006), pp. 55–83.

Seymour, M., 'Epistolary Emotions: Exploring Amorous Hinterlands in 1870s Southern Italy', *Social History*, 35:2 (2010); pp. 148–64.

—, 'The Culture of Credit in Eighteenth Century Commerce: The English Textile Industry', *Enterprise and Society*, 4 (2003), pp. 299–325.

—, 'Credit, Risk, and Honor in Eighteenth-Century Commerce', *Journal of British Studies*, 44:3 (July 2005), pp. 439–56.

Smail, J., 'Coming of Age in Trade: Masculinity and Commerce in Eighteenth-Century England', in, M. C. Jacob and C. Secretan (eds), *The Self-Perception of Early Modern Capitalists* (Basingstoke: Palgrave Macmillan, 2008), pp. 229–52.

Stott, G., 'The Persistence of Family: A Study of a Nineteenth-Century Canadian Family and their Correspondence', *Journal of Family History*, 31:2 (2006); pp. 190–207.

Tosh, J., 'From Keighley to St-Denis: Separation and Intimacy in Victorian Bourgeois Marriage', *History Workshop Journal*, 40:1 (1995), pp. 193–206.

Vickery, A., "'Golden Age or Separate Spheres?" A Review of the Categories and Chronology of English Women's History', *Historical Journal*, 36:2 (1993), pp. 38–414.

—, 'His and Hers: Gender, Consumption and Household Accounting in Eighteenth-Century England', *Past and Present*, 1, supp. 1 (2006), pp. 12–38.

Ward, W. R., 'Methodism and Wealth, 1740–1860', in D. J. Jeremy (ed.), *Religion, Business and Wealth in Modern Britain* (London: Routledge, 1998), pp. 63–70.

Webster, T., 'An Early Global Business in a Colonial Context: The Strategies, Management, and Failure of John Palmer and Company of Calcutta, 1780–1830', *Enterprise & Society: The International Journal of Business History*, 6:1 (2005): pp. 98–133.

Wilson J. F., and A. Popp, 'Business Networking in the Industrial Revolution: Some Comments', *Economic History Review*, 56:2 (2003), pp 355–61.

INDEX

Alston, John, 37, 149n55–7
America, 138, 175n28
Anderson, Joseph, 65, 71
Anderson, Wise and Company (Liverpool), 64
Anglo-Indian merchant houses, 66, 73
Arlett, William, 137
Austen, Jane, 118
Avia Steel and Tool Company Ltd, 140

Balliol College, Oxford, 136
banking failures, 109, 138, 163n60
bankruptcy, 66, 169n60
Barker, Hannah, 163n55
Batavia, 64
Bate, William and Henry, 139
Bates family (Liverpool), 19
Bates, Miss, 16
Bennett, Arnold, *Anna of the Five Towns*, 107
Bentley, Thomas, 56
Berenson, Edward, 5, 6
Best, Mr (Bolton), 88
Birmingham, 24, 31, 139
Black Country, 25, 33, 67, 111
Bloxham and Fourdriniers (London), 107
Bonaparte, Napoleon, 15, 129
Boulton's Soho Works, 25
bourgeoisie, *see* Victorian bourgeoisie
Boyce, Gordon, 19–20
British Tool and Engineering Company, 139
Brontë, Charlotte, 18
Burgess, Mr (Calcutta), 138
Burton's Mill, Middleton, 113
business
    and bailiffs, 108
    and economic forces, 127–8
    and family firms, 128
    and informal networking, 96
    and local investments, 108–9
    see also banking failures; bankruptcy;
        credit systems; entrepreneurs
business history, 4–5, 19, 57
Buxton (Derbyshire), 78, 91, 95, 125

Calcutta, 7, 24
    see also Palmer and Company; T. E.
        Thomson and Co.
Ceylon, 67
Chafer, Miss (later Wilkinson), 15, 54, 123, 156n92
Chapman, Mrs, 29
Chapman, Stanley, and merchant enterprise, 66, 159n24
Chapone, Hester, *Letters on the Improvement of the Mind*, 53, 144n30, 156n84
Chia, Robert, 60
Chubb and Co., 67, 159n32
class
    and ES's views, 112–13
    the middling sort, 3, 45, 56, 113–14, 123, 128, 130
    Victorian bourgeoisie, 107, 114, 116, 128, 130
Cobbett, William, 23, 113
Cohen, Deborah, 113–14
Colne (Lancashire), 1, 28, 29, 41, 86
commercial journeys, 24, 30–1
    and absence from home, 11–12, 55, 84–5
    and competitive conditions, 37, 150n56
    and geographic coverage, 31–2
    and JS's dislike of, 27, 82
    and network built by JS, 34
    and physical hardships, 82–3

commercial travellers, and stress, 161n25
Conger, Vivian Bruce, 118, 121, 145n51
Congregational Church, 106
Connell, C. Matheson, 66
Crane, Henry, 13, 72–3, 149n42
　　and business profits, 35
　　and death of JS's son, 73–4
　　and family friendship, 105, 106
　　and partnership with JS, 23–4, 30, 33,
　　　　34–5, 89
　　and Thomson, 69, 73–4
credit systems, 36–7, 107
　　bills of exchange, 82, 107
　　credit terms, 63, 70, 88, 159n37
customers, and JS, 30–3, 35–6, 38–9, 75,
　　101–2

Defoe, Daniel, 52
Dickens, Charles, 97
Dodds, P. (casual labourer), 34
Dreyfus, Hubert, 3

East India Company, 66
East Indies, 64, 65, 66, 70, 139
Edwards, Elizabeth (later Shaw), *see* Shaw,
　　Elizabeth (JS's mother)
Ellesmere, 32, 175n24
English, John (pin factor), 37, 148n41
entrepreneurs
　　and competitive conditions, 37–8
　　and entrepreneurial qualities, 3–4
　　and the family firm, 115
　　female entrepreneurship, 87, 129,
　　　　163n55
epistolary novels, 10, 13
Evan (JS's cousin), 27, 123

factories, 25
factors (middlemen)
　　and competition, 37–9, 127–8
　　and economic role, 23, 24, 30
　　and JS, 7, 34, 48
familism, 106
fatherhood, 80, 161n17
female entrepreneurship, 87, 129, 163n55
Finn, Margot, 72, 129–30
Flores, Fernando, 3
Franklin, Deborah, 121
French, Michael, 160n3

George Street, Wolverhampton, 114, 117,
　　170
Gibbons Bank, 163n60
Gisborne, Thomas, *An Enquiry into the
　　Duties of the Female Sex*, 52, 53,
　　155n55
Goodall and Alston (haberdashers), 37,
　　149n55–6
Goodall, Michael, 37, 149n55
Goodman, Dena, 18, 20–1, 46, 51
　　Becoming a Woman in the Age of Letters,
　　　　145n47, 155n73, 153n33, 153n41
Gordon, Eleanor, 80
Grant, Mrs, 113–14
Greenleaves, Henry, 119
Grill, Jean Abraham, 20

haberdashers, 37
Habermas, Jürgen, 21
Hamilton, Eleanor, 90, 141n8
Hanna, Martha, *Your Death would be Mine*,
　　12, 142n16
Hardwareman, 134–5, 138, 173n5, 174n6,
　　175n25
Harmonic Society (Wolverhampton), 105
Henderson and McKinley, 37
Henry Pooley and Thomas Walker (iron-
　　mongers), 26
Henry Stuart and Company, 139
Hobsbawm, Eric, 129
Holden, Isaac, 19, 21, 48, 117, 142n10
Holden, Sarah (née Sugden), 19, 21, 48,
　　142n10
Holland, 95, 165n2
Holt, Robin, 60
Hordern, Alexander, 116
Hordern and Company, 163n60
Hordern, Miss, 109

India
　　and British policy, 137
　　and British traders, 66–8, 73
　　see also T. E. Thomson and Co.
industrial revolution, 3, 24, 25, 26
　　and networking, 96, 106

J. & W. Hawkes (Birmingham), 139
Jenks Brothers Ltd, 139

Jenks, George Clement, 140
Jenks, Reginald P., 140
Jeremy, David, 105
John Shaw and Sons Ltd, 133–40
  anniversary pamphlet, 133
  cash reserves, 137–8
  centenary celebration, 134, 173n5,
    174n6
  and Hand Tool industry, 139
  limited liability company, 136
  and takeovers, 139–40
Jones, G., 66
Joseph Rodgers and Sons, 62, 63, 65
Journey Books, 30–1, 32, 102

Kay, A. C., 129
Kendal, 30, 31, 32
Kruger, Paul, 139

Laclos, Pierre Choderlos de, *Les Liaisons
  Dangereuses*, 10
Lancashire, 24
  and ES, 15, 28, 43
  and ES's family visits, 1, 77, 78, 89, 91, 92
  and JS's journeys, 31
  and Luddite riots, 113
Lancaster, Miss, 17
Latham, Jos (warehouseman), 34, 39, 89
Laws, E. (warehouseman), 33–4
Laycock, Mr, 29
Leamington Spa (Warwickshire), 95, 114
letter-writing, 13, 18
  epistolary relationships, 16–17
  and semi-communal letters, 12–13
  and the Shaws, 6, 9–12
    courtship, 7
    privacy, 13–14
    subject-matter, 15–16
    tone of JS's letters, 19
letters, as research sources, 6, 7
Linkin, H. K., 156n84
Lister, Anne, 104
Liverpool
  and JS, 31, 32, 102
  and William Shaw, 24, 25, 26, 31, 32
Lomax, James, 17
Lomax, Mary, correspondence with ES,
  16–17, 47, 153n40

Lomax, Mr, 29
Lomont, Miss, correspondence with ES, 16
London, 25–6, 95
  and Shaw and Crane, 108
Luddites, and riots, 113
Lyons, Martin, 16, 18, 20, 145n58

Macclesfield (Cheshire), 31
McCloskey, D., 130
McKendrick, Neil, 31
Manchester, 24, 32, 87
Mander, B., 105
Mander, C. N., and family business, 168n39
Mander, Miss, 103, 104, 105
marriage, 43, 45
  companionate marriage, 41, 42, 51,
    130–1
  and ES's views, 45–6, 47, 52–4
Marshall, Alfred, 25
Matheson, James, 66–7
Merchandise Marks Act, 138
Methodists, 47, 48, 49
  and wealth, 112, 113, 170n4–6
middlemen, *see* factors
Middleton (Lancashire), 113
Middlewich, 32
middling sort (middle classes), 3, 45, 56,
  113–14, 123, 128, 130
  see also class
Midgeley, Mrs, 45
missionaries, 71
Moore and Wright (Sheffield) Ltd, 139
Morton, Joseph, 35, 149n45
motherhood, models of, 80
Müller, Leos, 20

Nair, Gwyneth, 80
Nantwich, 32
Napoleon I, Emperor of the French, 15, 129
Nelson, R. K., 56
Nicholls, Arthur Bell, 18
non-conformists, 1, 2–3, 4, 112, 150n3
Northampton, 24
Nottingham, 37
Nussey, Ellen, 18

Onions and Company (Birmingham), 139
Osbourn, Joseph, 25

Oswestry, 32, 148n38
Overend, Gurney and Company, 138
Owen and Fendelow, 139
Owens, A., 115
Oxley House, Bushbury, 114, 115

Palmer and Company (Calcutta), 66, 67, 68, 73
patriarchy, 51, 79
Penn, 24, 146n5, 171n17
Perry, John and William, 38–9
Pireaud, Marie and Paul, 12
Plimley and Company, 139
Polwhele, Richard, *The Unsex'd Females*, 156n84
Pooley, Henry, 26
Proust, Marcel, 125

Queen Street Congregational Church, 106

Rawson and Holdsworth, 62, 63–4, 65
Rawson, Norton and Co., 65
religion
    and ES, 47–8, 111–12, 114, 153n43
    and JS, 47, 105–6
Rhodes, Cecil, 139
Richardson, Samuel, *Clarissa* and *Pamela*, 10, 13
Robert Wise and Company (Batavia and Singapore), 64, 158n18
Rochdale, 32, 62
    and ES, 28, 29, 102, 103, 118
Roper, Michael, 20, 145n60
Rothman, Ellen K., 56, 145n49
Ryton, Mr, 70

Sarah (servant to Shaw family), 14, 92
separate spheres thesis, 79–80, 80–1, 87, 130–1
Sesquicentum, 134, 138, 139, 140
Sévigné, Marie de Rabutin-Chantal, marquise de, 10
Seymour, Mark, 20, 21
Shackle, G. L. S. (economist), 61
Shaw, Charles E. (d.1942; grandson), 134–5, 137, 140, 173n5
    apprenticeship in firm, 135–6
    and Balliol, 136
    and British policy in India, 139

as Liberal MP, 137, 175n16
    world tour, 137, 138–9, 175n22, 175n28
Shaw and Crane
    articles of partnership, 149n42–3
    business partnership, 34–5
    business relationship with Thomson, 69
    and Chubb agency, 67
    credit and bills of exchange, 36, 107
    expansion to India, 7, 60–2, 63–4, 66–8, 71–2
    profits, 35
    and takeover, 38–9
    warehouse running costs, 33–4
Shaw, Edward Dethick (1821–86; son), 72
    and bequest from JS, 115
    business expansion, 134, 139
    illness and death, 136
Shaw, Elizabeth (Betsey) (b.1819; daughter), 72, 77, 91, 116, 125
Shaw, Elizabeth (JS's sister), 42
Shaw, Elizabeth (née Edwards; JS's mother), 24, 26, 27–8, 42
    advice to JS, 123
    and ES's visits, 103
    and marriage, 43
    relationship with children, 42–3
Shaw, Elizabeth (née Wilkinson)
    business
        attitude to speculation, 36–7
        involvement in business with JS, 87, 88–90
        and JS's commercial journeys, 78, 84–5
    courtship, 46–7, 48–51, 53
        engagement to JS, 13
        ES and JS as 'coscribblers', 9–10
        see also letter-writing
    family background
        and Colne, 25, 29–30, 86
        and family businesses, 28–9
        parents and siblings, 43–4
        and Rochdale, 118
    marital home, 87, 118
        furnishings and instructions to JS, 120–2, 172n39
        George Street, Wolverhampton, 114, 117
        Oxley House, 114–15
    marriage, 4, 5, 55–8, 92–3, 97

and birth of children, 72, 160n46
companionate marriage, 41, 51, 57,
  130–1
and dowry, 97–8, 99–100
family holidays, 95
home and motherhood, 129
views on marriage, 45–6, 47, 52–4
opinions
  on class, 112, 130
  on education, 103–4
  on Luddite riots, 113
  on Wolverhampton, 118
personal
  dress and fashion, 122, 123
  personality, 48, 119, 120
reading material, 52, 53, 122, 156n79,
  156n83
religion
  doctrinal differences, 47–8, 153n43
  and frugality, 111–12, 114
social networks
  correspondence with friends, 16–17,
    47, 153n40
  social life, 104, 105, 109–10
virtues and values, 130
Shaw, Ernest E., 135
Shaw, John (1782–1858)
  apprenticeship, 26, 27
  business, 6–7, 96
    attitude to speculation, 36–7
    credit and trust, 101–2
    ES's involvement, 87, 88–90
    fears and pressures, 82–3
    firm and family, 128
    investments, 97, 109
    items sold, 111
    and 'Journey Books', 30–1
    networks, 97
    overseas travel, 95
    views on business partnerships, 28
    Wilkinson family as customers, 97, 102
    see also commercial journeys; custom-
      ers; intermediation; John Shaw and
      Sons Ltd; Shaw and Crane; T. E.
      Thomson and Co.
  courtship, 46–7, 48–51, 53
    engagement to ES, 13
    JS and ES as 'coscribblers', 9–10

see also letter-writing
death of son John, 70, 73, 74
family background, 3, 42–3, 86
last will and testament, 116–17
marital home, 120–2, 124
  George Street, Wolverhampton, 114,
    117
  Oxley House, 114–15
marriage, 4, 5, 55–8, 92–3, 97
  and birth of children, 72
  companionate marriage, 41, 51, 57,
    130–1
  and ES's dowry, 97–8, 99–101
  family holidays, 95
personal, 168n46
  appearance, 122–3
  entrepreneurial qualities, 3
  family man, 90, 91–2, 124–5
  work ethic, 39, 77, 133–4
public service, 106
religion, 47, 105–6
views on home and domesticity, 117
virtues and values, 130
Shaw, John (1815–39; son), 72, 73, 125
  death in India, 70, 73
Shaw, John (JS's father), 26, 42
Shaw, John P. (grandson), 135, 136, 137
Shaw, Mary (b.1823; daughter), 72, 92, 116,
  165n84–6
Shaw, Mary (JS's sister), 12, 167n34
Shaw, Richard Edward (b.1827; son), 72,
  92, 116
Shaw, Thomas Wilkinson (1818–87; son),
  72, 91
  and bequest from JS, 115, 116–17
  business expansion, 134, 139
  death, 136
Shaw, William E., 135
Shaw, William (JS's brother), 24, 26, 42
  and JS, 24–5, 42–3, 146n5
Sheffield, 24, 32, 62
Shelmerdine and Co. (printers), 107
Shibden Hall, 104
Shropshire, 30, 95, 109, 138
Silk Triangle, 31
Singapore, 64
Skipton, 91, 95
Smail, John, 145n52, 146n10, 147n21

Smith, Bonnie, 119, 129
South Africa, 139
Sparrow, John Henry, 26, 27, 82, 115
Spencer, John (ES's cousin), 29, 98, 99, 100
Spinosa, Charles, 3
Stafford, 137, 175n16
Staffordshire, 5, 24, 25, 31
Steward, Mr, 103
Stobart, Jon, 24, 32
Stone, Lawrence, 51–2, 53, 54, 150n3, 151n5, 157n113
Sugden, Sarah (later Holden), *see* Holden, Sarah

T. E. Thomson and Co., 23–4, 60–1, 74, 75–6
  and credit terms, 69–70
  retail outlet in Calcutta, 67–8, 71
Thomson, Thomas Edward, 65–6, 71
  and Shaw and Crane, 68–9, 158n5, 158n23
Tosh, John, 21, 48, 56, 80
Toulman, Doctor, 103

urban development, 3, 23, 26, 32, 127

Vickery, Amanda, 16, 51–2, 54, 79–80
  'Golden Age or Separate Spheres?', 161n5–8, 161n14
  and letter writing, 18, 19
  and marital homes, 118, 123
Victorian bourgeoisie, 107, 114, 116, 128, 130
  see also class

Walker, Thomas, 26
Walton, Ben, 69–71
Walton, Miss, 44
Ward, W. R., on Methodists, 112
Weaver, Mrs, 104
Webster, Tony, 66
Wedgwood, Josiah, 56
Wedgwood's Etruria Works, 25

Wesley, John, 112, 170n6
West Indies, 139
Wilkinson, Betsey (ES's niece), 103
Wilkinson, Eliza (ES's mother), 43, 85, 86, 108
  business and buying trips, 87
  retirement, 163n46
Wilkinson, Elizabeth (later Shaw), *see* Shaw, Elizabeth
Wilkinson, John (ES's brother), 29, 44, 85, 86, 146n6
  and business partnership, 98, 99, 100
  and financial settlement, 98, 166n22
Wilkinson, Richard (ES's brother), 16, 25, 29, 166n12
  and daughter, 103
  and financial difficulties, 108, 169n59–60
  views on marriage, 43–5
Wilkinson, Sarah (ES's sister), 167n31, 170n67
Wilkinson, Thomas (ES's brother), 29, 30, 43, 45
  and ES, 53, 103
  and financial difficulties, 102
  and wedding, 15, 16, 123, 173n49
Wilkinson, Thomas (ES's father), 29, 30, 45
  and ES's dowry, 97–8, 99–100
  and finance for son's shop, 98, 99, 100
  and ill-health, 43, 86
  and JS, 48–9
Wilkinson, William (ES's brother), 45, 85, 108
William and Henry Bate, 139
William Sparrow and Sons, 26, 27
Wilson, James R., 175n23
Windle and Blyth (Walsall), 139
Wollstonecraft, Mary, 53, 156n84
Wolverhampton, 26, 31
  and businesses, 67, 69, 104
Wolverhampton Library, 106
Wolverhampton and Staffordshire Banking Company, 109, 174n9
Wrightson, Keith, 80

For Product Safety Concerns and Information please contact our EU
representative GPSR@taylorandfrancis.com
Taylor & Francis Verlag GmbH, Kaufingerstraße 24, 80331 München, Germany

www.ingramcontent.com/pod-product-compliance
Ingram Content Group UK Ltd.
Pitfield, Milton Keynes, MK11 3LW, UK
UKHW021611240425
457818UK00018B/497